D0081900

AGING NATION

AGING NATION

The Economics and Politics of Growing Older in America

James H. Schulz and
Robert H. Binstock

PRAEGER

Westport, Connecticut
London

Library of Congress Cataloging-in-Publication Data

Schulz, James H.
    Aging nation : the economics and politics of growing older in America / James H. Schulz
and Robert H. Binstock.
        p.   cm.
    Includes bibliographical references and index.
    ISBN 0–275–98415–X (alk. paper)
    1. Retirement—Economic aspects—United States.   2. Baby boom
    generation—Retirement—Economic aspects—United States.   3. Retirement—Political
    aspects—United States.   4. Retirement income—United States.   I. Binstock, Robert H.
    II. Title.
    HQ1063.2.U6S395   2006
    331.25′20973–dc22   2006026013

British Library Cataloguing in Publication Data is available

Copyright © 2006 by James H. Schulz and Robert H. Binstock

All rights reserved. No portion of this book may be
reproduced, by any process or technique, without the
express written consent of the publisher.

Library of Congress Catalog Card Number: 2006026013
ISBN: 0–275–98415–X

First published in 2006

Praeger Publishers, 88 Post Road West, Westport, CT 06881
An imprint of Greenwood Publishing Group, Inc.
www.praeger.com

Printed in the United States of America

The paper used in this book complies with the
Permanent Paper Standard issued by the National
Information Standards Organization (Z39.48–1984).

10 9 8 7 6 5 4 3 2 1

CONTENTS

PREFACE

The unfortunate tenor and direction of today's policy discussions regarding our "aging nation" is confusing and worrisome to most Americans. It has motivated us to write this book. After some 40 years of writing for academic audiences, our aim in this volume is to reach a much broader readership—the general public.

A variety of politicians, policy pundits, academicians, and journalists have characterized the aging of 76 million baby boomers as a crisis portending financial catastrophe. To be sure, the rapid aging of our population between now and 2030 presents substantial policy challenges. But the purveyors of gloom and doom see little hope unless radical changes are made. They argue that the Social Security and Medicare programs—widely recognized by Americans as essential ingredients today in providing income and health security for older people—will be unsustainable when baby boomers are elderly. With the stage set by their exaggerated crisis scenarios, they propose "solutions" that will likely leave millions of today's and tomorrow's older persons in dire straits.

During the decades in which we have each carried out research and analyzed policies related to the economics and politics of aging, we have witnessed many proclamations regarding so-called crises dealing with older people. So far, they have all turned out to be phony.

When Medicare was proposed (and finally enacted in 1965), leaders of the American Medical Association—a vigorous opponent of the legislation—made the ominous prediction that the program would quickly lead to "socialized medicine," causing a crisis in health care. They warned that most physicians in the United States would become salaried public employees, that government appropriated budgets would constrain the quality of care, and that Americans would lose the freedom to choose their own doctors.

No such thing happened, of course. None of the predictions came true. In fact, Medicare turned out to be a great boon to the American medical profession. It has, for example, financed the graduate medical training residencies of generations of physicians. And it has been a bountiful source of revenue for doctors and the entire health care industry.

Then in the late 1970s and early 1980s there was the so-called crisis in Social Security financing. An unusual confluence of double-digit rates of inflation with high unemployment created a projected financial imbalance in Social Security. The Reagan Administration proclaimed the program in crisis and headed for bankruptcy—setting out on a campaign to financially gut the program with a variety of cuts in revenue and benefits. Fierce public resistance to these actions stopped that effort.

In fact, despite the extensive crisis rhetoric at the time, it turned out that the financing problem was not terribly difficult to solve. President Reagan eventually appointed a bipartisan National Commission on Social Security Reform, chaired by Alan Greenspan, to develop a solution. The Commission came up with a package of modest, incremental reforms—enacted by Congress in 1983—that put Social Security on a very sound basis for many decades to come.

Still another crisis was perceived in 1986 when Congress outlawed mandatory retirement at any age for almost all jobs. Many employers foresaw economic disaster. They predicted that business payrolls would be overwhelmed and production clogged by large numbers of very old, highly paid workers whose skills and energy had diminished with age.

Yet, once again, the fears turned out to be unfounded. Relatively few older persons chose to work longer (and most that did were highly productive). Retirement remained popular (some say too popular). In fact, in the years that followed, the average age of retirement declined (and remains today at about 62). So much for that crisis!

Now we are faced with the "crisis" arising from the baby boomers' retirement. Is this crisis any different? Some say that it is. They point to the resulting unprecedented aging of the nation and the rising economic costs of retirement programs.

To us, however, the present shouts of "crisis" are also different from previous ones because of the massive uncertainty they are generating. The future elderly face an increasing number of years in "old age," but what that life will be like for them is unclear. There are proposals that at the extreme could very well lead to the destruction of the spectacular past gains in old age security—gains in well being that have resulted in what is often referred to as the Golden Years.

Repeated portrayals of the aging of the baby boomers as a major threat to the financial health of our nation are serving as a platform for radical policy proposals. Among these proposals are privatizing Social Security, establishing old-age-based cutoffs of health care, and demanding that older people retire later and work more.

Our view is that the insurance approach of spreading the risk—as embodied so well in Social Security and Medicare—is essential for preserving the gains that have transformed aging in America from a predominantly miserable stage of life to a decent experience for most. *Social* insurance is especially important now and for the future because the support from employer-sponsored pensions and retiree health insurance is on a dramatic downward spiral.

Our goals in writing this book go beyond simply challenging the pronouncements and conclusions of the doomsayers and their erroneous demographic determinism. There is currently a great deal of anxiety in the country, not only because of what the doomsayers and others say (and what they recommend). Much of the anxiety is also arising because of what is actually happening around us—"globalization," flat wages, permanently lost jobs, disappearing pension benefits, a skyrocketing federal deficit, disappearing government assistance, and a costly and unfair health care system.

Given these developments, we hope this book will help readers better understand the changes that are occurring nationally with regard to shifting demography and its impact on the elderly and their retirement decisions. Second, we want to help readers become more informed about the personal situations they are likely to run into as they prepare for retirement. And finally, we hope to contribute to the major dialogue (policy discussions) that must take place on the interdependent issues related to the economics and politics of aging.

There are now many fine books available on Social Security history, policy issues, and reform proposals. There are also many useful books on health care issues. In addition, there are a few good academic books on work and retirement policy, a few on private pensions, and a few on the politics of aging.

This book, the product of a collaboration between an economist and a political scientist, covers all these areas. In this regard it is unique. Of course, covering such a large number of topics in one book means we had to make many difficult choices about what to leave out. In these decisions we were guided by a desire to emphasize important basic information, avoid research jargon and highly technical discussions, and respond to the goals for the book as articulated above.

We would like to acknowledge a number of individuals who were kind enough to read and comment on all or portions of this manuscript at various stages of its being written: Merton Bernstein, James J. Callahan, Jr., John Cornman, Leonard Hayflick, James Horrigan, Chitra and Kumar Joug-dev, Eric Kingson, Laura Olson, Sara Rix, John Rother, Dallas Salisbury, John Turner, and John Williamson. Of course, none of these persons is responsible

Along with these illnesses comes the risk of enormously expensive hospital and nursing home bills. Such expenses can wipe out a lifetime of savings, including the equity in one's home that has been accumulated over many years.

Retirement also often means a loss of the social role that work confers, a key part of many people's identity throughout much of life. And to make matters worse, one may be socially labeled with a battery of negative ageist stereotypes—such as frail, fumbling, fussy, forgetful, and asexual.

But these are not "the worst of times." Forty or so years ago, the problems and risks associated with old age were much more severe than they are today—especially the financial risks of inadequate income and the overwhelming costs to families for health care. As we will point out in Chapter 3, before there was public and private insurance for income and health care, life in old age for the vast majority of elders was miserable and often dependent on the largesse of one's family and community.

Clearly that has changed. One of the greatest social achievements in the United States and other industrialized countries in the twentieth century was the transformation of old age from one of the worst times in the life course to a good time of life—in fact, in some cases, one of the best periods of one's life.

GREAT ACHIEVEMENTS

Starting with the Social Security Act of 1935, many of the challenges and risks associated with old age have been greatly moderated by public old-age retirement benefit programs. For many, there has also been pension and health insurance coverage through employer-sponsored programs. By the 1960s, Social Security and employer benefits had dramatically improved the financial situation of older people. In addition, the federal Medicare and Medicaid health insurance programs enacted in 1965 provided access to quality health services and long-term care for millions of older Americans. The result has been much less worry about financial support in old age, good health care, and a way of dealing with potentially ruinous health-care bills.

Overall, the past 40 years have witnessed a spectacular revolution in the quality of life for elderly Americans. For the vast majority of older people in the United States today, life in old age is characterized by

- Reasonably healthy and active lives, together with a national health insurance program that finances excellent medical care, with a large part of the costs paid for by health insurance.
- Generally adequate income (through Social Security, often supplemented by employer-sponsored pension plans) that enables one to avoid a desperate life of economic need and the stigma of surviving via family handouts and government welfare.

- Significant wealth, for many, arising primarily from a long-term but generally continuous increase in land and housing prices, supplemented in some cases by financial assets significantly protected (since the 1929 stock market crash) by regulation and insurance—with the value of these assets increasing over time with economic growth.
- Independent living arrangements arising out of financial independence, with a chance to practice "intimacy at a distance"—that is, an ability to remain close to one's children and socialize frequently with them but at the same time the ability to avoid the tensions and conflicts of living together (which most parents and children clearly prefer to avoid).
- A dramatic rise in the number of years in retirement, with ample opportunities to pursue a variety of leisure, volunteer, and second-career activities.
- Spearheaded by the 1965 Older Americans Act, the creation of special agencies for the elderly in every state and the development of a national network of basic services available to help meet special needs in old age, such as transportation for those who can no longer drive a car.

No wonder the term "Golden Years" became a part of American culture in the last half of the twentieth century!

FROM GOLDEN YEARS TO TARNISHED YEARS?

But now, there are indications that for baby boomers the Golden Years could become "the tarnished years." The unusually large size of the baby boom generation, in itself, poses problematic situations for the future of the public and private programs that provide benefits to older persons. Due mainly to the aging of boomers, there is the fear that there will not be enough revenue to fully pay benefits from the two major old-age "entitlement" programs, Social Security and Medicare. (They are called entitlement programs because spending on benefits is determined by specific program rules on who is entitled to benefits (and how much) rather than by annual Congressional budgetary appropriations that limit spending for most other federal programs.)

In addition, a variety of contemporary commentators whom we call the "Merchants of Doom" warn that there is great adversity ahead for all of us, *collectively*, arising from the fact that we are an aging nation. It is not just the growing numbers of older people. It is also the fact that the population of aged persons is rising sharply in relation to the number of people in *younger* age groups. As argued in *The Economist*, "A larger generation of old folk than ever before will need support for longer than ever before from a population of working age that is shrinking continuously in absolute size for the first time since the Black Death."[2]

The solutions that the Merchants of Doom offer to deal with our aging nation are nothing short of horrific. If adopted, they would wipe out most of the economic and social gains our nation made in the twentieth century related to life in old age. They urge the country to

- cut or eliminate Social Security;
- ration health care for older people;
- lower or terminate employer-sponsored pension benefits, make people work longer, and shorten the number of years spent in retirement; and
- require everyone to assume far greater individual responsibility, and the accompanying individual risks, for retirement financial planning and saving.

We are told there are no other sensible options.

Well, we beg to differ. The changing demographic structure of the population is relatively new and is challenging, but it does not necessitate a radical overhaul of our social institutions and a decline in our well-being during our later years. There is no need to drastically change the many positive aspects of old age that the current generation of old people enjoy. This book will explain why.

THE BABY BOOMERS

Baby boomers are a demographic anomaly. For more than a century, the overall trend in the fertility rate in the United States has been downwards. This decline was temporarily interrupted when 76 million babies were born in the 18 years following the end of World War II. The large number of babies born during those years created an exceptionally large and therefore most unusual generation. Over the years, this generation has challenged again and again our societal capacities, attitudes, and social policies.[3]

Throughout the course of their lives, boomers have experienced very different economic situations from those of their parents, and they also have had a large impact on many of our social institutions. When they were young they were greeted by overcrowded schools, schools overwhelmed by the sudden influx of record-breaking numbers of children. In response, school districts (using increases in property taxes) struggled to construct additional schools to accommodate them. (Of course, after the baby boomers passed through that stage of life, they left in their wake an oversupply of school buildings.) Similarly, when the boomers went on to higher education, colleges and universities found that they needed to substantially expand their faculties.

As the baby boom entered its working years, it had its unique experiences in the labor and housing markets. When the boomers entered the workforce they comprised an unusually large number of job seekers. This situation resulted in wages growing more slowly and a much greater competition for jobs than was the case for the generation before. Not surprisingly, boomers have also experienced relatively high rates of unemployment throughout their working years. In addition, the demand by boomers for housing has exceeded the supply, driving up prices so that they had to pay top dollar for their homes.

Now, the future impact of the baby boomers on government old-age benefit programs is a prominent feature of public policy discussions. The reason, of course, is that aged boomers will vastly increase the future number of individuals eligible for Social Security, Medicare, and other old-age programs. At present, the number of people aged 65 and older is about 35 million. In 2030, when all baby boomers will have turned age 65 or older, the number in that age category will have doubled to about 71 million. Consequently, the number of persons eligible, for example, for Social Security's retired worker benefits and for Medicare will essentially double.

WORRISOME PROJECTIONS AND TRENDS

It is now widely known that revenues scheduled to be collected under current Social Security financing provisions will not be sufficient to fully pay the retirement benefits due during the later years of the baby boomers' old age. Each year the trustees of the Social Security and Medicare trust funds are required by law to issue a report that projects the financial status of the programs over a future period of 75 years. (The six trustees are the U.S. Secretaries of Treasury, Labor, and Health and Human Services; the Commissioner of Social Security; and two "public members" appointed by the president and confirmed by the Senate.) Over the past several years these projections have consistently estimated that during the period when all baby boomers are eligible for Social Security, the program (unless changed in some way) will not be able to pay the full amount of benefits that are due. In their 2006 report, for instance, the trustees projected that in 2040 and the years thereafter, Social Security will only be able to pay 74 percent of scheduled annual benefits.[4] Not surprisingly, in mid-2005, a nationwide poll of nonretired adults revealed that 51 percent of them "did not think Social Security would have enough money to pay the benefits they expect when they retire; 70 percent of those under 45 felt that way."[5]

The outlook for Medicare is worse. To begin with, the projected date of the shortfall for Medicare's Hospital Insurance trust fund (also known as Medicare Part A) is much sooner than for Social Security. The 2006 trustees' report estimated that revenue for this program will be insufficient by the year 2018.[6]

people. The American polity responded to them by adopting and financing major age-categorical benefit programs, advantageous tax provisions, and various price subsidies. For the most part, eligibility for these benefits was not determined by need. Rather, we saw the creation of the New Deal's Social Security, the Great Society's Medicare and Older Americans Act (an omnibus social service program), special old-age tax exemptions and credits, and a wide variety of other measures enacted during President Nixon's New Federalism.

The result? The elderly received very special treatment; they were not subjected to the traditional screening applied to welfare applicants in order to determine whether they are worthy of public help.

During the 1960s and 1970s, advocates for the elderly identified just about every issue or problem affecting all or just some older persons. Most became a governmental responsibility for action through nutrition programs; legal, supportive, and leisure services; housing; home repair; energy assistance; transportation; employment assistance; job protection; public insurance for private pensions; special mental health programs; a separate National Institute on Aging; and so on. American society had learned the catechism of compassionate ageism very well and had expressed it through a great many policies designed to help "the aged."

"Greedy Geezers." But, starting in the late 1970s, the long-standing compassionate stereotypes of older persons began to undergo an extraordinary reversal. A watershed article entitled "Aging America: Who Will Shoulder the Growing Burden?" appeared in the *National Journal*, an influential publication in Washington public policy circles.[12] Older people came to be portrayed as one of the more flourishing and powerful groups in American society. This was the result, in part, of the many new government programs. But it was also the result of the growing number of elderly persons and false notions regarding their political behavior.

Suddenly older persons were attacked as too powerful and, at the same time, a burdensome responsibility. Throughout the 1980s and into the 1990s the new stereotypes, readily observed in popular culture, depicted aged persons as prosperous, hedonistic, politically powerful, and selfish. For example, "Grays on the Go," a 1980 cover story in *Time*, was filled with pictures of senior surfers, senior swingers, and senior softball players. The elderly were portrayed as America's new elite—healthy, wealthy, powerful, and "staging history's biggest retirement party."[13]

A dominant theme in such accounts of older Americans was that their selfishness was ruining the nation. The *New Republic* highlighted this motif with a drawing on the cover caricaturing aged persons, accompanied by the caption "greedy geezers." The table of contents' "teaser" for the story that followed announced that "The real me generation isn't the yuppies, it's America's growing ranks of prosperous elderly."[14]

This theme was echoed widely, and the epithet "greedy geezers" became a familiar adjective in journalistic accounts of federal budget politics.[15] In the early 1990s, *Fortune* magazine declaimed that "The Tyranny of America's Old" is "one of the most crucial issues facing U.S. society."[16] These themes concerning seniors have persisted and grown in public discourse over the years. For example, a 2003 story in *Slate* commenting on the costly new legislation that now provides Medicare prescription drug coverage for the elderly was titled "Meet the Greedy Grandparents."[17]

The initial precipitating factor for this reversal of stereotypes was probably the appearance of new concerns regarding Social Security's finances. In 1973 the trustees of the program's trust funds reported for the first time in the program's history a projected deficit, and in the years that followed the projections got worse. An unusual confluence of double-digit rates of inflation with high unemployment (together with problems related to the way benefits were indexed) created the problem. Opponents of Social Security were quick to seize on the problem as evidence that the program might not be able to pay promised benefits, and the media gave this view a lot of attention.

Ultimately the financial situation was addressed by accepting the recommendations of a bipartisan commission chaired by Alan Greenspan, which was assigned the task of working out a solution. These recommendations became law as the Social Security Amendments of 1983. The projections immediately changed for the better, but the public relations damage was done. This financial scare, along with some others that followed, resulted in growing concern among the public, and opinion polls began to show that increasing numbers of people doubted they would get promised benefits.

Two longer-term elements also contributed importantly to the reversal of stereotypes. One was the "graying of the budget," that is, a tremendous growth in the amount and proportion of federal dollars expended on benefits to aging citizens (which, in the late 1970s was about one-quarter of the annual budget and at that time comparable in size to expenditures on national defense).[18] Perhaps the earliest public comment on this trend was by David Broder of the *Washington Post* in 1973: "The significant, semi-hidden story in the ... federal budget is that America's public resources are increasingly being mortgaged for the use of a single group within our country: the elderly."[19]

By the late 1970s and early 1980s other journalists and a number of scholars began to notice and publicize the large proportion of the budget spent on old-age benefits. Economist Barbara Boyle Torrey, for example, pointed up this phenomenon by reframing the classical trade-off of "guns vs. butter" (a common metaphor used in introductory economics courses) to "guns vs. canes."[20]

Another element in the reversal of the stereotypes of old age was the "discovery" of dramatic improvements in the aggregate status of older

Americans, in large measure due to the impact of Social Security and Medicare. The success of these programs had improved the economic status of aged persons to the point where journalists and social commentators could—with only superficial accuracy[21]—describe older people, on average, as more prosperous than the rest of the population.

Intergenerational Equity. In this climate of opinion, public discourse became increasingly hostile to governmental programs benefiting older people. Moreover, the aged emerged as a scapegoat for a wide-ranging list of other American problems. In the mid-1980s, for instance, when it was widely (and erroneously) perceived that Japan had surpassed the United States as the dominant nation in the world economy, former Secretary of Commerce Peter Peterson suggested (believe it or not) that a prerequisite for the United States to regain its stature as a first-class economic power was a sharp reduction in public programs benefiting older Americans.[22]

But a new twist was added to making older people scapegoats for the nation's economic ills. Most of the problems for which older Americans were blamed were portrayed as issues of what was and still is called "intergenerational equity"—or, really, intergenerational *inequity*. At first, these issues of equity were propounded in a contemporary dimension. A number of advocates for children blamed the political power of elderly Americans for the plight of youngsters who had inadequate nutrition, health care, and education, and who also had insufficiently supportive family environments. One children's advocate even proposed that parents receive an "extra vote" for each of their children in order to combat older voters in an intergenerational conflict.[23] This construct of conflict between elders and children was given considerable respectability and momentum in 1984 when demographer Samuel H. Preston, then president of the Population Association of America, erroneously argued that rising poverty among children was the direct (cause-and-effect) result of rising benefits to older people.[24]

Widespread concerns about spiraling American health-care costs were also redirected, in part, from health-care providers, suppliers, administrators, and insurers—the parties that were responsible for setting the prices of care—to elderly persons for whom health care is provided. A number of academicians and public figures, including politicians, expressed concern that health-care expenditures on older persons would soon absorb an unlimited amount of our national resources. It was argued that the elderly were already crowding out health care for others, as well as a variety of additional worthy social causes.[25] A prominent bioethicist, Daniel Callahan, even argued that denying life-saving care to persons aged 80 and older is necessary, desirable, and just.[26]

The construct of intergenerational equity also has a future dimension, focusing on *the impending changes* in the age structure of American society that will be brought about by the aging of the baby boom. One aspect of this issue was highlighted by what was called "generational accounting" analyses. This analytical approach was developed by Boston University economist Laurence Kotlikoff.[27] Though highly controversial,[28] generational accounting statistics have received considerable attention. Kotlikoff projects a bleak financial return from government old-age programs. He argues that future generations of older people will do less well than contemporary older people in terms of the taxes they pay for income security purposes relative to the subsequent lifetime payments they will receive through public programs.

These and other concerns about the future were highlighted by the efforts of an organization that called itself Americans for Generational Equity (AGE). AGE was formed as an interest group in 1985, with backing from the corporate sector as well as from a handful of congressmen who led it. The organization recruited some of the prominent "scapegoaters" of older people, such as demographer Samuel Preston and bioethicist Daniel Callahan, to its board and used them as spokespersons. According to its annual reports, most of AGE's funding came from insurance companies, health-care corporations, banks, and other private sector businesses and organizations that are in financial competition with Medicare and Social Security.[29]

Central to AGE's credo was the proposition that tomorrow's elderly baby boomers will be locked in conflict with younger generations with regard to the distribution of public resources. AGE's basic view was that the large aggregate of public transfers of income and other benefits to older persons was unfair. These transfers, they argued, are financed through inequitable and burdensome taxes on the contemporary labor force—transfers of a magnitude that are unlikely to be available to generations in the future.

AGE disseminated this viewpoint from its Washington office through press releases, media interviews, a quarterly titled *Generational Journal*, a book by one of its members,[30] and periodic conferences on such subjects as "Children at Risk: Who Will Support an Aging Society?" and "Medicare and the Baby Boom Generation."

AGE faded from the scene at the end of the decade. This was primarily the result of internal strife among its key leaders and the disgrace of a principal founder, Minnesota Republican Senator David Durenberger. (In 1990, Senator Durenberger was formally and unanimously "denounced" by a vote of the U.S. Senate for illegal conduct related to the receipt of outside income.)

In 1992, AGE's dismal message regarding the economic and social consequences of maintaining Social Security and Medicare in an aging society was taken up by another organization called the Concord Coalition. The president and a founder of the Concord Coalition is Peter Peterson, who has been an executive in the investment management and financial services industry for many years. The organization is dedicated "to educating the public about the causes and consequences of federal budget deficits, the long-term challenges facing America's unsustainable entitlement programs [read Social Security and Medicare], and how to build a sound economy

Alan Pifer and Lydia Bronte, the editors of an influential 1986 book *Our Aging Society: Paradox and Promise*, sought to alert policymakers and other readers to the problems that might be caused by what they termed *a demographic revolution.* Given the projected future population structure, they asked, "Would such [an aged] society, or anything approaching it, be viable?"[36]

The alarming tenor of this question is typical of most writing on this topic, then and today. The literature on the impact of population aging is now quite large. The writers that we call the Merchants of Doom customarily begin articles and books on the future of aging by pointing out the declining ratio of workers to dependents, linking these changing "dependency ratios" to a so-called economic and political "crisis" looming on the horizon. They see the crisis arising from three trends. First, as we discussed above, there is the long-term decline in fertility rates, which means that the national *proportion* of older persons continues to grow. Second, there is the trend of sharply increasing *absolute numbers* of older persons who will be eligible for old-age programs. And third, there is the substantial increase in average life expectancies at older ages, which means that persons eligible for old-age benefits will be receiving them for longer periods than in the past.

Average life expectancy at age 65, for example, increased by 31 percent from 1950 to 2002. Today, a 67-year-old woman can expect to live on average over 18 years. So when the youngest of the baby boomers has her 67th birthday in 2031, she may very well (given upward trends in longevity) collect Social Security benefits for over two decades (through the year 2050 or longer).[37]

What are the consequences of these demographic changes? If one heeds the Merchants of Doom, the consequences are quite threatening, even frightening, for older people and society in general.

One of them, bioethicist Daniel Callahan, is concerned about health-care expenditures for older people of today and tomorrow. In 1987 he wrote a widely read and influential book titled *Setting Limits: Medical Goals in an Aging Society.* In it he characterized the older population as "a new social threat" and a "demographic, economic, and medical avalanche ... one that could ultimately (and perhaps already) do [sic] great harm."[38] Accordingly, he proposed limits on life-saving health care for elderly persons.

An eminent liberal economist, Lester Thurow, former dean of the school of management at MIT, has constructed an ominous scenario from the demography of population aging. He envisions a revolution: "A new class of people is being created.... It [the elderly class] is a revolutionary class, one that is bringing down the social welfare state, destroying government finances, altering the distribution of purchasing power and threatening the investments that all societies need to make to have a successful future."[39]

Investment industry executive Peter Peterson has written a number of articles and books that present apocalyptic visions of the aging society. One of his latest works is a book titled *Gray Dawn: How the Coming Age Wave Will Transform America—and the World.* The jacket and the title page immediately convey his distressing interpretation of the worldwide consequences of population aging by displaying the following call to arms: "There's an iceberg dead ahead. It's called global aging, and it threatens to bankrupt the great powers. As the populations of the world's leading economies age and shrink, we will face unprecedented political, economic, and moral challenges. But we are woefully unprepared. Now is the time to ring the alarm bell."[40]

Such doomsaying has not been confined to academics, journalists, and other commentators on public affairs. Politicians have also been among the Merchants of Doom. One of the earliest public officials to weigh in with gloomy perspectives on the aging society was Democratic Senator Bob Kerry of Nebraska (now president of The New School in New York). In 1993, when President Clinton was attempting to secure passage of legislation to raise taxes, he needed one more vote in the Senate. Kerry had not committed himself, so he had bargaining leverage with the president. He used it to get Clinton's promise to create a Bipartisan Commission on Entitlement Reform, with Kerry as its chair, in return for the latter's vote on taxes. Entitlement reform, of course, meant Social Security and Medicare reform. To no one's surprise, the Kerry Commission report depicted continuing government financing of pensions and health-care costs for older people as *an unsustainable economic burden* for our nation.[41] Since then, other national politicians have expressed similar concerns about the future of old-age benefit programs.

President George W. Bush strongly entered the fray when he began his second term in 2005, particularly with respect to the future of Social Security. In a campaign without historical precedent, he personally undertook a speaking agenda, described by the White House as "60 stops in 60 days," to decry the status of the Social Security program. He repeatedly asserted that the program was immanently headed for disaster—that it soon would be "flat bust,"[42] and that it was "headed toward bankruptcy."[43] He blatantly ignored the fact that the shortfall, estimated to be around 26 percent, was not projected to begin until the 2040s—more than three decades hence. To undermine confidence in Social Security financing, President Bush undertook a "photo-op" trip to an office building in Parkersburg, West Virginia, home of the U.S. Federal Bureau of Public Debt. There he ceremonially opened a file cabinet holding the U.S. Treasury bonds that have accrued as reserves in the Social Security Trust Funds and declared these U.S. bonds to be worthless; he described them as "just IOUs" and asserted that "there is no trust fund."[44]

This characterization will surprise most people, because U.S. government bonds have long been considered the most creditworthy and safest financial asset that one can hold. But these financial securities held as trust fund privatization of Social Security into personal investment accounts; a third called for investing some of the Social Security trust fund in the stock market (instead of the current investment in U.S. bonds.)[50] Each plan called for investing tens to hundreds of billions of additional dollars in the private sector. Needless to say, many denizens of Wall Street were pleased.

These and subsequent proposals for partial privatization, from both Republicans and Democrats, *have transformed the politics of Social Security reform*. The rapidity with which privatization gained political acceptability was underscored in the spring of 1998 when the Senate passed a resolution calling for private investment accounts to be part of any Social Security reform package.[51] By that summer, President Clinton was seriously considering some form of equity investment as part of Social Security reform.[52]

President Bush picked up this theme during his 2000 election campaign, and in his first year in office he appointed a President's Commission to Strengthen Social Security. The president made sure that only people who supported privatization of Social Security in some form were appointed to the Commission. Not surprisingly, the Commission's report argued that the long-term financial solution was to introduce privatization.[53] But once again there was no unanimous agreement; the Commission's final report presented three alternative strategies.

The fact that the Commission members could not agree and the events related to 9/11 pushed the Commission's report into the background. But, as indicated above, the president was not to be deterred. He made privatization a top priority on his domestic policy agenda as he began his second term. Many groups in the American business community quickly supported the President's efforts, joining a newly created Coalition for the Modernization and Protection of America's Social Security. By early April 2005, the coalition included 116 business associations and interest groups.[54]

"SOLUTIONS" THAT INCREASE RISK?

Political scientist Joseph White has written a book titled *False Alarm: Why the Greatest Threat to Social Security and Medicare is the Campaign to "Save" Them*.[55] His title succinctly conveys some of our concerns about the tenor and direction of today's policy discussions regarding our aging nation.

First, the Merchants of Doom are overstating the problems that population aging creates for Social Security, Medicare, and other old-age programs. Everyone agrees there are financing problems, but they are not caused solely (or primarily) by demography and the baby boomer phenomenon. As the Center on an Aging Society at Georgetown University has demonstrated, "demography is not destiny,"[56] especially with respect to public policies; policies continually change—especially over periods exceeding 20 years. Economist Henry Aaron of the Brookings Institution reminds us that projections in the arena of public policy *almost invariably prove to be wrong*.[57]

A number of factors can render obsolete today's projections regarding the future of old-age programs and opinions about their economic consequences. For example, a higher rate of economic growth could eliminate the Social Security shortfall by exceeding the relatively conservative rate that the Social Security trustees have postulated in making their projections. Or, the present political climate that emphasizes cutting taxes, rather than raising them, could change, making it politically more feasible to use taxes to deal with shortfalls. Consider that President Clinton, not many years ago, succeeded in raising taxes in his first year in office to meet national needs. Not only did he get reelected, but raising taxes did nothing to harm, and may have helped trigger, one of the most prosperous periods in American history.

Second, the radical solutions being offered by the Merchants of Doom would put the old-age benefit programs that helped to make old age the Golden Years at much greater risk than they presently are. For instance, if a portion of the present payroll tax is diverted to set up individual accounts for investment in the market, the projected shortfall in Social Security will occur much sooner than the trustees have projected. This would not only affect the financial security of many baby boomers, but also older people who are already receiving Social Security.

Third, a major reform offered by the doomsayers is to put much more responsibility for retirement financing back into the hands of individuals. If they have their way, ultimately the bulk of retirement savings will be invested in private accounts, with almost all the risks (and there are many) associated with such accounts falling on the individual. Given the risks and complexity of financial planning (and the problems associated with unscrupulous retirement hucksters), the economic future for older people would likely to be very different. Instead of today's financial security in old age, the Merchants' approach could head us in the direction of massive financial insecurity.

Finally, through their apocalyptic warnings the Merchants of Doom are diverting societal attention from reform measures that would enable baby boomers to experience the same moderation of old-age risks that older persons of the past 40 years have experienced. At the same time, they are unnecessarily undermining confidence in and political support for the present system that has served recent generations of older persons so well. If confidence in the present approaches can be maintained, there is much that can be done to deal with the problems that are projected without radical and risky reforms.

THIS BOOK

Many years ago, when the authors of this book told people that we dealt with public policy and aging, they often said: "What does public policy have to do with aging?" Today, hardly any American would ask such a question. Rather, the many journalists, academics, and politicians that we term Merchants of Doom are tireless in warning of very bad times ahead and calling for major changes in policies on aging. They constantly seek to sell us myths that predict extraordinary crises arising from the aging of the baby boomers, resulting (they envision) in the serious disruption of public policies and dire economic, social, and political consequences for the nation.

The Merchants of Doom inspired us to write this book because their gloomy scenarios about the future contain gross exaggerations and, in our opinion, unnecessarily frighten people. Moreover, their assertions about the future promote highly unsound changes in public policy that may do great harm to the country's citizens. They claim, for example, that Social Security will collapse and must be replaced in whole or part. They tell us that policies to deny health care for elders at older ages will be necessary. They argue that future generations must work much longer before they can retire. They say that we should prepare for a politics of class conflict arising between the old and the young. And their special message to baby boomers is that they must bear the brunt of the burden through these cutbacks in pensions, health care, and retirement years.

Certainly we cannot say too many times that there are problems surrounding old age and that policies on aging can be improved. But we do not think that the future is as bleak as the Merchants of Doom would have us believe. Our aim in this book is to help readers sort out the truth from the myths. In doing this, our focus is on the economics and politics of aging. Income is not the only resource contributing to our economic and general welfare in old age.[58] But as Mollie Orshansky (who developed the official U.S. poverty index) has observed, "While money might not be everything, it is way ahead of whatever is in second place."[59]

Given dire predictions about the future, some would have us turn back the clock and shift more responsibility for old age to individuals and their families. However, in this book we will explain why, whether we like it or not, the days of major individual and family provision for old age are gone. As never before, the older people in industrialized nations are now, and will remain, highly dependent on the retirement income and service programs sponsored by their employers and governments. One result is that politics and government play a major and growing role in determining the outcome of what life will be like for us in old age.

The question of a nation's ability to support various age groups and generations at "appropriate levels" is very complex. We argue in this book that much of what is written today on the issue is too simplistic, misleading, and overly pessimistic. There is no doubt that population aging complicates the decisions facing baby boomers and other generations to follow. We argue, however, that the future costs of an aging population and our ability as individuals and a nation to meet these costs depend fundamentally not on demography but on the general *economic health* of the nation and the quality of the programs addressing issues of old age.

In a growing and prosperous country like the United States, almost anything is possible. The major economic issue we need to confront, therefore, is whether we can keep growing and whether we want growth to provide a higher standard of living in our retirement years at the expense of a lower standard in our younger years. We all (governments, businesses, families, and individuals) have to make many major choices. Although trade-offs in governmental and family budgets must be continually made in the short run, rising incomes in retirement are closely related over the long run to the sacrifices we are willing to make in consumption during our earlier years. Focusing our attention almost exclusively on demographics and rising pension costs is a wrong approach. This is especially true if the goal of such a focus is primarily to scare the public as a political way of getting policies and programs changed to better serve certain ideological and/or monetary ends.

Finally, when we try to develop sound aging policies by focusing on people only when they are old, we are missing a critical perspective. Aging is a lifelong phenomenon, with the outcome in old age dependent on decisions made about life at all ages during the life course. Thus, whether we like it or not, the "economics of aging" begins for most of us quite early in life.

In this book, we look closely at how demography and politics are changing the world that baby boomers are aging into. We explain why the demographic aging of our population will cause few major problems and, hence, why demography will have little to do with our future economic prosperity.

If not demography, what? We look in Chapter 8 at what will probably be the most important (and most difficult to solve) domestic issue of the twenty-first century: Who will get quality health care in the United States and how will we deal with skyrocketing health-care costs. While the nation is busy debating the future of old-age pensions and proposed radical change through privatization, there have been no major proposals to address the problems of health-care coverage and costs (while they are getting dramatically worse by the hour).

To the extent that health-care costs are currently addressed, the focus, once again, is on the wrong issue—looking primarily at rising Medicare and Medicaid costs. In truth, the factors causing the rise in the costs of these two programs are, for the most part, the same factors responsible for the rise in overall health-care costs for all age groups. Therefore, as a report by AARP (formerly the American Association of Retired Persons) correctly argues: "It is necessary to address system-wide issues in order to succeed in containing public-sector health care costs. Simply put, the problem is not Medicare and Medicaid—it is our entire health care system, which requires reform and our immediate attention."[60]

Other chapters in this book explain why retirement pensions are so important in modern societies and the problems posed by replacing traditional pensions with "personal pensions." If this trend continues, there will be a big

CHAPTER 2

The Phony Threat of Population Aging

The Old Folks: The myth is that they're sunk in poverty. The reality is that they're living well. The trouble is there are too many of them—God bless 'em.

—Jerry Flint, *Forbes*[1]

Crisis mongering and fact throwing ensure the supply of American public 'problems' will be enormous.

—Marmor, Cook, and Scher[2]

Welcome to the demographic "crisis." In the words of respected economist Lawrence Kotlikoff, welcome to the world of "the coming generational storm."[3]

As we discussed in Chapter 1, a rapid transformation of "the elderly's" public image took place in the late 1970s and 1980s. Post–World War II improvements in Social Security and private pensions reduced the number of elderly living off welfare or supported by their children. For the first time in the nation's history, a majority of the elderly could live independently, with incomes above the poverty level.

But this positive change came at a cost. Public and private pensions began transferring large and ever growing amounts of money to the elderly just at a time when the numbers and proportion of elderly in the population were rising significantly.

At the same time, demographers, policy analysts, and journalists gave increasing attention to what the future would be like when the baby boomers became old. Given the already large costs of income transfers to older person, many were alarmed by the prospects of the many boomers joining the ranks of the elderly. And many observers of public affairs raised issues of equity between generations.

In 1994, journalist Robert J. Samuelson summarized the evolving intergenerational controversy as follows: "Everything about an aging America tells us it contains the seeds of huge social and political problems. Is it fair to impose such large tax burdens on workers to pay for retirees, many [of] whom are now (and will be in the future) relatively healthy and well off?"[4]

Good question. To answer it, we need to begin by looking more closely at the evolving population structure in the United States and its economic and political implications.

WHY WAS MALTHUS WRONG?

In 1798 a young scholar by the name of Thomas Malthus wrote *An Essay on the Principle of Population.* He sought to show that, given "the laws of nature," it is impossible for countries to develop economically with its citizens having equal access to the necessities of life. He argued that a country cannot increase its means of subsistence (economic output) as fast as the country's population will increase. According to Malthus, populations will always expand to the limits imposed by a lagging means of subsistence.

As demographer David Price points out, "These ideas were not original with Malthus; they had been clearly enunciated by others, including Adam Smith (1776), whose work he knew well."[5] The major contribution Malthus made to the discussion was to focus on, and write extensively about, the social and economic limits to economic welfare that were imposed by population growth. In this regard, Malthus' arguments fed into the intellectual and political debate of the time about how best to promote what Adam Smith called *The Wealth of Nations.*

Malthus predicted an "inevitable" increase in population that would "inevitably" make everyone in a country poorer. Moreover, he argued that some would be poorer than others. Significant social inequality would arise, he wrote, with the emergence of an underclass perennially afflicted by misery and vice.

Events of the day seemed to prove him correct. After nearly two centuries of relative stability, the population in England began to grow. And as economic journalist David Warsh points out, population doubled between 1780 and 1800, prices soared, and poverty dramatically increased. "There were mutinies and riots and summonses to revolution."[6]

Political conservatives seized on Malthus' population determinism. They used it as an argument against developing social policies to help the poor— since according to Malthus, poverty could not be prevented. Others criticized his views. They saw them as undermining attempts to develop policies and programs that would help the lower classes. Increasing numbers of people saw the need to deal with the often horrible pain and insecurity associated with the birth of industrial capitalism and the unpredictable vicissitudes of market-dominated economies.

Of course, Malthus' predictions proved to be wrong. Even as the pain and insecurity rose, the country was beginning the great transformation called "the industrial revolution." The populations of the industrializing countries did increase dramatically over the years, but at the same time economic growth surged ahead even more dramatically. The resulting economic prosperity raised the living standards for all age groups and has done so at all socioeconomic levels. And in industrialized countries, it has eliminated most, but not all, of the most abject poverty.

Where did Malthus go wrong? Certainly it would have been difficult for him to foresee the spectacular increases in productive capacity that arose out of the Industrial Revolution, which included a dramatic mechanization of food production. His focus was only on agriculture and mining, the country's two principal economic activities before industrialization.

Nor did he anticipate the related decline in women's fertility that occurred with the changing nature of their social roles. Women's new roles were the result of the disappearing agrarian society, rising incomes, better access by women to education, changes in attitudes about reproduction, emergent birth control options, and a growing variety of attractively paid work opportunities for women.

Among the many new results of this changing reality was a slow but steady decline in the average number of babies born to women in England, the United States, and other industrializing countries. In the United States, the fertility rate fell steadily during the first half of the twentieth century, rose briefly during the postwar "baby boom" years from 1946 to 1964, and then began to fall again. The fertility rate (measuring the average number of births for a woman throughout her childbearing years) reached a historic low of 1.7 children by the mid-1970s. It then increased slightly—finally seeming to level off to around 2.1. Thus, we find that the United States' current rate coincides with the rate at which the average number of births results over the long run in a steady (constant) number of people in the population. This rate is called "the replacement rate" by demographers (see Figure 2.1).

Here then is the source of the demographic aging of our nation. As eminent demographer Ansley Coale explains, "Whether a national population is young or old is mainly determined by the number of children women bear.... The high fertility population has a larger proportion of children relative to adults of parental age as a direct consequence of the greater frequency of births.... On the other hand, prolonged low fertility produces a small proportion of children and a large proportion of the aged—a high average."[7] That is, the fertility rate has a much greater impact on the age structure of the overall population than the other major factors shaping our demographic profile—living longer and immigration into the United States.

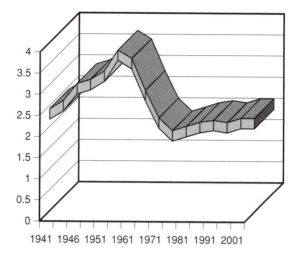

Figure 2.1. Total fertility rate, 1941–2001. Note: Rate is the average number of children that would be born to a woman during her lifetime. *Source:* Data from the U.S. National Center for Health Statistics.

In 2005, the elderly aged 65 and over were about 12 percent of the population, with 4 million over the age of 85 and 50,000 who were centenarians.[8] The U.S. Census Bureau projects that by 2030, the share of the 65+ population will have risen to around 20 percent. And if one gets out the magic looking glass, stretches current trends, and makes some reasonable demographic assumptions, the Census Bureau says we might see at the turn of the century a country with nearly one-quarter of its population aged 65 or older.

THE THREE DEMOGRAPHIC TRENDS

Thus, the twentieth century witnessed the beginning of a gradual "graying" of the population which will continue far into the future. We saw it coming. For decades now, experts have forecast the impending population change and raised concern about possible problems.

Once again, as in Malthus' days, we are being confronted with a kind of demographic determinism. We are warned, for example, of "The Gray Peril." It is customary for doomsayers to begin any writing on the future of aging by mentioning "the crisis" looming on the horizon, resulting from three trends. First, as we described above, there is the long-term decline in fertility rates, coupled with a steady rise in average life expectancy. Second, there is the dramatic decline in the average age of retirement (discussed at length in Chapter 7). And finally, there is the trend of *sharply increasing* numbers of older persons as a result of the impending retirement of the baby boom generation. It is true that all three trends contribute to what is called the "population aging" (many say "population crisis") of America.

Almost all writings on population aging start by projecting the results of current demographic trends into future decades. They then point out the important impact that the resulting population structure may have ("is going to have") on the economy and relations between generations. The debate about population aging is dominated by dire prophesies:

- Every future worker will have to support too many retired people.
- Social Security will go bankrupt and will not be there when younger workers retire.
- The *entire* federal budget will ultimately have to go to pay for entitlements.
- Government support for older people at more than minimal levels will come at the expense of our children and grandchildren.
- Population aging will destroy our nation's global competitiveness, perpetuating the curse of low growth and a shrinking economic pie.

The predictions of calamities by the Merchants of Doom have fallen on receptive ears, in part because they argue that the survival of some of our most important social and economic ideals is at stake. They warn that population aging will seriously undermine our efforts to compete in the new global marketplace—threatening future economic growth, and hence, the "American dream" that each generation will have a standard of living better than its predecessor. In fact, the seriousness of the situation has been characterized by *Forbes* magazine with the frightening image that we will end up "consuming our own children," with a resulting progressive immiserization of future generations.[9] And, as if that were not enough, many experts argue that one of America's most popular institutions, Social Security, is unsustainable and will become a "bad deal" for future generations—if it is able to survive at all. No wonder these Merchants of Doom have gotten the attention of politicians and ordinary citizens.

Given the emotional, nonanalytical, apocalyptic nature of these predictions—one might be tempted to dismiss them out of hand and search for a more balanced discussion of the issues. But these predictions cannot be dismissed so easily, since today they represent the currently accepted opinion of most policymakers and much of the American population.

For decades there has been a kind of holy war designed to "wake up" and "educate" Americans to the supposed dangers resulting from the aging of the U.S. population. This campaign actually promotes the *intergenerational conflict* many of the doomsayers predict (but which most would agree does not yet exist). And by encouraging confrontation between age groups over the distribution of the nation's output, it undermines the already tenuous national sense of community and social solidarity.

DEMOGRAPHY IS NOT DESTINY

If you want to understand the issues surrounding possible generational conflict and economic crisis arising from population aging, we agree that the place to start (but not end!) with is demographics. Those who talk about the unsustainable economic "burden" of the elderly, for example in terms of pension and medical costs, invariably point to the importance of the nation's changing population structure to support their views. Thus, researchers from the Urban Institute (a Washington think tank) warn: "The real bottom line is adjusting to lower mortality and fertility rates. In a world in which people live longer and have fewer children, we have to stop imagining that those children will be able to support their parents during ever-longer retirements. Thinking that this [coming crisis] is just a Social Security issue is like believing that Cinderella's only issue was her shoe size."[10]

A recent report published by the National Academy on an Aging Society cautions, however, that "demography is not destiny."[11] We agree. Demography is the place to *start,* but one cannot stop there. In this chapter we suggest that the fears of AGE, Samuelson, *Forbes,* and other Merchants of Doom are overstated, that the nature of the "demographic aging problem" is also frequently misstated, and that many of the complexities of analysis related to this issue are often ignored. More importantly, as we argue later in this chapter, the future economic well-being of the whole population (of all ages) has very little to do with "population aging" and much to do with technological change, investments in people (education) and businesses (plant and equipment), management skills, and many other *nonaging* factors—factors that in large part determine the rate of economic growth.

POPULATION DECLINE

The first policy lesson from past demographic studies is that the major factors affecting population change (such as the fertility rate) are almost impossible to project accurately. Few, if any, of the major demographic changes of the past century were foreseen by population experts. There have been many demographic surprises over the years—changes intimately related to social and economic developments.

For example, to the surprise of most demographers, the largest numerical population increase in the history of the United States occurred over the past century (1900 to 2000). The nation grew by 205 million, from 76 million in 1900 to 281 million in 2000—far greater than anyone predicted.[12] At the moment, the population of the United States is aging, but it is certainly not yet shrinking; it reached 298 million in 2006.[13]

Similarly, the world population is increasing rapidly. It was about 6.5 billion in 2006. That is over 3.5 times the size of the world population at the beginning of the twentieth century and roughly double its size in 1960.

"Never before has the earth sustained such a large human population."[14] And never before has there been such pressure and drain on the planet's ecosystems and resources.

Hence, it is surprising that currently, in contrast to the past, population *decrease* is the main concern in many nations. Given the dramatic drop in the number of children women are having in various countries, the absolute number of people in some countries has started to actually decline—including in Japan, Germany, and Russia. In Japan the 2005 population of about 127 million was 19,000 lower than what it was in 2004.[15] And in Germany, the population has been declining since 2003, together with a massive shift of population from areas of former East Germany to the more prosperous western part of the country.

Between 1992 (shortly after the dissolution of the USSR) and 2003, the Russian population declined by about 4 million people. Moreover, the population is projected to decline further, a total of 19–21 million between the years 2000 and 2025.[16] Russian president, Vladimir Putin, has described the decline as a "creeping catastrophe."[17] The reason for Russia's sharp decline, according to the National Bureau of Asian Research, is "remarkably low birth rates" and "terrifying high death rates."[18]

Fertility rates in most European countries have been much lower than in the United States. The U.S. fertility rate is close to 2.1, the rate required to keep the population steady. In contrast, Spain, Italy, and Greece (which have the lowest fertility in Europe) have rates between 1.1 and 1.3.[19] Between 2000 and 2050, "the population of the 27 countries that should be members of the EU by 2007 is predicted to fall by 6%, from 482m to 454m. For countries with particularly low fertility rates, the decline is dramatic. By 2050 the number of Italians may have fallen from 57.5m in 2000 to around 45m [in 2050]."[20]

Even in most developing countries, populations are aging, often quite rapidly. However, rather than being pleased that the problems and threats from "overpopulation" are moderating, the slowdown and ultimate decline in population size is beginning to worry many people. Some see it as a prelude to a decline in various nations' geopolitical clout. Businessmen are concerned about shrinking markets. But the most often voiced concern is that population decline goes hand in hand with lower growth and economic decline, effects compounded by population aging.[21]

VOODOO DEMOGRAPHICS

Whether it is population decline or just "population aging," the discussion in most of the recent books and articles on the economic impact of population aging are highly speculative. They are supported by very little sophisticated research. There have been frequent examinations of *demographic* statistics but almost no *economic* analysis of the evolving situation. A kind of "voodoo demographics" has developed that raises the specter of an intolerable economic burden arising from growing numbers of older people—resulting in the emergence of intergenerational conflict.

Most of these dire predictions rely heavily (often exclusively) on "dependency ratio" statistics. Dependency ratios crudely measure the ratio of working age individuals to those people in the population, of any age, who are not working. Dependency ratios are useful for indicating changes in the age composition of the population over time. This enables policymakers to make crude estimates of the speed at which economic support relationships have changed in the past and are expected to change in the future. But they must be used with great caution. As explained below, it is important to remember that the validity of dependency ratio analysis rests on a number of key, often suspect, assumptions.

The Aged "Dependents". The most frequently cited (but most misleading) statistic is the *aged* dependency ratio. This is the ratio you are likely to read about in newspapers and magazines. The ratio is the number of individuals who are age 65 or older divided by the number of people "of working age" (20 to 64)—the result then multiplied by 100. Using the age distribution of the population, it is a crude measure of the number of workers potentially available to support the elderly population. That is, it is a ratio that attempts to measure the number of older persons in the society, assumed not to be producing output, relative to those assumed to be doing the producing.

Almost every prediction of demographic doom starts with this basic statistic. For example, in 2000 the aged dependency ratio was 20 (i.e., 20 elderly persons for every 100 people of working age). It is projected that this ratio will rise eighty years later to a little over 40 in 2080.[22]

A related statistic often cited is a measure of Social Security dependency. In the year 2040, given current Social Security law, there will be only 2.0 workers per Social Security recipient—in contrast to the current level of 3.3 workers per recipient.[23] The United States has a partial pay-as-you-go Social Security financing system. Most payroll taxes go immediately to meet current obligations. The Social Security dependency ratio tells us that in the future there will be a declining number of workers paying payroll taxes relative to the number of retirees receiving benefits.

The truth, however, is that aged dependency ratios are simplistic, one-sided, and misleading. As Brookings Institution economist, Henry Aaron, argued almost two decades ago, it is clear that "statistics showing that the working age population is going to suffer a heavy burden because the number of elderly is going up are so misleading as to verge on deception. To be sure, the number of elderly will rise and so will the ratio of the elderly

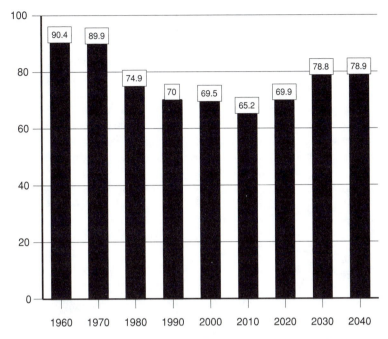

Figure 2.2. "Dependents" per 100 Workers Aged 20 to 64. *Source: 1977 Annual Report of the Board of Trustees of the Federal OASDI Trust Funds*, as presented in National Academy on an Aging Society. *Demography Is Not Destiny.* Washington, DC: The Academy, 1999.

to the nonelderly adult population. But [at the same time] the proportion of children is going down."[24]

Count Children Too. In almost all industrial countries of the world, the *total* dependency ratio (which combines both young and elderly "dependents") is actually quite low, much lower than in the past, and much lower than currently exists, for example, in many developing countries (with large numbers of children).[25] That is, we have already experienced periods in our history when the total dependency ratio was higher than the projected future ratios that the Merchants of Doom are worrying about. Moreover, the "total dependency ratio" (i.e., a ratio that includes nonworkers at all ages) has been declining in the United States. Projections indicate that this ratio will soon begin rising (around the year 2010). However, if the projections are correct, *it will never surpass the high levels reached around 1960* when most of the baby boomers were "dependent" children (Figure 2.2).

Some say in this context, children are analytically irrelevant and not a problem, because they are mostly supported by their parents. But in terms of economic demands on society's resources, it is numbers and consumption that count, not who pays. Of course, who pays is an important political issue (which we discuss later).

Count All Workers. But the total dependency ratio also leaves something to be desired. Some elderly and teenagers work; some adults in the so-called "working years" cannot or do not. Thus, an even better measure of dependency is one where the ratio takes into account who is *actually in the labor force* for all age cohorts. Projections of this "labor force dependency ratio" (measuring those who are not in the labor force against those who are) indicate that for all ages the labor force dependency ratio is expected to decline until around the year 2010. After that year, the ratio increases but again does not surpass the high levels reached in the early 1960s. When we look at people working and not working in all age groups (children, youths, middle-aged adults, and the elderly), increases in the numbers of aged not working are to some extent counterbalanced by declines in the number of nonworkers in the other age groups. Projections indicate that the total *labor force* dependency ratio *declines* from about 15 in 1960 to about 11 in 2020. From 2000 to 2020, the total ratio is influenced by the baby boom generation and rises only slightly.[26] So, again, what is the problem?

The problem is the active efforts of many individuals and groups to convince us that there is a crisis that needs radical solutions. The aged dependency ratio is nearly always the first statistic presented to identify the supposed crisis we face and to confirm the need for a solution based on private market programs. Many Merchants of Doom, with strong affinities for, and specific ties to, large private sector interests—Peter Peterson is a good example—use aged dependency ratio statistics to hype the dire consequences of population aging.[27] This misleading framework lays political groundwork for arguments to privatize Social Security and Medicare.

The Need for Economic Analysis. There is an even more important matter to consider when constructing dependency ratios. An economic analysis of the impact of population changes is crucial but technically a far bigger challenge to estimate than simply presenting demographic dependency ratios. One of the most important limitations of typical dependency ratio statistics is the assumption made that per person costs associated with different types of "dependent persons" are the same. As we have discussed above, there may be a generally offsetting demographic decline in the number of children as the number of older people increases. But what does that mean in economic terms? Is the amount of the economic resources consumed in a year the same for babies as for old people? For preschoolers? For teenagers? For college students? For mothers at home with their children?

Obviously not. Individuals consume (use up economic resources) at different rates at different stages of the life cycle. Dependency measures need to take that reality into account.

In an earlier book, *Economics of Population Aging*, Schulz (with others) reported on their research where demographic data are weighted to reflect the "private support costs" associated with different age groups of nonworking persons and to show the potential effect on economic growth.[28] Based on this extension of the demographic statistics to include economic differences, the research concludes, first, "that the economic impact of demographic aging is not as bad as those doomsayers who use simplistic dependency ratios would have us believe"; and second that, "as in other areas of social policy, relatively small increases in economic growth rates have the potential to substantially moderate the ill effects of other factors that have a negative impact." In fact, these economists conclude from their research that the future overall economic "support burden" in the United States will be less in the years 2030–2050 than it was during 1950–1970.[29]

Economic Growth and Population Change. This brings us to the matter of economic growth. Most important of all is the fact that nearly all reported dependency ratios fail to take account of economic growth—growth that will lower the support "burden" associated with rising aged dependency. For example, look at how our national economic output has been changing over time. In 1964, the parents of the baby boomers enjoyed a per capita GDP of $12,195. Assuming less than two percent annual growth, the retired boomers and their children will be living in a country where the year 2030 per capita income (inflation adjusted) will be almost three times as large ($35,659).[30] Other issues aside, in which period would you rather be living?

Without doubt, growth matters. It really matters! So what is the effect of population change on economic growth? Is it a big negative factor?

Economists have been debating this question since the field of economics first began. One of the nation's top experts on population economics, Richard A. Easterlin, has done research that indicates that population growth is not necessary for economic growth. Analyzing economic data over the past 100 years for the United States and ten European countries, he finds a generally consistent *inverse* relationship between trends in economic growth and population growth—that is, economic growth has generally risen at the same time that population growth was falling. As Easterlin points out, this "is just the opposite of what one would have expected if declining population growth were exerting a serious drag on the economy." Moreover, based on the historical data, Easterlin concludes that "one would be hard put to argue that dependency had much to do with the dramatic post-1973 drop in economic growth rates, and, not surprisingly, it is never mentioned in scholarly attempts to explain this decline."[31]

This is a very important conclusion, one that warrants more detailed examination. In the next section we look at the factors important for economic growth and the small role that Social Security and population aging play in the process.

SAVING, ECONOMIC GROWTH, AND POPULATION AGING

Economists have given a lot of attention to the role played by saving in the economic growth process. If saving, for example, is reduced by population aging, then economic growth might be negatively affected as a result of lower investment.

The potential impact of demographic aging on saving and growth has been a major issue in the debate over Social Security for many decades. Contemporary calls for privatization of Social Security are motivated in part by a desire to ensure that retirement pension programs do nothing to diminish saving and growth.

Why do economists think saving is so important for growth? Here is the way one Nobel Laureate economist, James M. Buchanan, explained the growth process in an article directed at noneconomists:

> The act of saving allows for a release of resources into the production of capital rather than consumer goods. This increase in capital inputs into the market operates in essentially the same fashion as an increase in the supply of labor inputs. The increase in capital expands the size of the economy and this, in turn, allows for an increased exploitation of the division and specialization of resources. The economic value of output per unit of input expands, and *this result ensures that all persons in the economic nexus, whether they be workers, savers, or consumers, are made better off and on their own terms.*[32] [emphasis added]

Buchanan's certainty that saving expands production is not shared by all economists, however. The literature on the determinants of economic growth is extensive, complicated, and often highly sophisticated—but also highly controversial, and generally inconclusive. One would never know that, however, from reading the policy prescriptions given by so many economists today. The complexities and inconclusiveness of economic theory and empirical work on economic growth are generally ignored when it comes to making policy recommendations.

It is not that saving does not matter. Economists today are generally unanimous in pointing to the value of increased saving in order to increase investment and promote economic growth. The overemphasis given by some economists to saving results in part from a long tradition in economics. Both traditional neoclassical growth theory and much of the more recent growth theory focus on the role of saving and investment. As economist Robert A. Blecker points out: "Since the late 1970s, mainstream macroeconomics has been dominated by a conservative policy consensus, which emphasizes raising national saving rates and avoiding government intervention in financial or labor markets."[33]

Thus, it is not surprising to find great concern about Social Security among those economists who believe that this major government program reduces aggregate saving and thereby reduces economic growth. For example, University of Michigan economist Edward M. Gramlich, after chairing the 1996–1997 Social Security Advisory Council, wrote:

> In the end the most profound impact of Social Security on the economy, for good or ill, is its impact on national saving and investment. In the long run the most important policy-controlled determinant of a country's living standards is its national saving ratio, according to neoclassical growth models of the sort that were developed by Robert Solow.... The United States now saves an extraordinarily low share of its national output. The disappointing aspect of this low national saving is that as long as it persists, living standards are not likely to rise very rapidly in the future.[34]

The research on Social Security and saving is inconclusive. Yet Gramlich assumes Social Security means lower saving. And, therefore, he asserts that this lower saving translates into slower growth and results in a slower rise in living standards. Note that there are no ifs, ands, or buts in the Gramlich quote reproduced above. Low saving equals low growth! Therefore, in the Advisory Council he chaired, Gramlich argued for mandatory "individual accounts" managed by the government, as a supplement to Social Security retirement benefits.

As we will show below, these simplistic and dogmatic articulations of the sources of economic growth ignore decades of research and debate following Nobel Laureate economist Robert Solow's insightful, but seriously deficient, early modeling of the economic growth process. There are many important factors determining the rate of growth of a nation's economy.[35] To imply that saving is the only one, or that it is the most important one, is simply bad economics.

Unfortunately, Gramlich's views are highly representative of the current views of so many other economists. For example, eminent Harvard economist and former chairman of the President's Council of Economic Advisers, Martin Feldstein, has written many articles promoting privatization of Social Security. He asserts, for example, "There is, however, no doubt that the net effect of the transition from the PAYGO [pay-as-you-go] funding of the Social Security] system to the prefunded PRA [Personal Retirement Accounts] system would be a rise in national saving *and therefore* a larger capital stock and a higher level of real national income."[36] [emphasis added]

It is our opinion, however, that this almost exclusive attention to saving produces a highly biased view of the question. It is one that seriously distorts the policy discussions about population aging, economic growth, and elderly income support policies.

Why do economists think saving is so important? To paraphrase the explanation by James Buchanan (quoted above), the answer given is that saving is necessary if there is to be investment by businesses in new factories and equipment. Saving is defined as the amount of current income that is not spent (not consumed) on finished goods and services over some specified time period. As Buchanan points out, the economic resources of a nation (its land, labor, and capital) are limited and can be used to produce goods that are consumed and used up or, alternatively, to produce goods that can be used to produce greater quantities of goods in the future ("capital goods"). Saving is necessary for investment, and investment potentially results in new productive capacity that can be the basis for economic growth in future years. So from an economic growth perspective, saving is a good thing. Clearly in times of robust employment, it is better than no saving or low saving.

But the definitional relationship— saving *always* results in investment *always* results in growth— is too simplistic for making policy decisions. This view of saving is a far cry from the real world. There is not just one factor (saving) or two factors (saving and investment) that are the key determinants of growth. While saving and investment are necessary, they are not sufficient enough for us to be sure that the rate of growth will be adequate to achieve any set of goals. There are many other factors that are as important—or perhaps more important. Paradoxically, all economists know this, which makes one wonder why so many of them have chosen to ignore the other factors (discussed below) when the question of population aging comes up. As Columbia University economist Richard Nelson (who has served on the Council of Economic Advisers and is a specialist on economic growth) observes, "The key intellectual challenge to formal growth theory. . . lies in learning how to formally model entities that are not easily reduced to a set of numbers, such as the character of a nation's education or financial system or the prevalent philosophy of management."[37]

THE SOURCES OF GROWTH

One of the giants of economics, Alfred Marshall, wrote many years ago in his *Principles of Economics*: "Knowledge is the most powerful engine of production; it enables us to subdue nations and satisfy our wants."[38] His statement reminds us that the job of dealing with any economic strain arising from the baby boom and population aging does not rest solely on increasing saving.

All one has to do is look around at businesses that succeed and fail to see that saving is only one of many factors important for innovation and growth. Twenty-five years ago, America was the leader in tire production around the world, and Akron, Ohio was the tire capital—with four of the five biggest tire companies in the country. As an article in the *Economist* points out: "Now only one of those firms, Goodyear, remains both American and a market leader. Akron was undermined by Americans' enthusiasm for longer-lasting radial tyres [sic] after the 1973 oil shock. The problem was not that Akron's firms did not know how to make radial tyres; the technology was decades old. What they were unable to do was *adjust their business model*, which relied on short-lived tyres." [emphasis added][39]

The American tire industry did not decline because of a lack of available saving; these companies were huge and had been profitable in the past, with lots of retained earnings available for capital investments. What was missing was the right combination of entrepreneurial judgment, risk-taking, and successful managerial skills.

In the same *Economist* article, there is a discussion of the many reasons why businesses have been thriving in the Silicon Valley:

> To an unusual degree Silicon Valley's economy relies on what Joseph Schumpeter, an Austrian economist, called "creative destruction." Some modern writers have rechristened the phenomenon "flexible re-cycling," but the basic idea is the same: old companies die and new ones emerge, allowing capital, ideas, and people to be reallocated. An essential ingredient in this is the presence of entrepreneurs, and a culture that attracts them.
>
> Research has increasingly concentrated in clusters ... where there is "something in the air" that encourages risk-taking. This suggests that culture, irritatingly vague though it may sound, is more important to Silicon Valley's success than economic or technological factors.[40]

The *Economist* also points out that there has been no shortage of saving (in the form of venture capital for investment). Funds continue to flow into the Silicon Valley, fluctuating with general economic conditions.

Economic journalist David Warsh recently wrote a detailed history about the evolution of economic growth theory. He argues that "the most recent discovery, the one that has not been obvious [to economists] all along, is that, in a rapidly converging global economy, capital will by and large take care of itself (with an occasional nudge from central banks)."[41]

The early neoclassical growth models that Gramlich refers to focused exclusively on labor and capital—ignoring as *explanatory* factors the impact of how businesses are organized, technological change, and the growth of knowledge over time.[42] For many years, economist Richard Nelson, among others, has pointed out the complexities of growth and the key role played by factors other than saving. He argues that many economists' models treat businesses as if they were machines that can be turned on and off with the flick of a switch. These economists ignore empirical research that clearly documents the fact that businesses are social systems—systems that are often resistant or unresponsive to management commands.[43] What might be called "management style or entrepreneurship," for example, can make a big difference in the success or failure of a firm.

What about "knowledge"—the education of the workforce and the development of a scientific base for facilitating and stimulating the use of new technologies? As Alfred Marshall and many other economists have pointed out, it is vitally important to spend sufficient societal resources on human capital, and government policies on education clearly have been responsive to that goal. "All over the world it is taken for granted that educational achievement and economic success are closely linked—that the struggle to raise a nation's living standards is fought first and foremost in the classroom."[44]

In the more recent theoretical work of Stanford economist Paul Romer, a broader concept of the economics of knowledge (and through it innovation) has been put forward and has been credited with major importance. For Romer (and others), knowledge, education, technological change, and entrepreneurship together form a powerful set of factors promoting economic growth. Years ago, the Austrian School of economists (such as Joseph Schumpeter, Ludwig von Mises, and Friedrich Hayek) recognized this in their writings. And this tradition or focus (i.e., a strong emphasis on the role of knowledge and discovery) has continued within the modern Austrian "school of economics"—what the Austrians call "entrepreneurial discovery."[45] It is a focus sorely missing (until recently) in American mainstream economics.

Again, we want to emphasize that we are not saying that economists in the United States have completely ignored the role of technology, risk-taking, and entrepreneurship. Rather, we argue that the importance of these factors is frequently missing from, or downplayed, in most Social Security policy discussions.

Our discussion here has only skimmed the surface in describing the many factors important to promoting economic growth; the list of factors is very long. Our primary purpose, however, is to merely show that not only is most of "the-burden-of-the-elderly" literature overly simplistic, it encourages us to look for solutions in the wrong places.

In summary, increasing economic growth rates is a very complex task and one still not well understood. Yet, good public policy requires recognizing those complexities and articulating them to the general public. Today, as ever, the most important determinants of the future economic welfare of people (of all ages) are those that influence the rate of growth: technological change, entrepreneurial initiatives and risk-taking, managerial skills, government provision of infrastructure, saving, investment in human and business capital, labor-force participation levels, and so on. *The debate over how best to run an economic system is concerned with far more than is-sues of aging (or Social Security).* In fact, Social Security and the aging of populations have relatively little to do with the outcome.

University of London economist Richard Disney's book, *Can We Afford to Grow Older?*, is a comprehensive and careful review of the relevant liter-ature on "the economics of aging." He concludes that "there is no 'crisis of aging.' Although many countries now exhibit dramatic demographic transi-tions, talk of a 'crisis of aging' is overblown..." And "there is no evidence of adverse effects of aging on aggregate productivity. Microeconomic and macroeconomic studies have failed to uncover any convincing evidence that differences in demographic structure between countries and over time are a major factor in determining productivity levels."[46]

THE POLITICS OF POPULATION AGING

But even if the economic requirements are manageable, the changing com-position of the support burden has major political and corporate policy dimensions. Parents directly pay for most of the expenditures on children (education in the early years is usually the big exception). In contrast, the elderly receive much of their economic support through employer-sponsored programs and government programs supported by various taxes. Much of the concern about the future burden of the elderly should be interpreted as concern about governments' ability to tax (that is, voters' willingness to pay higher taxes). Also, as we discuss in Chapter 5, there is concern about em-ployers' growing efforts to transfer most of the responsibility (and risk) to their employees for meeting the needs of groups like the aged who in today's world rely heavily on payments outside the family. In this era, when tax reductions (rather than increases) are being presented as the only option, the politics of population aging is very much in doubt.

lodged together with criminals or people with totally different needs. Yet the poor farm was the only option for the elderly, unless they had a family capable of taking care of them.

In a little more than a 100 years there has been a dramatic change in what happens to us when we grow older. This chapter is about that change.

THE MISERY OF BEING OLD IN EARLY AMERICA

Before Social Security and pensions, life in old age among older Americans was typically not very pleasant. When early America was basically agrarian, many of the older people who owned land did relatively well—at least until their health turned bad. Most historians agree, however, that with the coming of industrialization there was a fairly steady decline in the status and circumstances of the elderly.[4] Landless workers were at the mercy of a very harsh but highly productive market system that rewarded and punished people according to their usefulness to the production process. Older workers were unable to easily compete in the new industrial environment and were often "discarded"—forced to survive on economic resources other than from jobs in the market economy. More often than not, they sank into economic deprivation.

Suppose an older person had inadequate money, income, or savings and was unable to survive independently. In early America, one of three things typically happened. Most were taken care of by their children. If that was not possible, in colonial times the town that older persons lived in took over their remaining land and other assets and then "boarded them out" to some family in town.

In fact, believe it or not, "it was not unusual to auction off the needy... to the lowest bidder."[5] The successful bidder agreed to provide room and board for a specific period, usually a year. The successful bidder was then permitted to put the person to work without pay—in return for providing food, shelter, clothing, and health care. Thus, the quality of life of many elderly was largely dependent on the kindness, fairness, and economic situation of their "masters."

Yes, this system was actually a form of indentured servitude. "It sounds a lot like slavery—except that it was technically not for the pauper's entire lifetime."[6]

In such a world, imagine the fear and horror associated with growing old and poor. Sociologist Jill Quadagno helps us understand what it was like by describing the plight of one aged couple living in Massachusetts in the eighteenth century. Their story is not fiction but one depressing example of what could, and often did, happen to many older people in early America:

> Barnet and Sarah Campbell, an aging couple, applied to the town for poor relief, expecting to receive outdoor relief [that is, money assistance while continuing to live in their home]. Instead, the Overseens of

the Poor ordered them to the workhouse. Barnet Campbell protested before the Berkshire County Sessions court, arguing that "instead of that kindness and tenderness which Old Age and impaired health required and that provision and support which human nature Demands, [we] have been treated with ... roughness, threatened with the workhouse, whips and chains ... and left without any support." To prove that he was not among the idle poor, he obtained depositions from twenty-three friends who testified to his good moral character and frugal nature. Although the justices agreed that the Campbells did not deserve confinement in the workhouse, the overseers refused to grant them outdoor relief.[7]

Starting in the middle part of the nineteenth century, poor older people might be sent to these "workhouses." These institutions were hailed by the elite as a more efficient, effective, and cheaper way of dealing with the poor. The principal aim of these institutions was *not* to help people in economic distress. Instead, according to the officials who supported them, the principal function of workhouses was to reform and cure the poor of their bad habits and character defects—the habits and defects assumed to be the main causes of their poverty.

Even in the nineteenth century, the amount and type of welfare assistance was subject to the vagaries of public officials. State and local governments were reluctant to provide money to the elderly so that they could continue to live a relatively normal life in the community. Moreover, the local welfare setup was rife with corruption, often depleting most of the already minuscule funds made available by the community to help the aged and other needy.

Eventually the workhouses began to wind-up, but they were replaced by new institutions. Instead of workhouses there were now poor farms (like the Minnesota one described above), "almshouses," and "asylums." Some of these institutions were administered in a fair and caring way. Others, however, were houses of degradation, disease, near-starvation, and corruption. It is hard for us to believe today that the responsible officials often crowded people who were simply poor (young and old) into the same building with the mentally ill, other ill or seriously disabled persons, and even criminals.

Bruce Vladeck, former head of the U.S. Health Care Financing Administration (1993–1997), describes the early history of elderly care in his book *Unloving Care: The Nursing Home Tragedy*: "Although poverty among the elderly was often depicted as the product of 'imprudence' in failing to set aside adequate savings, there seemed to be general agreement that chronic illness constituted a legitimate exception to the structure of Puritan 'deservingness.' A major theme in the growing criticism of the almshouse system was the way it housed frail older people ... cheek to jowl with the retarded, insane, and immoral."[8]

It was not until the Progressive Era of the early twentieth century, however, that the administration of welfare began to shift from the hands of the often corrupt local officials to state agencies that, it was hoped, would be less corrupt. And for the first time, there was a significant amount of discussion about helping the aged with something called a "pension."

The first pensions in the United States were the payments made to veterans of the Civil War. The legislation to authorize these Civil War pensions was enacted in 1862. Later, some people voiced the view that all older people should receive a pension payment similar to the Civil War pensions, payments in a form that preserved the dignity and self-respect of the elderly. Some argued that pensions could be constructed that would place "no greater burden on the community as a whole" than the prevailing welfare system.[9] Initially, however, these proposals got nowhere.

Throughout the nineteenth century, the resources of people when they reached old age continued to be minimal. Thus, it is no surprise to find that in 1900, more than 60 percent of persons aged 65 and older in the United States were living with their children. They were simply too poor to live independently and stayed with children to avoid having to go into the horrible institutions created by the government.[10] It was with the establishment of Social Security in the 1930s that the notion of a right to a pension through work first became a reality for many older Americans.

But Social Security was not an American invention.

THE INVENTION OF SOCIAL SECURITY

It was the year 1881. On a cold winter night in early February, 500 guests gathered in Berlin, Germany, for an evening of exchanging pleasantries, a buffet dinner, and, of course, the customary political gossiping.[11] The party was hosted by members of the German parliament. However, one man dominated the scene—Chancellor Otto von Bismarck.

About 30 years before that evening, the young Bismarck had emerged onto the political scene. He entered during a period of dramatic European upheaval that followed the French Revolution (1789–1798) and what was called the "1848 revolution." The so-called revolution of 1848 was not one event but many events. It took the form of many attempts by liberals all over Europe. From 1815 to 1848, they sought to protect for commoners the newly won freedom and privileges acquired after the French Revolution. They struggled against a reactionary nobility bent on recovering its former social position and power.

At this time, "Germany" was not in any sense a nation; rather, it was a collection of over thirty states, all of which were under pressure to grant greater freedom to the lower classes. For example, in 1844 the politicians of the various German states were shaken when weavers rioted in Silesia, and the governing authorities repressed this uprising in a brutal, bloody fashion. The Silesian textile industry, prosperous for over a century, could no longer compete with the technologically advanced mills of England. Rebuffed in their requests for higher wages and suffering from a lack of food due to poor crops, the workers massed and marched. Clothed mostly in rags, living in dilapidated shacks, and forced to exist on the black flour and inferior potatoes normally fed to livestock, the weavers (joined quickly by other artisans and day workers) ravaged the homes of the textile "aristocracy."[12] Three infantry companies quelled the uprising, killing many of the workers and imprisoning many others.

In the Prussian capital of Berlin, more muted but widespread and escalating protests occurred—the protests reaching a zenith in March of 1848 with troops firing on a huge demonstration and killing two people. Barricades were erected, fighting erupted in the city, and casualties on both sides continued until the troops were ordered to retreat.[13]

"The year 1848 was a defining one for Bismarck."[14] Born Otto Eduard Leopold Graf von Bismarck, he had studied law in Berlin and Göttingen. He was a dedicated conservative and concerned about the uprisings in Prussia. In 1848, Bismarck decided to run for parliament and was elected in 1849. His speeches in the Prussian parliament immediately earned him a reputation for intelligent reasoning, a passionate love for his country, and having a vision of Prussia's long-term needs. In a short time the government appointed him to a variety of diplomatic and ministerial positions, with his reputation growing year by year.

In 1862, the King of Prussia, Wilhelm I, appointed Bismarck prime minister. While in this post, he took forceful and dramatic military action that cumulated in the successful unification of Germany. First, the northern German states were joined together into the North German Confederation—after wresting away authority over them from Denmark and Austria. He then provoked France into war, with the southern German states joining the northern states in the conflict. With the defeat in 1871 of the French (in the Franco-Prussian War), King Wilhelm I was crowned Emperor of Germany, and Bismarck was made the first Chancellor of a unified Germany. Reflecting on his achievements, Bismarck declared: "I am bored. The great things are done. The German Reich is made."

But that comment was certainly hyperbole. Bismarck remained in the post of Chancellor for nearly two decades more. An astute politician and a commanding speaker, he was blessed with bountiful diplomatic skills. These traits, and above all his forcefulness in peace and war, earned him the nickname of "the Iron Chancellor." During his many years as chancellor, Bismarck presided over the transformation of Germany into one of the most economically and militarily powerful countries in the world.

Somewhat surprisingly, Bismarck also turned out to be a leader in the development of social legislation. How was it that this extremely conservative man (described in his early years as an arch-reactionary and "wholly backward-looking") became the father of social insurance, initiating one of the most forward-looking pieces of social legislation in Western history?[15]

new approach was to rely heavily on a more systematic and reliable social welfare protection mechanism—the widespread introduction of what are called "pensions."

Pensions of one sort or another appear throughout much of early European history—for example, during the Roman Empire.[22] Mostly these pensions, however, were only for government workers, especially the military. Starting with Bismarck's Germany, however, pensions expanded to cover large segments of the population (including the "common people") and took on a variety of unique characteristics. Bismarck's social insurance scheme was established in 1889. During the next 25 years his approach was adopted in one form or other in many European countries, for example, Denmark (1891), Belgium (1894), France (1903), Britain (1908), and Sweden (1913).

THE POLITICS OF CRAFTING U.S. SOCIAL SECURITY

The year was 1934. The place was Washington, DC. On November 14, with the nation in the thralls of a cataclysmic depression, President Franklin D. Roosevelt addressed a National Conference on Economic Security. The conference was set up by top officials in the Roosevelt administration charged with developing policies that would address the desperate economic security needs of workers. During his speech, Roosevelt stated: "I do not know whether this is the time for any Federal legislation on old age security. *Organizations promoting fantastic schemes* have aroused hopes that cannot possibly be fulfilled. Through their activities they increase the difficulties of getting sound legislation, but I hope that in time we may be able to provide security for the aged—a sound and a uniform system which will provide true security." (emphasis added)[23]

These are not the words one would expect to hear if Roosevelt was to give priority to the needs of the nation's elderly. What did Roosevelt mean by "organizations promoting fantastic schemes"? There were many.[24] But the one receiving the most attention at the time was a national pension plan promoted, not by a politician, but by an obscure physician—Dr. Francis E. Townsend.

Dr. Townsend joined the ranks of the Great Depression unemployed when he lost his job as assistant medical officer in Long Beach, California. Face to face with one of the worst aspects of the depression, Townsend was moved to action. This was not just the result of the growing personal insecurity he faced; it was also generated by the horrible things he saw around him in his community. For example, looking out of his bathroom window one morning, Townsend saw three old women rummaging in a garbage pail for scraps to eat. "From that moment the old man's crusade was on," writes political scientist James MacGregor Burns, a Pulitzer Prize-winning

Figure 3.1. Dr. Frances E. Townsend (right) confers with Sheridan Downey, U.S. Senator for California. *Source:* U.S. Office of War Information, National Archives.

biographer of Roosevelt. "He came up with a plan that—to old people at least—was spine-tingling in its sweep and simplicity."[25]

The basic idea of Townsend's plan was relatively simple. The government would provide a pension of $200 per month to every "retired" citizen age 60 and older but with the stipulation that the money was to be spent within 30 days (in order to stimulate the economy). The pensions were to be funded by a 2 percent national transaction or sales tax.

The first step taken by Townsend was to write a letter to the *Long Beach Press-Telegram* in early 1933 proposing his sweeping and daring plan. The letter produced an immediate and major positive reaction, one that spread quickly across the country, surprising even Townsend. As hard as it is to believe, within a year there were over 1,000 Townsend clubs. And within 2 years of sending his letter to the newspaper, this unemployed medical officer found himself the head of a "movement" with 7,000 Townsend clubs all over the United States.[26] Active in these clubs were more than 2.2 million members, urging that the Townsend Plan become the nation's old age pension system! Clearly, at the time older people were "ripe for organization and politics."[27]

Although the Townsend Movement never achieved its objective of a universal flat pension, the movement itself had a major political impact. The plan created a "bitterly divisive issue. For many of its aged adherents, the Townsend Plan became a matter of faith, a new version of the millennium."[28] There were two major reasons why so many older Americans actively supported the plan. One, of course, was the promised money, which was to target a group quite desperate for financial help. However, the other reason why older people—particularly small-town Middle Americans—were so enamored by the plan was because it offered them a chance to help save their country. They were told that by receiving pension money and spending it immediately, they would create a powerful economic stimulus. That is, everyone receiving a pension would be required to spend the money within 1 month. This monthly surge of spending, Townsend promised, "would create so much demand for goods and services that millions of new jobs would blossom and America would climb right out of the Depression."[29]

In stark contrast to the support of the elderly, most economists harshly criticized the Townsend plan and called its economics the epitome of *naïveté*. But it was not just economists that opposed the plan. For many different reasons, organizations across the ideological spectrum opposed the plan; communists, socialists, business organizations, and the American Federation of Labor all announced their opposition. And President Roosevelt strongly opposed it, because he hoped to create a government pension plan that was not a handout, but instead one that was "earned."

One paradoxical result of the Townsend Movement, however, was that it clearly helped to marshal political support among voters for federal pension legislation to help the elderly, and it strongly encouraged President Roosevelt to act sooner rather than later in taking action to deal with the problems of the elderly.

As we indicated above, at the November 1934 Conference on Economic Security, Roosevelt was noncommittal about taking quick action on the issue of old age security. J. Douglas Brown, who was an economist and dean at Princeton University, was part of the group writing the Social Security legislation. He reports in his book on the history of Social Security that some of Roosevelt's staff were dismayed by the president's noncommittal remarks in November. These staff members, including Brown, took what he calls "desperate measures"—secretly encouraging both criticism on this issue by the media and a call for action from supportive business executives.[30]

A bad press, encouraging business leaders, and the growing threat of the Townsend "handout" program galvanized Roosevelt into action. Particularly upset by several hostile editorials, Roosevelt soon sent a message to Congress requesting that they act quickly on his Social Security legislation. And by the end of 1935, Social Security was a reality.

Helping to get the legislation passed quickly was perhaps the most significant political impact of the Townsend Plan. "The threat posed by the plan weakened conservative opposition to the more moderate proposals encompassed in the Social Security Act."[31] Initially the Republicans in Congress joined with organized business to oppose the legislation as reckless. In addition, some of the Democrats in Congress opposed the Act but for a different reason. They thought that the benefits under Social Security would be too low.

A Contributory Program to Deal with the Unexpected. Attacked from the left and right, Roosevelt's approach to basic old age economic security was to steer a path right down the middle. He made it clear to his advisers that Social Security was to be modeled after private insurance and private pension plans. Roosevelt said, "If I have anything to say about it, it [Social Security] will always be contributed, and I prefer it to be contributed, both on the part of the employer and the employee, on a sound actuarial basis. It means no money out of the Treasury."[32] Roosevelt made it very clear that he wanted the financing of Social Security to come from payroll taxes rather than from general government revenues.

Many of Roosevelt's advisers argued against payroll taxes, but Roosevelt was adamant. In explaining his decision some years later, Roosevelt made a statement that is now one of the most famous quotes in the history of Social Security. "I guess you're right on the economics," he said. "But those taxes were never a problem of economics. They are politics all the way through. We put those payroll contributions there so as to give the contributors a legal, moral, and political right to collect their pensions and their unemployment benefits. With those taxes in there, no damn politician can ever scrap my social security program."[33]

Roosevelt wanted Social Security modeled after private pensions. But there was to be an important difference. A public plan would have the full powers (legislative and taxing) of the federal government behind it. This meant that unlike private pension programs, the government plan (instead of going bankrupt) could, in fact, deal with future *unexpected* developments and emergencies (i.e., the surprises of economic history) and *guarantee* that promised benefits would be paid. Looking back over time, we can see the difference. The history of private pensions includes many, many stories of

And let there be no mistake, the issues of adequacy and dignity in dealing with inadequate income continue today. For example, over the last few decades as high as 40 percent of the eligible elderly have not applied for benefits under the means-tested Supplemental Security Income welfare program (available to very poor aged, blind, and disabled persons).[42] Research has found that this is, in part, because of the arduous application process applicants are put through. But it is clear that it is also the result of the stigma people feel is attached to the program—a program that does not even ensure for those attaining eligibility an income above the poverty level.[43] American dislike of means testing for the general population is one big reason why the Social Security approach was so strongly welcomed by most Americans in the 1930s.

SOCIAL SECURITY BECOMES A REALITY

When the Social Security bill first reached the floor of the House of Representatives, all Republicans except one voted to recommit the bill to committee (and thereby hopefully kill it). Their opposition, together with the opposition of those who preferred the Townsend Plan, threatened to defeat the program. The Democratic chairman of the Ways and Means Committee, "Fighting Bob" Doughton, pleaded with his fellow Democrats. "We cannot go all the way at one journey," he said; "We are doing more than has ever been done in any piece of legislation for unfortunate people."[44]

Ultimately, with steady pressure from the Roosevelt-aligned House leaders, the House of Representatives voted down the Townsend Plan, 206 to 56.[45] But because of the political strength of the Townsend Movement and the general concerns throughout the nation regarding the plight of the elderly, most Republicans (fearing voter reprisal) ultimately voted for the Social Security bill. The Social Security Act passed the House in April 1935 by the overwhelming vote of 371 to 33 (and the Senate in June by a vote of 76 to 6).

When Roosevelt signed the law on August 14, he said: "We can never insure one hundred percent of the population against one hundred percent of the hazards and vicissitudes of life, but we have . . . [given some protection] against loss of a job and against a poverty-ridden old age."[46]

ECONOMIC SECURITY, NOT THE MAXIMIZATION OF RETURN

Today, maximizing financial returns on individual or personal investments is very much in vogue. Proponents of privatizing Social Security often frame the discussion in terms that emphasize the importance of creating *individual* investment accounts, *individual* equity in programs, and the promotion of investment options that allow *individuals* to seek the best returns on their retirement savings.

That was not the main concern in the 1930s, and we think it is not the main concern of most Americans today. Rather, security and help dealing with risk were the most important tasks that Social Security addressed at its creation. As we indicated above, it is the desire for *economic security with dignity* that is the number one goal of most people. Opinion polls over the years have shown that what people have wanted most is a high degree of certainty that promised benefits will be there when they retire. And they want to be sure that they will not be forced to go through the demeaning process of begging money from their children or (worse yet) from some government welfare agency or private sector charity. Such certainty was impossible to attain in the years before Social Security came into being. Government income support policies before Social Security relied heavily on families and on welfare programs of the worst kind.

In this regard, Roosevelt argued that families could not protect themselves from a variety of economic risks without help from government. Although people, since earliest times, have attempted to mitigate or eliminate economic insecurity by banding together in groups (guilds, tribes, communities, etc.), the approach often does not work. The major problem with the family (and various other group associations) is that the number of people involved is often relatively small. Thus, there is always a danger that sheer accident will bring the proportion of earners to nonearners in a family or group to a level at which the group cannot function economically.[47]

The economic situation in the 1930s was especially serious and shook the basic fabric of American society. With regard to the elderly, three things happened. The proportion of dependent elderly rose dramatically—probably exceeding 50 percent by 1935.[48] In addition, rising unemployment (that exceeded 12 million people in the depths of the Depression) seriously affected the ability of families to support aged relatives in need. Also, existing private charities and private pension plans were overwhelmed by events, with most of the private pensions collapsing and unable to pay promised benefits.

PENSIONS NOW OR IN FORTY YEARS?

When a nation or an employer starts up a new pension plan, a fundamental choice must be made. The population of the nation is, of course, of various ages when the plan starts: some people are young, and some are older; some are working, and some are retired. So at the beginning of any new public or private pension program, retiring people will have spent little of their working life covered by the program. Only after a transition period of about 40 years will all the people retiring have worked their entire lifetime under the pension plan. Given this reality, there arises an important question. What should the pension be for people with few years of coverage, that is, for those people retiring during the *transitional period*?

The way that question was answered for the Social Security program in the United States has major implications for the financing of the system today. When critics currently talk about Social Security being unsustainable and providing a low rate of return, we need to understand these assertions in the historical context of the transitional period.

As we discussed earlier, Roosevelt demanded that the financing of the system be from payroll taxes paid by employers and employees (with no government contribution). Employees would build up rights to benefits based on these contributions, and the size of their benefits would be related to the *level of earnings* upon which they paid taxes and the *number of years* payroll taxes were paid. But this approach left the problem of what to do about those employees that were nearing retirement—those individuals who would have an insufficient contribution record to be eligible for a reasonable benefit amount.

In the eyes of the founders, one basic objective of Social Security was to reduce the number of people that would have to seek welfare. Therefore, there was widespread agreement that benefits for the early waves of retirees under the system should be much greater than the contributions they had paid into the system. There was no agreement, however, on how to finance that decision. The Committee on Economic Security's plan called for government contributions from general revenues to be paid starting around 1980. As we indicated above, Roosevelt strongly opposed using general revenues. And the President's view prevailed when Social Security was passed. The initial legislation called for higher payroll tax levels in the early years and the accumulation of a large reserve fund.

But the higher taxes and large reserves never occurred in the early years. Both Democrats and Republicans in Congress repeatedly raised benefits and repeatedly delayed raising payroll taxes. The result, effectively, was the abandonment of the reserve fund approach. Instead, the financing of Social Security quickly evolved into a modified pay-as-you-go system. Why?

Perhaps the most important reason was politics. With the success of the Townsend Movement there was widespread political support, especially in Congress, to grant significant pension benefits to persons reaching retirement age during the initial years (or start-up) of pension programs—benefits "not paid for." As Martha Derthick writes in her classic book, *Policymaking for Social Security*, payroll taxes "made social security highly attractive to Congress as an institution. With a slight tax on many, Congress offered the promise of future benefits to all taxpayers and gave current benefits to several million of the aged in amounts far out of proportion to the social security taxes they had paid."[49]

This is how it worked. To become eligible for Social Security benefits, an individual must have a certain number of calendar "quarters of coverage" to be credited as a result of paying payroll taxes.[50] Congress initially set the required quarters very low for older workers close to the retirement eligibility age. This resulted in these workers receiving benefits that far exceeded what could be "actuarially purchased" from their relatively few years of contributions. Thus, ever since the Social Security system began, the vast majority of "transitional" retirees have received far more retirement benefits than they ever paid contributions into the program. New groups (such as the self-employed and farm workers) that were covered in the 1950s and 1960s also were granted similar benefits—what are sometimes called "windfall gains."

If that is the case, you may well ask whether this was a big mistake. Why did Congress grant these generous benefits (relative to payroll contributions) for early participants in the system? Was it all just "politics"?

No, there were other important reasons. First, most of the early participants needed the benefits. Without them, a majority of the elderly would have had incomes way below the poverty level. Remember, a financial catastrophe had occurred. Many individuals had seen their lifetime savings disappear or decline dramatically during the Great Depression. In addition to the fear of voter retribution, Congress, aware of families facing serious economic plight, sought to create a program that in future years would ameliorate such problems and to do it in a way that would *avoid forcing people to confront the stigma of needs-tested public assistance.*

Second, Congress at the time was confronted with historically high unemployment rates, and Social Security became one of many New Deal laws seeking to respond to the need for job creation and relief for those out of work. It initially set the threshold for benefit eligibility very low to encourage older workers to leave the labor force. The law also made receipt of benefits conditional on meeting a "retirement test." In the original 1935 act, benefits were *not* to be paid to persons receiving any "covered wages from regular employment." And later unemployment during downturns in the postwar period again encouraged Congress to expand coverage and set liberal eligibility requirements.

Third, some economists pointed out that any significant reserve accumulation during the depression would take a lot of money out of the hands of spenders and be a drag on the economy. At a time when the Great Depression strongly shaped people's attitudes, this point carried heavy weight and raised many fears.[51]

Fourth, most Republicans were strongly opposed to the planned accumulation of reserve funds. For example, Senator Arthur H. Vandenberg, a Republican member of the Finance Committee, berated the Roosevelt Administration on the floor of the Senate. Accumulating a reserve fund of $47 billion, he said, "is the most fantastic and the most indefensible objective imaginable. It is scarcely conceivable that rational men should propose such an unmanageable accumulation of funds in one place in a democracy."[52] M. Albert Linton, president of Provident Mutual Life Insurance, was also strongly critical: "The politician has but scant appreciation of the significance of a reserve fund and of the necessity of foregoing the expenditure of

protection. In fact, as we discuss in the chapters to follow, rather than becoming smaller, this economic insecurity is growing.

As journalist Thomas L Friedman observes in his book, *The World Is Flat,* "The crisis is already here.... The flattening of the world is moving ahead apace, and barring war or some catastrophic terrorist event, nothing is going to stop it. But what can happen is a decline in our standard of living, if more Americans are not empowered and educated to participate in a world where all the knowledge centers are being connected."[58]

According to Friedman, the world has been flattened by a long list of new developments. There is the emergent *dominance* of competitive markets, the computer revolution, empowering business software, the Internet and its search engines, "supply chaining," global collaboration and competition, the digitalization of data and jobs, and other components of (for lack of a better word)globalization. The result is a world of unbelievable economic potential and, at the same time, a world where every business and employee faces tremendous risks.

Gene Sperling, President Clinton's National Economic Advisor, points out that "In 2000, about half the companies that had comprised the 100 largest industrial firms in 1974 had either gone bankrupt or been taken over." We have entered an era of "a never-ending global economic Olympics" where every leading business and its employees are now less secure.[59] For example, the Business Employment Dynamics Survey of the U.S. Bureau of Labor Statistics found that in 1999, "fierce competition destroyed an astounding 32.9 million private sector jobs, the equivalent of more than 20 percent of our workforce."[60]

Social Security is one of the key programs that significantly moderates some of those risks. It is still popular because, first, it can be counted on; Social Security has never once missed mailing out the millions of checks that go out each month to eligible beneficiaries. More importantly, Social Security was built on a number of fundamental propositions that continue to have widespread support:

- It is both efficient and more secure to build collective mechanisms for old age support based on the insurance principle—that is, bringing people together to take advantage of the laws of large numbers to keep down costs and raise security.
- Both parents and children prefer that the major economic support for old age be from other sources than the family.
- Family members also prefer that support be provided in a way that preserves the dignity of the individual. That is why contributory Social Security programs so successfully replaced the demeaning means-tested programs that preceded them.
- There is a broad consensus that there is a need for social mechanisms that take into account both the shortsightedness (the myopia that

most people readily admit to) in financial planning and the fact that most people desire to delegate retirement planning to experts—given the complexity of this decision making and the fact that most people would rather do other things with their time.

- While there is a role for private collective action, it is recognized that only governments can ultimately secure the benefits promised in old age—given the economic vicissitudes of global, regional, and community shifts in economic opportunity in the face of such things as changing product demand, technology, the competitive *milieu*, and macroeconomic events associated with recession and inflation.

None of these fundamental propositions has changed significantly over time. They are the underlying basis for political and economic decision making in the area of social policy related to our growing older. It is important to begin any debate on changes in our policies by recognizing them.

We have come a long way in the search for security with dignity. When Bismarck and Kaiser Wilhelm first developed Social Security, they were seeking to promote political stability and economic security, and their actions were in large part self-serving. Little did they realize the long-term changes their social welfare innovations would trigger. For today, the "common people" (especially older people) in industrialized nations enjoy a security that was unthinkable a century ago. We in the United States should be proud of that achievement, as proud as we are of our mothers and apple pie!

CHAPTER 4

. . . .

Dealing with Risk

Hesitation increases in relation to risk in equal proportion to age.

—Ernest Hemingway[1]

Private insurance often works well, but it has inherent drawbacks. Profit-making insurers simply can't offer reasonably priced protection to high-risk groups, provide affordable insurance for the less affluent or require that everyone have coverage. Only government can.

—Jacob Hacker[2]

The Great Depression of the 1930s was *not* the first serious economic crisis the United States faced. Severe economic downturns occurred, for example, in the 1840s and again in the 1890s. During the depression of the 1890s, unemployment was widespread, and Americans began to realize that in an industrialized society, the threat to economic security represented by unemployment could strike anyone—even those able and willing to work. One reaction to this realization was that workers began to protest, often as a group. Perhaps the most quixotic and notable was the group that came to be known as "Coxey's Army."[3]

Jacob Coxey was an unsuccessful Ohio politician and industrialist who, in 1894, called on the unemployed from all over the country to join his "army" that was to march on Washington. The response was huge; tens of thousands of unemployed workers assembled when the march began. By the time Coxey's army finally made it to Washington, however, only about 500 hard-core believers remained. Upon arriving, Coxey himself was promptly arrested for walking on the grass of the Capitol Building, and the protest fizzled out.

Although the march failed, Coxey's Army was a harbinger of issues and concerns that would arise in the future—concerns spawned by the new types of insecurity arising as the nation changed from its agrarian orientation toward becoming an industrial powerhouse. Social Security and the other pension programs that were ultimately established were not merely mechanisms to pay out money on a more or less regular basis. They were (and are today) also ingenious schemes for effectively dealing with one of the most pervasive problems of the modern world. They were designed to "insure" for citizens the availability of sufficient economic resources to live reasonably well when they became old or disabled and no longer able to work. It became clear to many in the newly emerging industrial societies of Europe and America that without pensions this problem was virtually unsolvable in a reasonable way for the average individual.

THE ROLE OF PENSIONS IN MARKET ECONOMIES

Economists generally refer to pensions as an important device for "smoothing consumption" over the life cycle—dealing with various income-disrupting events, such as job loss, problems of old age, or the premature death or severe disability of a family's breadwinner. For instance, in contrast to farmers, urban workers face the difficulty, inconvenience, and outright inability to put aside sufficient physical output (such as food) to tide them over in old age. Pensions are a way of exchanging claims on the economy's *current* output of products and services for claims on *future* output that workers and their families need when they are old and no longer working.

Pensions can also help to deal with the risks in a market economy that adversely affect individuals and create social problems. With the shift to economic systems dominated by "free markets" and competition, the types of risk facing workers changed radically. As we mentioned in the last chapter, competitive markets continually threaten workers' jobs: new production methods dictated by technological change, shifts in consumer preferences, new sources of productive inputs, and so forth. The insecurity arises from the reality that a firm's profits, and often its very existence, are at risk if the firm ignores the demands of competition, changing technology, new production methods, and/or changing output "needs." The firms' reactions to these changes usually result in a need to make changes to the workforce, sometimes radically. Thus, the built-in incentives of the market not only promote efficiency, innovation, and economic growth but also create unemployment, bankruptcy, social disruption, and economic inequality.

The contemporary economic and political commentator James Fallows has expressed it well: "Capitalism is one of the world's more disruptive forces. It can call [through market forces] every social arrangement into question, make cities and skills and ranks merely temporary. To buy into it is to make a commitment to permanent revolution that few political creeds can match."[4]

The story of tradeoffs between economic production efficiency and social stability has been told many times over the years.[5] What has not been given sufficient attention, however, is the extent to which manpower and retirement policies for older workers have been shaped by the more general issues of economic policy. Historically, the problems arising from markets have had a powerful impact on the nature of our social welfare system and have promoted the development of pensions.

For Bismarck (and many of his emulators), pensions and other social reforms were seen as a way of commanding the loyalty of the workers and, by doing so, creating an alliance against the bourgeoisie property and business owners. But in the more liberal European democracies (such as Belgium, England, France, and the Netherlands), pensions in the form of Social Security tended to grow with industrialization, together with the spread of the voting franchise in the late nineteenth and early twentieth centuries.

The Economic Risks of Old Age. Over the years, the word "pension" has been used to describe a variety of payments. Any employer or government can pay out some money to individuals and call it a pension. Today, however, when we think of pensions, we think of programs with a number of special characteristics.

The key attribute of many public and private pension programs is *the pooling or spreading of risks* by creating collective organizations or programs that bring together individuals and resources. Spreading risk reduces the harm that might affect any one individual.

To understand better the role played by pensions, let us begin with the financial planning situation facing almost all individuals. One of the most difficult tasks an individual faces in modern society is dealing with the economic risks of old age and planning for retirement. Dealing with the unpredictability of the economic situation over time and one's job security is only one of many problems. We all must confront retirement planning.

Immediately problems arise:

- One doesn't know with certainty when she or he will die.
- One doesn't know exactly what future preretirement income will be.
- One doesn't know what basic "retirement needs" will be.
- One doesn't know exactly when one will retire.
- One cannot easily predict the future rate of inflation and, hence, its impact on retirement financing.

- One cannot easily predict the future rate of economic growth, which affects the return on investments and whether one's economic situation in retirement will make it possible to keep up with the generally rising standard of living.

The number and magnitude of the problems listed above indicate that individual retirement planning is a very difficult job and that the risks associated with it are very high. Not surprisingly, a survey of baby boomers in 2003 found, for example, that over one-third (39%) were not able to report that they were confident in their ability to prepare adequately for retirement.[6]

There is no doubt that the personal decision-making process involved in preparation for retirement is a very complex one. Let us look at the uncertainties listed above in more detail.

First, not knowing when you (or maybe a spouse) are going to die is a major complicating factor in figuring out the amount of money you will need in retirement. To be sure you do not run out of money you need to know the number of years for which income is required. Because that is not generally possible, attempting to provide for retirement entirely by *individual* actions alone brings great risk of having too little money at some point in old age.

The second problem is that one does not know what one's total earnings and other income will be over a lifetime. We do not know if, when, or how long we will be unable to work—given such happenings as child-bearing, ill health, or disability (either short-term or long-term). Other uncertainties are the possibility of unemployment, finding oneself in an obsolete job, or facing job discrimination from an employer who thinks all older workers are "over the hill." Also, recurrent periods of recession (and inflation) are outside the control of the individual and are very difficult to predict; yet such developments have a significant, if not dominating, impact on the amount of lifetime earnings and other income individuals receive and on the purchasing power of income and assets when they are spent.

A third problem arises from not knowing what one's retirement needs will be. A major factor here is the great uncertainty that exists with regard to the state of one's health when one gets old. Will chronic or serious illnesses develop (and when)? Will nursing care be required? Will institutionalization be necessary? Not only is health status directly related to medical costs, it also affects retirement mobility—influencing recreation and transportation expenditures.

Yet another set of retirement planning issues arises if one is married. There is uncertainty as to whether the family unit will break up through divorce and uncertainty about how long each spouse will live. Pension benefit rights for a surviving spouse often change if the eligible worker dies. Thus, the amount of money a *spouse* will need or will have in retirement depends to a major extent on the lifetime marital history, an essentially unpredictable matter. In fact, such issues are currently among the major factors responsible for the high rate of poverty among unmarried older women, which in 2001 was 21 percent (exactly double the rate for all persons aged 65 and older).[7]

A fifth problem occurs because of the variability in the age at which people retire. Although most individuals have a large measure of control over when they retire, in some cases the decision is based on events beyond their control. Among these factors are deteriorating health, pension rules, early retirement options made available by employers (sometimes accompanied by management and/or union pressures to retire), and discriminatory practices that affect hiring, promotion, and firing of older workers.

Perhaps one of the most difficult retirement preparation problems is that we do not know how much inflation will occur before and during retirement. To the extent that an individual accumulates assets (or pension rights) for the retirement period that do not automatically adjust in value for inflation, he or she is faced with the likelihood that these assets may shrink in value—perhaps being of little worth later in the retirement period.

Finally, some individuals preparing for retirement may be concerned about changes in their *relative* economic status in retirement. After one retires, the real incomes of the working population will almost certainly continue to rise over the years. If the retiree wants to keep up with the general rise in living standards, he or she will have to make some estimate of the economic growth that will occur during retirement. Additional funds must then be provided before retirement that can be drawn upon to keep a person's economic status rising along with that of everybody else. Some people will decide that they do not want to bother dealing with this issue; they will be content just to keep their retirement standard of living constant. Some may even prefer to allow it to decline. Nevertheless, this is an important issue that should not be overlooked in retirement planning. There is a choice to be made, and it should not be made passively, simply because individuals are unaware of the nature of that choice.

Using Pension to Deal with the Risks. Pensions can be an efficient and effective way of dealing with many sources of economic insecurity and risk. For example, the first problem in our list of unknowns (above) was that an individual does not know exactly when he or she will die—that is, how long a retirement period to provide for. This means that a conservative person (or family) preparing for retirement must assume the "worst"—a long life—and put aside enough money to take care of that eventuality. Alternatively, one must be prepared to rely on private or public charity if one lives "too long" and one's own economic support is exhausted.

Fortunately, there is a much better way to deal with the unknown life expectancy problem. The decision-making process is simplified and uncertainty reduced through an "insurance" arrangement. Many public and private pensions provide collective protection by covering under the same plan a large number of employees whose actual individual life expectancies are unknown—some living short, others medium, and, still others, long lives. This type of collective pension program provides an attractive option—grouping together individuals and their pension claims and operating in accordance with average expectations provided by what statisticians call "the law of large numbers." If the number of individuals in a pension program is sufficiently large, mortality tables of life expectancy can be constructed that show estimates of *average* life expectancy at particular ages. Retirement preparation costs can then be geared to average life expectancy, with the "excess" payments of individuals who die before the average age going to those who live beyond it. The result is that no one has to pay more than they would need to put aside personally if it were known with certainty that they would live for a period of years equal to the average life expectancy.

The second problem, discussed earlier in connection with individual retirement preparation, is the lack of predictability of future income. For example, unexpected chronically low earnings, ill health, or periods of unemployment (as a result of a wide variety of different factors) may make sufficient saving for retirement very difficult or even impossible. Also, health or employment problems may force an individual to retire unexpectedly and much earlier than was originally planned. Again, risk pooling using large numbers of people can help us deal with the problem.

Of course collective arrangements for risk sharing are not new. Throughout history individuals have relied heavily on family ties to provide protection from economic insecurity in old age. Even today in the United States, the family still remains an important source of economic and social support for many older persons when they become seriously ill; and in some other countries—particularly those that are less industrialized—the family still remains the major source of economic protection and security in old age.

As we noted in the previous chapter, the *major problem with the family (and many other group associations) for sharing risk is that the number of people involved is relatively small*. As economist Kenneth Boulding has observed, "It is when the 'sharing group' becomes too small to ensure that there will always be enough producers in it to support the unproductive that devices for insurance become necessary. When the 'sharing group' is small there is always a danger that sheer accident [illness, crop failure, unemployment, and so forth] will bring the proportion of earners to nonearners to a level at which the group cannot effectively function."[8] That is the main reason why relying on ourselves or on our family often does not work.

Thus, the need for better collective arrangements to deal with the economic problems of old age has always been with us. The earliest available statistics on the economic status of the elderly prior to the establishment of pensions indicate that most of the aged in the United States were poor, and that, in fact, many were completely destitute. The reasons why risk-sharing pension programs were not developed earlier in the United States are not entirely clear. Indeed, by the time America adopted social insurance, there were thirty-four nations already operating some form of social insurance program (about twenty of these were contributory programs like Social Security).[9] In explanation of the American timing, various writers have pointed to the *relative* economic prosperity throughout America's history, the country's decentralized governmental structure, and (most importantly) a relatively unique emphasis on individualism in American political ideology.[10]

Why Compulsory Pensions? Individual self-reliance and voluntary preparation for retirement—together with family interdependence—dominated the early discussions of old age security provision. It is now generally accepted, however, that this is not the appropriate cornerstone of an income maintenance policy for the aged. Instead, there is widespread support for relying on pensions and, in particular, making public pensions compulsory. Economists Joseph Pechman, Henry Aaron, and Michael Taussig, in their classic book on Social Security, discuss one of the most important reasons:

> There is widespread myopia with respect to retirement needs. Empirical evidence shows that most people fail to save enough to prevent catastrophic drops in post-retirement income ... Not only do people fail to plan ahead carefully for retirement, even in the later years of their working life, many remain unaware of impending retirement needs. ... In an urban, industrial society, government intervention in the saving-consumption decision is needed to implement personal preferences over the life cycle. There is nothing inconsistent in the decision to undertake through the political process a course of action which would not be undertaken individually through the marketplace.[11]

Action to respond to the myopic behavior of individuals (i.e., their lack of foresight and poor planning) is often referred to as the *paternalistic* rationale for compulsory pensions. However, it can be argued that compulsion is also appropriate from a *self-interested* point of view—a device for making sure that everyone "pays their own way." Economists call this the "free rider" issue. Economist Kenneth Boulding explains the problem this way:

> [If an individual] were rationally motivated, [he or she] would be aware of the evils that might beset ... and would insure against them. It is argued, however, that many people are not so motivated, and that hardly anyone is completely motivated by these rational considerations, and that therefore under a purely voluntary system some will insure and some will not. This means, however, that those who do not insure will have to be supported anyway—perhaps at lower levels and in humiliating and respect-destroying ways—when they are in the nonproductive phase of life, but that they will escape the burden of paying premiums when they are in the productive phase. In fairness to those who insure

voluntarily, and in order to maintain the self-respect of those who would not otherwise insure, insurance should be compulsory.[12]

Over the years, a number of research studies of this issue have been carried out. They conclude that without compulsory Social Security (or its equivalent), a substantial fraction of the population would be inadequately prepared financially for retirement.[13] That is, it is clear that large numbers of the population, if left on their own, are likely to undersave for old age. In fact, research by Stanford University economist B. Douglas Bernheim and others concludes that even with Social Security, most members of the baby boom generation are currently not saving enough to ensure adequate income during retirement.[14]

Finally, there is a more controversial role that can be played by pensions, especially compulsory pensions. They can be used to alter an unsatisfactory distribution of income. Distributional problems result within nations from their historic patterns of unequal wealth ownership. And, in market-oriented economies, they are caused by the ups and downs (rewards and penalties) of competitive markets that are used to efficiently guide economic activities.

Every country relying heavily on markets alters the resulting income distribution in order to achieve what it considers to be a more just society. Common interventions include welfare programs, medical assistance, public education, progressive income taxes and other special tax provisions, minimum wage laws, and a variety of "social benefits."

One such intervention is the establishment of public pension programs that can be designed (in terms of eligibility, benefits, and financing provisions) to shift greater income into the hands of various needy or "deserving" groups. Although income can be redistributed in many ways (with various advantages and problems associated with each), pensions have been valued over the years as a good strategic way to supply the needy elderly with income. Pensions are a socially acceptable way to do this because they preserve the dignity of the individuals. The pension approach contrasts dramatically with means-tested benefit programs that are often intrusive, expensive to administer, and underused by those eligible for them because of the welfare stigma associated with them.

Redistribution is a very important attribute of Social Security in the United States. Although there is controversy about it, the Social Security old age program was designed to redistribute some of its revenue from higher to lower earners. Benefits are determined by a "weighted benefit formula" that favors workers with lower earnings. There is also a contribution cutoff point, which limits the benefits of highly paid individuals. A special minimum benefit, spouse benefit, widow's benefit, and protection for a worker's young children all have an element of redistribution—given that average life expectancy varies by income level. Few people realize how valuable some of these benefits are. For example, an average wage earner with a family who is covered by Social Security has benefits equivalent to a $400,000 life insurance policy and a $350,000 disability policy.[15]

Finally, as we discussed in the previous chapter, there is redistribution among generations as a result of giving "start-up" benefits to workers. Remember that workers close to retirement in the early start-up years of the program received significant benefits, even though their years in the program were few and their total payroll contributions extremely small.

Legislating Mandatory Social Security. J. Douglas Brown, who helped draft the original Social Security pension program for the United States, writes in his book on the history of Social Security, *An American Philosophy of Social Security*, that the drafting group never seriously considered anything other than a compulsory program. The drafting group did worry, however, about whether a national compulsory program would be constitutional.

Hoping that it might be possible to avoid a court test of the constitutionality of Social Security, the drafting group did consider briefly a plan that would have permitted elective Social Security coverage by states and various industrial groups. The drafting group rejected it, however. According to Brown, the plan was "so cumbersome, ineffective, and actuarially unsound that no further attempt was made to avoid a head-on constitutional test of a truly workable system."[16]

As it turned out during the debates that followed, the principal argument for compulsion was a financial one. An optional coverage program would have made it actuarially impossible to project both costs (benefits) and revenue for the program. It was feared that this problem would create financial instability and make it difficult to guarantee adequate, equitable, and improved benefits as Social Security developed.

The original Social Security Act required participation by all workers in commerce and industry except those working for railroads. Railroad workers were exempted because the federal government had already enacted pension legislation on their behalf in 1934. Although this original legislation covering railroad workers was later declared unconstitutional, new (but still separate) railroad pension legislation was enacted in 1935 and 1937.

A number of other groups were specifically excluded from early Social Security coverage—the major groups being farm workers, the self-employed, and federal government employees (including military personnel). Over the years, as coverage was extended to these groups, optional coverage was introduced for certain other groups: employees of nonprofit institutions, state and local governments, and most clergymen. But in each case, coverage was not optional for the individual, depending instead on the collective decision of an organizational unit. (Today Social Security coverage is mandated for almost all of these "optional coverage" groups.)

The situation with respect to *private* pensions in the United States is not very different. Most of the workers who were covered (or not covered) by the early private pension plans achieved that status not through personal choices but by employer decisions. That practice is currently changing, however, with the rise of a special type of pension plan. These plans, called defined contribution plans, are discussed at length in Chapter 6.

Pensions Around the World. The decision of the United States to have a compulsory national public pension program is in no way unique. There is only one country in the world with a Social Security old age pension program that has designed a large amount of voluntary coverage into the program. In Great Britain workers must participate in a basic social insurance plan that provides a flat-rate benefit, but employers and/or individual workers can opt out of a second-tier earnings-related national pension by establishing employer or individual plans. Like the United States, many countries have special public pension programs that cover certain broad groups of workers (especially government employees) but exclude other groups (such as farm workers, the self-employed, or employees of very small firms).

Almost all of the compulsory pension programs throughout the world are public. There are some countries, however, that rely heavily on mandatory private provision. Australia, for example, has no social insurance program, relying instead on a relatively generous means-tested public program, together with mandated private pensions.[17] Switzerland combines a first-tier social insurance program with mandatory employer-sponsored plans with specified minimums. Chile terminated its social insurance program for "new hires" in the early 1980s and mandated that 10 percent of every worker's earnings be deposited for retirement purposes into individual accounts managed by private investment institutions (regulated by the government).

THE NEW RISKY SOCIETY

Like compulsory Social Security, many defined benefit company pensions in the United States have established large risk pools. However, their future role in moderating individual risk has become problematic in the early twenty-first century. For a variety of reasons (discussed in Chapter 5), private sector employers have been shifting from defined benefit plans to defined contribution plans. Unlike the traditional defined benefit plans that spread the financing of life cycle risks across large groups of company workers, these newer plans are *personal* retirement accounts. Each employee is left with the challenge of individually investing pension assets well enough to deal with the financial risks associated with financial planning for retirement. Each personal "pot" of pension assets is subject to the overall ups and downs of the market, as well as market-timing issues and the outcome of investment decisions made by the individual. In some instances, under the new approach, the employees' defined contribution holdings are funneled in a variety of ways into company stock of his or her employer. Such was the case with the Enron Corporation, whose stock (because of management deceit at the very top) collapsed in 2001, wiping out the pensions of its employees.

As we noted in our opening chapter, recently there has been growing interest, strongly encouraged by President Bush in 2005, in converting all or part of Social Security into such personal retirement accounts. The rewards from such accounts for *some* individuals might be greater than from compulsory participation in the social insurance mechanism of Social Security. But for *others*, the results could be devastating. With private defined-contribution plans, the timing and selection of investment decisions, market cycles, and the timing of retirement are all major hazards. One of the major impacts of converting Social Security into personal retirement accounts is that much of the risk would be shifted from the collectivity of all Americans, where today it is shared and moderated, to one individual—YOU!

But even as the baby boomers and their children face the increased risks associated with personal retirement accounts in the private sector, and possibly in the public sector through Social Security reform, they also face other economic uncertainties as they grow older. Fortunately, a big difference between today and the Great Depression of the 1930s is that programs and laws have been put into place to help people deal more effectively with the many economic problems and to mitigate some of the worst possible outcomes. The foundation of the post-World War II society in the United States is a series of mechanisms that have been developed to deal with the worst impacts of the many financial risks companies and individuals face throughout their lives.

Already by the end of the nineteenth century, American lawmakers had acted to protect businesses through limited liability laws, bankruptcy regulation, and banking reform. In the twentieth century, the New Deal era produced Social Security protection that became a lynchpin in the protection of individuals. It is important to remember, however, that President Roosevelt also focused on other areas where risks were high. For example, he supported important financial and banking reforms designed to help both businesses and individuals.

Roosevelt spent his whole first week in office, for example, dealing almost solely with the housing upheaval confronting the country. Few things are scarier to ordinary citizens than the threat of losing their home. In early 1933, foreclosures were occurring in the United States at a rate of more than a thousand a day.[18] To deal with this crisis, the Home Owners' Loan Corporation was established. It was the first of many laws over the years designed to facilitate home ownership and shield owners from some of the many risks that hit them during exceptionally bad times and for which they were not responsible.

In addition, there was the establishment of the Securities and Exchange Commission to regulate the securities market and the Federal Deposit Insurance Corporation to insure bank accounts. Adding to this important protection legislation was the establishment of workers' compensation, new welfare programs, unemployment benefits, and legislation promoting and protecting unions. Clearly, we have had a history, as described by journalist Peter Gosselin, in which the leaders of the nation "spent most of the twentieth century adding to the economic protections that Americans could count on—and reducing the risks they had to tackle alone."[19]

No longer. During the last two to three decades, we have witnessed what political scientist Jacob S. Hacker calls "the great risk shift."[20] Let us briefly describe some elements of this shift. First are the fluctuations in income that are much greater than in the past.

Fluctuations in Income. In 2005, the *Los Angeles Times* launched an investigation into the nature and extent of rising insecurity in the United States. The paper hired economic consultants to analyze survey data that followed a group of Americans over a number of years (using the "Panel Study of Income Dynamics" at the University of Michigan). They concluded that nowhere is the risk shift of the last quarter century more apparent than in the widening swings in working families' incomes: "Although average family income adjusted for inflation has risen in recent decades, the path that most households have followed has hardly been a steady line upward—the historical norm for most of the post-World War II era. Instead, a growing number of families have found themselves caught on a financial roller coaster ride, with their annual incomes taking increasingly wild leaps and plunges over time."[21]

The Ups and Downs of the Stock Market. The ups and downs of financial markets remain with us today, but the swings are greater. Remember the dot-com bubble that burst in 2000? Just as in the 1930s, people who were millionaires on paper because of high stock prices suddenly found much of their wealth gone. There is no doubt that while over the very long-run stock prices on average have gone up, historically there have also been long periods where stock prices have remained low.

Private Employers Shift Pension and Medical Care Risks. As we have already indicated, a revolution has occurred in the private pension area. As the *New York Times* put it in 2006, "The death knell for the traditional company pension has been tolling."[22] The security and relative certainty of benefits under defined benefit plans has been replaced by the uncertainty and risk associated with defined contribution plans. In 1980, over 80 percent of workers with an employer-sponsored pension plan had a defined benefit plan. By 1998, that percentage had dropped to less than 50 percent and continues to fall rapidly.[23]

Similarly, the extensive health insurance coverage sponsored and usually paid by employers (at least in part) is shrinking.[24] In 2004, 16 percent of Americans, some 46 million persons, were not covered by any health insurance. Lack of insurance has been increasing, not decreasing in recent years, with the number of uninsured increasing by six million individuals between 2000 and 2004.[25] (Due to Medicare and Medicaid, less than 1 percent of older persons are uninsured.)

In addition, for those covered by health insurance, growing numbers of employers over recent years have required workers to pay an increasing share of the premiums. Currently, 80 percent of unmarried workers and 90 percent of workers with family coverage are required to pay part of their health care insurance costs. On average, a worker with family coverage pays almost one-third (28 percent) of the premium.[26]

Many health plans sponsored by employers also offer some supplemental insurance coverage to about seven million company retirees.[27] But here again, the general trend is down. A study of firms with 200 or more workers found that the percent of firms offering such benefits fell from 66 percent in 1988 to 34 percent in 2002.[28]

More Exporting of Jobs Abroad. As we discuss in Chapter 7, getting a job when you are old is not easy. If you are older, the barriers to employment remain significant. Moreover, today one must add to the traditional list of barriers the growing practice by American business of exporting jobs to other countries, what is often called "off-shoring." It used to be that workers with lots of seniority and white-collar workers were relatively safe from layoffs and terminations. That is no longer true. Recent downturns in the economy have resulted in a much broader spectrum of workers being adversely affected. A survey by the Conference Board of employers in the late 1980s found that 56 percent of major corporations agreed that "employees who are loyal to the company and further its business goals deserve an assurance of continued employment." But today, *only 6 percent* of corporations agree with that statement![29]

EVALUATING PENSION PLANS

For individuals who want to evaluate public and private pension plans, what factors should be considered in addition to any risk-sharing provisions? With an institutional arrangement as complex as pensions, one can generate a long list of plan features that might be studied. Opinions differ widely on which are most important. Moreover, there is little agreement on the relative weights to assign each feature when judging a particular pension plan. Below we set out some important characteristics of pension plans that would probably appear on everyone's list.

As you read about this list of factors, once again you might feel over-whelmed by how complicated the pension issues are that we face. This is not fun reading.

The Adequacy of Pension Benefits. Any discussion of a particular pension plan's adequacy must explicitly recognize the variety of means available to the individual (or society) to achieve the objective. Any particular public or private pension plan is rarely designed to be the sole source of retirement income. How much are individuals expected to accumulate for their old age through personal savings? Are all individuals *able* to save for old age? What non-cash programs (such as health insurance) are available to provide economic support? How large are both public and private pension benefits? Who is currently covered by each? Who should be covered?

There will never be complete agreement about the appropriate roles for the various means of providing income in old age—collective pension schemes are only one major way. Rather, there will usually be continuing political debate and private discussion among bargaining groups over these matters. Out of such debate and discussion come decisions on pension legislation, employment contracts, and employer/government policies. Then it is possi-ble to evaluate their economic implications for retirement income adequacy. And the contribution the resulting pensions will make to a particular indi-vidual's or group's goal can be estimated.

The Certainty of Benefits. One can examine particular pension plans and estimate the degree of uncertainty associated with the *promised* benefits. At least six major contingencies should be evaluated:

- *Plan termination*: What provisions exist to ensure that the plan will survive economic or political adversity, such as a change in govern-ment policy (affecting public pensions) or bankruptcy of the firm (affecting private pensions)?
- *Political risk*: Are the levels of benefits promised so high that it is unlikely that the promise can be kept in later years, given actuarial projections, and (as a result) the likelihood that plan provisions will be changed?
- *Investment risk*: To what extent will benefits ultimately paid out be dependent on the financial performance of invested funds and the skills of the investors?
- *Inflation*: How well are the workers' future benefits and the pension recipients' actual benefits protected from general increases in the level of prices?
- *Loss of rights*: What happens at various ages to pension rights if a worker involuntarily or by choice stops working or changes jobs?

- *Inadequate survivor provisions:* Are survivors' benefits automatically provided or can they be elected? Who makes the decision (the worker or both the worker and the spouse) in cases where coverage is optional?

Flexibility. The larger the pension program in terms of people covered, the greater the differences in the circumstances and preferences of these participants. It is desirable for pension plan provisions and rules not to be too rigid. The introduction of greater flexibility, however, usually results in greater administrative costs (discussed below). And by complicating the program, flexibility often makes it more difficult for participants to be knowledgeable and to understand details of the program.

Nondiscriminatory Coverage. The determination of eligibility for pension coverage is a very complex, but it is an important factor in assessing pension options. Most people would agree that individuals in similar circumstances (e.g., working for the same employer) should not be arbitrarily excluded from coverage under a pension plan or excluded because of age, sex, race, and other demographic characteristics. But the actual determination of who should be included is often difficult because of a variety of administrative, technical, political, and economic considerations. For example, should workers be excluded from protection because they do not (or cannot) work full time or because they work at home?

Equity. Whether a pension program is perceived as fair depends in large measure on how the program treats different individuals and how these individuals think they *should* be treated. The major issue around which equity questions usually cluster is financing. For example, how much do benefits cost the individual in contrast to other benefit recipients. Under what terms do people pay but not receive benefits? Some pensions emphasize "individual equity," where benefits received are closely related to payments or taxes paid. Other pensions, especially public pensions, are designed to also redistribute some income among recipients, providing additional help to those considered needy.

Administrative Costs. Apart from the benefits paid out by a pension program, the level of administrative expenses can significantly influence the amount of benefits you ultimately receive. These costs can be separated into the following categories:

- *Marketing expenses:* if pensions are not compulsory, there are typically advertising, sales commissions, and other marketing expenses to acquire clients.

- *Fund management charges*: expenses associated with financial research, market analysis, remuneration to financial managers, transaction fees, profit returns to financial management firms, etc.
- *Business maintenance costs*: record keeping, client communication and reports, and general administrative expenses.
- *Adverse selection contingency charges*: costs imposed on annuity purchasers, assuming that "adverse selection" will occur (that is, those people who expect to live longer will be more likely to take out annuities).
- *Costs of switching*: charges that result from switching money from one fund account to another, early plan termination, investing in multiple funds, or the maintenance of inactive funds, etc.

Simplicity and Ease of Understanding. It is important that individuals know whether they are covered by a pension plan, what the conditions of benefit entitlement are, what benefits they (or their family) can or will receive, what the risks of losing benefits are, and various other facts about the plan. Over the years a large amount of evidence has accumulated that indicates a great lack of knowledge and much misinformation among workers in the United States with regard to their own expected pensions, both public and private. As the number and variety of pension programs grow and many of these programs become more complicated, this problem will also grow. Therefore, in reviewing existing programs or proposals for pension changes, the complexity of the program needs to be considered. An assessment should be made of the resultant impact on the employees' ability to understand the pension program and to incorporate it realistically into their preretirement planning.

Integration. A particular pension plan is almost always only one of a number of collective programs operating to provide economic security. It is not sufficient to view a particular pension program in isolation from these other programs. For example, eligibility or benefit determination under one program is sometimes related to benefits received from another program. Employer-sponsored pensions paid to workers are sometimes reduced based on the size of the Social Security benefits they receive.

FINDING SOMEONE YOU CAN TRUST

Given the old and new risks, what are the implications for individuals who want to provide themselves with adequate income in retirement? When people talk about giving individuals more control over their retirement savings, they often make it seem like this can be done easily. That is certainly not true.

Managing one's retirement finances before and during retirement is one of the most challenging life tasks one will face. For example, as we discuss later, even Nobel laureates in economics report that they have not managed their retirement finances as well as they would have liked. Some even admit they have made serious mistakes in managing their money.[30]

Remember that retirement planning is such a challenge in large part because of the many risks and challenges we have enumerated and because of the huge amount of knowledge and information needed to make informed choices and safeguard one's wealth. Unfortunately, these are not all the problems. Remember from our discussion of pensions earlier in this chapter that much of the basic information you need will NEVER be available until it's too late—such as most of your labor force history, and your ages of retirement and death.

Moreover, most of us have a natural inclination to avoid thinking about old age and death until they are close upon us. Hence, many of us give very little systematic thought to the financial issues of old age until we come face to face with them—when it is usually too late. Also discouraging us from early thinking about retirement preparation is the flood of criticism about the adequacy, financial viability, and equity of Social Security and private pensions (regardless of their merits), which creates confusion and distrust among us.

In the new world of retirement planning, one must make major investment decisions about large, sometimes huge, sums of money. Ready to help with those decisions are a growing numbers of investment salesmen, brokers, and financial counselors.

But one must be wary and wise in seeking help. It is common to hear about frauds that have wiped out the personal savings of older people. However, at a hearing of the U.S. Senate Special Committee on Aging, the securities administrator for the state of Maine, Stephen Diamond, spoke about additional dangers. He warned that focusing on the frauds that get media attention ignores a much bigger and more basic problem:

> Investment abuses are not always the work of con artists who are engaged in criminal fraud.... In Maine, the elderly lose more money from abuses committed by licensed persons selling lawful products. Much of this results from what I call ... soft-core fraud, or from broker incompetence.[31]

For example, over 23,000 investors were sold $250 million worth of unsecured bonds in the Lincoln Savings/American Continental scandal of the 1980s.[32] Many were elderly persons investing retirement savings.

If you're like most people, you may be a bit overwhelmed by all the issues related to evaluating pensions and assessing their impact on your future retirement. As Ben Stein says in his book, *How to Ruin Your Financial Life*,

"Let's face it. It's a bit upsetting to think about money. It involves mathematics, and maybe you were never very good at math. It involves discussions of the future, and as we've already come to realize, those discussions can be supremely boring and frightening."[33]

Enter the professional financial advisor. But, as indicated above, finding a good, reliable financial advisor is not an easy task. A number of key steps can be taken, however, that will dramatically reduce the possibility of major problems:

- Take the time necessary to find a good person; one should not simply follow the suggestion of a relative or friend. Asking people for suggestions is a reasonable place to begin, but it is no substitute for an in-depth investigation of options.
- Interview more than one advisor. The first person that you talk to is almost certainly going to sound good, especially since you have no basis for comparison.
- Prepare a list of questions. Ask the potential advisor about his or her investment philosophy, their planning approach, the methods that will be used, the extent of their training, whether they are "certified" (and by whom), the final product that will be provided, and the fees you will have to pay.
- A planner's prior work should be assessed by asking to see copies of plans done for other people and talking to some of the planner's recent clients. (Although the planner is not going to refer you to dissatisfied clients, you will find it useful to learn what prior clients see as the planner's strong and weak points.)
- The background of an advisor should always be investigated thoroughly, checking for prior legal or certification problems. At a minimum, you should ask for a copy of both parts of Form ADV (the background materials that most advisors file with the Securities and Exchange Commission).

Before talking to a financial planner, you need to do some preliminary organization of your financial information, and you also need to think about your financial goals. For example, preparing a list of current assets and liabilities is a must.

At this point, many readers will ask, "Can't I deal with the problem of finding a good and trustworthy adviser by hiring someone who is "certified"? Unfortunately, the answer is yes and no. Neither the U.S. Securities and Exchange Commission (SEC) nor any other state or federal government agencies *directly* regulate people calling themselves "financial planners" or certify any of them. In fact, almost any nonfelon can become a "Registered Investment Advisor" with the SEC by making application and paying a fee (regardless of the person's financial planning knowledge).[34]

Although anyone can call himself or herself a financial planner, there are many organizations that give people special certification titles.[35] Requirements for these titles vary greatly. Certification can be earned through some programs in a couple of days; in one, it takes more than a year.[36] But beware. Once a "stamp of approval" is given, there is almost no evaluation or "policing" of performance. In fact, there is little, if any, follow-up of any kind—although several certificate-granting organizations have programs to investigate complaints.

WOMEN AND FINANCIAL PLANNING

Many studies show that both men and women lack basic knowledge about financing retirement. However, it is particularly hard for some women to manage the financial planning challenge. Adequate income in retirement is especially difficult for some women to achieve. This is because of the common sex biases in the workplace, the complexity of women's roles, their longer life expectancy, lower pension coverage, inadequate survivors' benefits, and a long tradition of women not managing the family finances.

Current midlife and older women are at a special disadvantage. Given traditional gender roles over their lifetimes, they have had less income and accumulated less wealth. Often they have left managing the money to someone else and have made the care of others a higher priority than planning and saving for their own future. When women become involved in issues of investing and financial planning, whether by choice or necessity, some become profoundly uncomfortable and feel unprepared.

A Brandeis University survey of 500 women aged 50 and older found that women do not feel knowledgeable about "the investments that count."[37] The survey asked women about seven types of financial assets and how they rated their understanding of them. While comfortable with CDs and savings bonds, the women surveyed reported low understanding with regard to other investment opportunities. For example, mutual funds are designed to allow people with even small amounts of money to invest in a greater range of investment opportunities, while reducing risk and the amount of sophistication that is required to make sound decisions. Yet less than one-third of the women surveyed indicated they had a significant understanding of this type of investment.

In companies today there are increasing numbers of 401(k) defined contribution plans, requiring workers to make individual investment decisions. To make informed decisions related to the money going into these plans, workers obviously need to understand the various trade-offs between return and risk among various investments. However, most of the older women surveyed felt that they lacked the personal expertise to perform this critical task.

EMPLOYER ASSISTANCE

Employers, labor leaders, and specialists in aging all bring different perspectives to the question of how we should deal with and improve preretirement planning. However, they all generally agree on one primary goal. There is a need to generate a greater awareness among workers and their spouses of the problems and potentials of old age. And they generally agree that assistance should be available, where appropriate, in preparing for successful retirement. Many companies have some kind of program designed to ease the transition to retirement for their employees. In a number of cases, however, employees receive little more than booklets with general retirement and benefit information. There are some companies, however, that organize formal programs. These programs often last two or more days and cover company benefits, health-care cost issues, Social Security, legal considerations, and topics on financial planning (taxes, investments, and estate issues). Unfortunately, sometimes the people who deliver this information come from outside the company but have a financial interest in specific products or services.

In the United States, the big challenge is for us: (1) to increase the availability of unbiased and accurate preretirement education to persons seeking such information; (2) to improve the number and quality of available programs; and (3) above all, to encourage people to begin preparing for retirement at a relatively early age. Individual financial planning for retirement is a difficult and complex matter; it may be one of the most difficult things you will ever have to deal with. Moreover, planning shortly before retirement (even 10 or 15 years before) is usually too late.

WILL SOCIAL SECURITY BE THERE FOR ME?

To this point our discussion has focused on "why" Social Security and other pension schemes exist and how to evaluate them. We have not discussed "how" they are financed. Yet everyone knows that there are serious financing problems that must be dealt with. With regard to public plans, the Merchants of Doom, from President Bush on down, keep reminding us of the problems in horrific terms. It is not surprising, therefore, that almost half (44%) of baby boomers in a 2003 survey said that they were not confident that Social Security would "still be available" when they retired.[38]

Certainly the financing issues have not been ignored. There are now countless books (and other writings) describing the long-term problems and suggesting solutions.[39] What is clear to most experts, based on the data and extensive debate to date, is that the financing problem with regard to Social Security retirement pensions does not require radical changes to be solved.

Everyone agrees that the only solutions for Social Security are a rise in payments, a cut in benefits, or (more likely) some combination of the two.

Conservatives generally support a cut in benefits—for example, by changing the procedures for calculating benefit amounts. Alternatively, reforms that focus on increasing revenues include: raising the employer and employee shares of payroll taxes (for example, by just 1 percentage point each, which would keep the system fully solvent for 75 years);[40] raising or completely eliminating the salary and wage ceiling on the Social Security portion of the payroll tax ($94,200 in 2006) so that higher-paid employees would contribute more revenue;[41] dedicating to the financing of Social Security the revenue from a 3 percent surcharge on all income over $200,000.[42]

Another proposal we think is highly worthy of discussion has been developed by Robert Ball, the longest serving Commissioner of Social Security (1962 to 1973). Ball proposes that the future shortfall in Social Security be met by taking three actions. First, very similar to the proposal above, the maximum earnings level upon which payroll taxes are assessed would be increased to its historic level (90 percent of covered earnings). Second, some of the funds in the Social Security trust funds would be invested in equities, rather than 100 percent in federal government bonds. Third, the estate tax exemption level would be frozen at the 2009 level of $3.5 million, and tax revenues on estates over that level would become dedicated revenue, to be used only for paying Social Security benefits.

Ball bases the rationale for this approach in part on the early history of Social Security and the unlikely possibility of using general revenue instead of the estate tax. Ball argues:

> Like most of the founders of Social Security, I once assumed that general revenues would eventually be used to make up for [the] initial deficit of contributions. The idea still makes sense, since there is no good reason why the cost of getting the system started should be met entirely by the future contributions of workers and their employers. But there are no general revenues available because of the president's [George W. Bush's] policies which have resulted in projections of deficits rather than surpluses as far as the eye can see.[43]

Nearly everyone agrees that it is important that we reach political agreement on an approach to deal with the financing gap and the specific changes to be made. While there is not a financial crisis now or in the near future, spreading the changes over a long period of time makes them politically and economically more palatable.

Believe it or not, as problems go, the financing problems regarding Social Security retirement benefits are relatively easily solved; there are many *economic* options that are not horrendous. However, the politics related to reform is extremely uncertain—given the agendas of the various Merchants of Doom, given the fact that bipartisan cooperation has ended in Washington, and given the huge imbalance that currently exists in projected government revenues relative to necessary and appropriate future expenditures (mainly as a result of tax cuts and a projected $1.3 trillion long-term cost resulting from the Iraq war).[44]

DEBATING THE PENSION MIX

It has been over a century since Bismarck set the world on the path of providing pensions for old age to most of a nation's citizens. If we look at the pension programs currently existing in various industrialized countries, we find that there is a tendency to rely heavily either on public pensions or on some sort of private/public combination *with extensive regulation of the private sector.* In countries that rely heavily on private pensions, the tendency is for the private and public pension programs to be closely coordinated by a large number of complex legislative and administrative mechanisms and regulations. In France (perhaps an extreme example), it is difficult to make a distinction between Social Security and the widespread private pension programs, given the elaborate coordinating mechanisms that have been established.

In the United States, both public and private pension plans have assumed a growing share of responsibility for providing retirement income needs. Reliance on this collective approach will continue to be important, and we hope it will not be significantly diminished in the future. But having said that, it is not yet clear how this collective responsibility ultimately will be divided between public and private institutions.

Although there is broad agreement today regarding the social value of pensions, there continues to be a lot of debate over what kinds of pensions should be used and whether they should be publicly or privately managed. As we discussed in Chapter 2, one context for this debate is demographic change. The Merchants of Doom see population aging as creating the need to abandon the old types of pensions and replacing them with other types. We do not agree.

With regard to the choice between defined benefit plans like the present Social Security program and defined contribution programs, such as 401(k) plans, we agree with Alicia Munnell, Director of the Boston College Center on Retirement Research: "Neither defined contribution nor defined benefit plans are intrinsically superior; they involve a number of trade-offs. The question is which is most appropriate for the basic level of income."[45] As Munnell points out, shifting the Social Security approach to the use of defined contribution personal accounts would (1) destroy the current predictability and surety of benefits, (2) reduce the social contract that supports the redistribution of some Social Security revenues, and (3) open up Social Security to a whole host of new problems that plague existing defined contribution plans in the United States and abroad. These problems are the focus of our next two chapters.

. . . .

CHAPTER 5

The Company Pension: Altruism or Self-Interest?

Private retirement income programs constitute a patchwork quilt—a patch here, a bit of padding there, some beautiful plush velvet squares beside a threadbare spot—that covers, at best, half the bed.

—Merton and Joan Bernstein[1]

If you have a corporate defined-benefit pension that's fully funded, feel free to stand up and dance a jig. The problem is, it's difficult to know for sure.

—Ben Stein & Phil DeMuth[2]

The baby boomers approaching old age have grown up and worked in a society very different from the struggling nation of the Thirties. One big difference was the mushrooming growth of employer-sponsored pensions.

Once Social Security was in place, employers and unions turned their attention to ways of supplementing the relatively meager benefits provided by this new public program. Pension plans set up by private companies had appeared by the end of the nineteenth century. And although between 3 and 4 million workers were participating in private schemes prior to the establishment of Social Security, coverage was concentrated in a few old, big businesses, and benefits were very limited.

In the 1940s and 1950s things changed dramatically. Private employer coverage rose rapidly as a result of the growing recognition, especially by unions, of Social Security's very low benefits and the consequent need for retirement income supplementation. And, as we discuss below, it was a time when employers found pensions to be an effective tool for dealing with manpower issues. So, by the time the baby boomers began entering the labor force, employer-sponsored pensions were quite common.

But pension coverage began to level off by the 1970s and has remained a relatively constant percent of the labor force ever since. Not only did coverage slow, but the basic nature of pensions began to undergo modifications, and with them, employers' responsibilities began to lessen, dramatically.

THE BIG CHANGE

Today, employer-sponsored pension plans cannot be counted on as a reliable and adequate source of supplemental income for future retirees receiving modest Social Security benefits. All too frequently, we have witnessed major companies in financial distress that have decided to abandon, reduce, or radically change their pension commitments. Other employers, as part of their financial strategic planning, have frozen their traditional pension plans for current workers and have shifted the major responsibility for adequate pension income from the company to their workers.

In the context of such developments, many boomers and other retirees in the future face a much less certain retirement income situation. In the worst cases, employees who have been "covered" by pensions during most of their working life may end up with nothing, or very little, in the way of pension benefits. For increasing numbers of retirees, the very modest payments from Social Security may well be their primary source of retirement income or, for some, their only source.

Yet, President Bush and other Merchants of Doom continue to "beat the drums"—purveying the message that Social Security is unsustainable and will soon go broke. Of course, their message has undermined public confidence in the program, which is exactly what they want to do. Creating this fear and confusion among the public is part of a political strategy by many of the Merchants to gain acceptance of the notion that we should turn parts of our public program into private "personal accounts." These personal accounts would parallel developments in the private pension arena that place much of the responsibility for adequate retirement income—in the form of market investment decisions—on the individual worker.

In this chapter, and the one that follows, we will look closely at the roles private pensions have played over the years, the way that their nature has been changing, the problems they pose for both employers and employees, and the impact they are likely to have on prospects for adequate retirement income in future years. Included in these discussions will be a review of how workers have faired in two other countries where national programs of personal accounts have been established.

Together, this chapter and Chapter 6 should make it clear that many boomers, and many of those who will follow them, may not be able to count on high pensions in their retirement years. This unfortunate reality increases the importance for retirees of being able to count on Social Security benefits that are as least as good as those today's elders receive.

"SAVE WAL-MART A SUBSTANTIAL SUM OF MONEY"

In 2005, M. Susan Chambers worked for Wal-Mart as executive vice president for benefits. Concerned about her firm's rapidly rising employee benefit costs, Chambers (on behalf of management) wrote an internal memo to Wal-Mart's Board of Directors. In the memo (leaked to the *New York Times*), Chambers proposed various ways to hold down spending on pensions and health care. Among the recommendations was a proposal to hire more part-time workers and to discourage unhealthy people from joining the company's workforce. Specifically with regard to pensions, her memo stated: "We should reduce our overall investment in the profit sharing and 401(k) program from approximately 4 percent of wages to approximately 3 percent of wages. Doing so would bring the program more in line with retail offerings and would save Wal-Mart a substantial sum of money."[3]

How was the money to be saved? In large part by only making company contributions into individual employees' 401(k) plans if the employee also contributed into the plan. This would be a big change from Wal-Mart's practice at the time of making *automatic* contributions, whether or not the employee contributed. Wal-Mart knew from the experience in many other American companies that if participation were optional, many workers, especially low-wage workers, would not contribute to a retirement pension account. The result would be that those employees who did not participate would lose the company's retirement contribution, and Wal-Mart would save money.

THE EMPLOYER-SPONSORED PENSION

Over the years, the pensions sponsored by employers have played an important role in retirement income security. But, as illustrated by the Wal-Mart example, there is a strong trend today by employers to reduce the role they play in the retirement income situation. There is little doubt that this trend will have unfortunate implications for baby boomers and lots of other workers.

In 1962, most of the income received by the elderly came from Social Security; employer-sponsored pensions accounted for only nine percent of all elderly income (see Figure 5.1). In 2002, most of elderly income still came from Social Security, but the percent coming from pensions had more than doubled, to 20 percent.

As employer-sponsored pensions (and a variety of other savings vehicles) have grown in importance, problems associated with them have also grown. In fact, the problems have been so serious that rather than a reliable source of

risk of providing the guaranteed level of retirement benefits. Plans typically provide a choice as to how benefits are paid out, often in a lump sum but sometimes as an annuity.

WHY EMPLOYER-SPONSORED PENSION PLANS?

Employers started pension plans for two principal reasons. First, there was an altruistic motivation. It was the desire of many employers to help "faithful workers" deal with the economic problems that arose when they could no longer work or, in some cases, no longer meet the pace or physical demands of their jobs. Actually, pensions helped in two ways. They *helped the worker* finance a potentially extended period without earnings—which ultimately came to be called "retirement." But second, pensions *also helped employers* deal with an awkward and unpleasant situation—the act of "turning out" a worker into an uncertain economic situation as he or she approached old age. In both the early twentieth century-era of small businesses and the later era of big business, employers found pensions useful in dealing with this unpleasant aspect of retirement. In both smaller and larger firms, employers found it difficult to make a "retirement decision" they knew would likely have tragic results: laying off, for example, a 60-year-old worker who might never find another job.

It is important to realize, however, that the creation of pensions that provided workers with an opportunity to retire was not just a paternalistic or caretaking action by businesses. Its function, in fact, was often precisely the opposite. Many employers wanted to get rid of older workers; decisions had to be made and communicated. Pensions helped. As historian William Graebner points out, "The pension was expected to free those who made personnel decisions from the fetters of personalism, to transform a human situation into a bureaucratic one."[6]

For this and other reasons, many employers developed pension plans *to promote their own interests*. They saw that pensions could be used to (1) help in the retention of the workers they viewed as most desirable, (2) promote greater efficiency in the workplace, (3) help adjust the company's workforce to shifting demand, and (4) facilitate the retirement of workers no longer considered suitable for employment.

Historically, the first pension benefits were offered typically on a "take it or lose it" basis. There were little or no rewards to workers who left firms "early" for other jobs. Nor was there a pension "bonus" given to those workers who wanted to continue working beyond the employer's designated retirement age.

As unions emerged, still another use for pensions was found. Some employers incorporated pensions into a broader strategy designed to contain labor unrest and weaken the union movement. Most early company pension plans, for example, "included clauses prohibiting workers from striking on penalty of forfeiting all pension rights."[7]

The early history of private pensions, therefore, is one that makes clear that employer-sponsored plans were basically a tool of management—one way to assist employers in dealing with manpower/personnel issues.[8] Altruism, although it existed among some employers, was certainly not the major consideration for most when the early pension plans were designed.

When the Great Depression came in the 1930s, private pension plans (along with most everything else economic) were financially devastated. Plan reserves disappeared; employers disappeared; and many workers found their future or current pension benefits gone. But despite these events, employer-sponsored pensions came to be accepted as a key part of the American retirement income system.

Yet there remained many problems with them.

THE COVERAGE PROBLEM

Want to have adequate income in retirement? Then most people will need more income than they will get from Social Security. Old Age and Survivors benefits, even with the sizable benefit increase Congress legislated in 1972 (and many other smaller ones), were never intended to provide more than a basic "floor of protection." It was clear from the beginning that Social Security would need to be supplemented by employer-sponsored pensions and/or personal savings. Social Security "replacement rates" for most workers are low.[9] Retiring workers with low earnings levels get most of their preretirement income replaced by the Social Security benefits they received. But the replacement rate falls dramatically as earnings rise. This opens up a gap that needs to be filled by other income sources. Hence, over the years there have been many actions by the federal government to provide sufficient incentives for employers and individuals to plan for retirement and set up supplemental pension/savings accounts that would effectively deal with retirement needs over and above Social Security.

But none of the incentives enacted has worked very well. Today, even with all the tax incentives offered by the government, a very large proportion of Americans are not covered by an employer-sponsored pension or by their own personal savings account. As a report by the U.S. General Accounting Office points out:

Since the 1970s, only about half of the nation's [full-time] private wage and salary workers have been covered by employer-sponsored pensions. Although it is difficult to predict whether any particular worker currently in the labor force will ultimately earn a pension benefit, at present only about 52 percent of retirees receive pension income. Over

the past 25 years, considerable attention has been focused on mod-
ifying pension law, in part to improve coverage and ultimately retirement income adequacy, yet a significant portion of the workforce
remains without pension coverage and the opportunity to earn pension
income.[10]

As a matter of fact, pension coverage rate was lower in 2002 than it was in
1979.[11]

WHO IS COVERED?

DB plans dominated the early growth in pension coverage. By 1975, the
number of workers in DB plans had reached about 27 million, compared
to 12 million in defined contribution plans.[12] In those days, workers with
defined contribution coverage were predominately in small companies where
the costs of administering DB plans were viewed as prohibitive.

Today, the sad fact is that for every full-time worker covered there is
one *without* any pension coverage. The term "pension covered" is typically
used by analysts to refer to all workers in a company or government agency
who have a pension plan, whether or not all employees actually *participate*
in the plan. In fact, however, some workers in a company may not be
eligible to participate in an existing plan (for example, part-time workers
are often excluded). Other workers cannot participate until they reach a
certain age (typically age 21) and achieve a minimum tenure on the job
(typically one year). Published statistics on coverage vary greatly because
different definitions are used to define the relevant population. The Center
for Retirement Research at Boston College reports 2002 coverage of 64
percent for *government and private* "eligible" workers, together, but only
39 percent for *private sector* full- and part-time workers.[13] Even among these
broad categories, coverage varies greatly among different kinds of workers.

A major proportion of workers not covered by a pension are in two
industries: wholesale and retail trade and the service industry. But the best
factors to use in predicting coverage are union status and the size of the
employing firm. A very high proportion of full-time workers without pension
coverage are nonunion and work for firms with a relatively small number
of employees.[14]

It has been especially difficult to extend private pension coverage to employees in small firms.[15] Among the factors that have been cited to explain
the low coverage are:

1. The high costs per employee of establishing and maintaining a private plan.
2. The lack of pressure for pension benefits from employees of small
   companies.

3. The fact that small businesses are often relatively young and, on average, short-lived.
4. The tendency of small employers to see pensions costs as "coming out of their pocket."
5. The emphasis in small firms on individual self-reliance in financial matters.
6. The often unstable and insecure financial status of many small businesses.

Given the experience to date, it is pretty clear that a very large proportion of the American wage workforce is not likely to be covered by an employer pension—ever! This is the case despite great interest over the years in a wider variety of mechanisms to provide retirement income other than the traditional DB and DC plans. Let us look more closely at the range of pension types.

TYPES OF COVERAGE

Private sector pension plans vary greatly. In fact, there is even disagreement among experts over just what type of arrangement should be called a "pension." Let us look at three such controversial arrangements.

Profit-Sharing Plans. Most estimates of nationwide pension coverage include workers who are covered only by a "deferred profit-sharing plan." Yet profit-sharing plans are very different from traditional DB plans. Contributions into profit-sharing plans usually vary with the amount of a particular company's profits and consequently are more directly tied to the ups and downs of the economy and the fortunes of a particular firm. Hence, profit-sharing plans—less certain with regard to the ultimate payout—are more problematic than DB plans as a means of insuring adequate retirement benefits for the millions of workers with *only* this type of coverage. In contrast, DB pension plans make a benefit promise that is generally independent of fluctuations in the economy or the prosperity of a particular business enterprise (as long as it stays in business).

The pension history at the Sears and Roebuck Company (now just called Sears) is a good example of the problems that can arise. Initially, the company provided retiring workers with only profit-sharing payments that were invested in Sears stock. In the 1970s over 20 percent of Sears common stock was owned by Sears employees through the company's profit-sharing plan. In the company's high profit years of the 1960s and early 1970s, employees experienced through the plan huge investment gains (on paper), as the price of Sears stock soared. Some became "paper millionaires." But later, as new companies like Wal-Mart entered the highly competitive retail market,

year. Traditional DB plans, in contrast, increase a worker's pension accrual during the last years on the job when wages and salaries are usually higher than earlier in working careers.

An argument over whether these plans constitute age discrimination against older employees is working its way through the courts and is discussed further in the next chapter. Because of protests from older workers, some companies are giving their employees a choice between the old-style DB plans and a cash balance plans. But not all companies give their workers this option.

EXTENDING COVERAGE: IRAs

Created to extend pension coverage in the private sector, individual retirement accounts (IRAs) were considered by some people to be one of the most important mechanisms to do so. In a message to Congress on December 8, 1971, President Richard Nixon proposed that pension legislation be enacted that would allow and encourage people without group pension coverage to benefit from favorable tax provisions for retirement saving. Such legislation was ultimately enacted as part of the private pension reform legislation—the Employee Retirement Income Security Act (ERISA)—that became law in 1974.

President Nixon's proposal, and the subsequent legislation signed into law by President Gerald Ford (in 1974), permitted wage and salary earners to set up their own individual retirement plans (IRAs) *if they are not covered by any other qualified pension plan*. In addition, the 1974 pension reform legislation liberalized existing limitations on contributions to retirement plans (called Keogh plans) that are contributed to by self-employed workers. Then the Economic Recovery Act of 1981expanded IRA eligibility to all workers.

IRA and Keogh contributions are tax-deductible on federal income tax returns for most people. The ceiling on annual contributions to IRAs is $4,000 for eligible individuals under age 50 and $5,000 for persons older than 50, through 2007. All IRA accounts can accumulate investment earnings taxfree. However, once the money is taken out of an IRA account it is then taxable as income. The amount of money accumulated in these accounts is now quite large. In 2004, there was $3.48 trillion worth of financial assets held in IRA accounts.[23]

When President Nixon proposed the original IRA legislation, he argued that it would encourage people to save and that public policy should reward and reinforce this type of activity. In transmitting the legislation, he said:

Self-reliance, prudence, and independence are qualities which our government should work to encourage among our people. These are also the qualities which are involved when a person chooses to invest in a retirement savings plan, setting aside money today so that he will have greater security tomorrow. In this respect pension plans are a direct expression of some of the best elements in the American character. Public policy should be designed to reward and reinforce these qualities.

Whether the IRA mechanism has in fact increased total savings over the years is still being debated, but the general consensus is that it has not. Statistics indicate that many of those who have invested in IRAs (typically higher earners) would probably have invested those same funds in other vehicles for personal savings.[24]

President Nixon also argued that this legislation would be responsive to the inequity that existed between those people who were covered by private pensions and those who were not. People covered by private pensions receive favorable tax treatment because contributions made by the employer on their behalf are not taxable. These private pension contributions are only taxable at the time they are paid out, often at a lower tax rate because an individual's or couples' income in retirement is typically lower than income when working.

These were President Nixon's two principal arguments in favor of such legislation. An additional argument in favor of IRAs is that by encouraging people to save for retirement individually, one allows them greater control over their investments. They can decide what they want to invest in and the amount of risk they want to take. In contrast, members of a collective DB plan usually have nothing to say about the investment policy of the plan. Often the gains of good investment accrue only to the employer. But those employees who are sophisticated about financial matters might be able to do better on their own, it is argued, especially if they are willing to take more risks. Some evidence indicates, however, that many individuals often invest too conservatively, when given responsibility for managing retirement funds.[25]

As we indicated above, the proportion of *lower-paid* workers who take advantage of the IRA opportunity for tax-sheltered saving is much smaller than that of more highly paid persons. The fear that such tax-exemption proposals would turn into tax loopholes for higher-income people was the principal argument voiced in Congress against the legislation when it was proposed and continues to be an argument made today, based on actual experience showing that participation in IRA plans rises dramatically with income level.[26]

ROTH IRAs

A new IRA option was initiated in 1998—the Roth IRA. It is available to everyone whose "adjusted gross income" on their federal tax return is below specified levels (in 2006, $95,000 for single individuals and $150,000 for couples). The maximum annual contribution to a Roth IRA in 2006 for persons under age 50 was $4,000 (or 100 percent of compensation, if less). If age 50 or over, the maximum rose to $5,000.

The most important difference between a regular IRA and a Roth is that unlike regular IRA contributions, Roth IRA contributions are not tax-deductible. Despite this, Roth IRAs are generally more advantageous, since no taxes are levied on both the resulting investment income (similar to regular IRAs) and also any income paid out after five years or more (*unlike* regular IRAs). Because the investment income growth component of an IRA (not the contribution component) is typically the largest part of the final payout, many people, especially those investing at younger ages, will come out ahead using Roth IRAs rather than regular IRAs. However, which IRA is best also depends to a degree on an individual's or couple's tax bracket at pay-in and pay-out, and on the number of years of contributions.

THE PASSAGE OF ERISA

Pension coverage is only one issue that has arisen related to private pensions. With the growth of employer-sponsored pensions came many other problems. Many of these problems arose from the fact (as we discussed above) that these pensions were designed to meet the manpower needs of employers. So, for example, many of the early pension plans had vesting provisions that helped achieve employer goals but were inequitable and hostile to the welfare of workers. Vesting refers to pension plan provisions that give a participant the right to receive an accrued benefit, regardless of whether the employee is still employed with the granting company at the time the designated years of service or eligibility age for benefits are reached.

In the early days of employer pensions, employers often designed plans so that only workers who remained with the company until the date of early or normal retirement received a pension. Vesting provisions were nonexistent in many early plans; you received a pension only if you stayed with the company for a full working career. Other plans vested benefits only after many years. In some of the worst cases, workers were terminated just before becoming eligible for vesting. Suppose your pension rights in a particular company were scheduled to vest after 30 years of continuous employment. You could be terminated, for example, by the company after 29 years of work and not receive any pension benefits. (This was not common, but it did happen.) What was common, given the intricacies of the early vesting provisions, was for workers to think they were covered by a pension plan and to anticipate a benefit—only to discover when they reached old age that they were eligible for nothing!

Vesting provisions were not the only issue. Another major problem was the loss of pension security as a result of (1) inadequate employer pension funding, (2) misuse of the pension funds controlled by employers, or (3) the termination of plans because of business closures, bankruptcy, or other reasons. In 1968 a White House Task Force on Older Americans estimated that only about ten percent of individuals who were "covered" by pension plans had ever received any benefits.[27]

Still another problem resulted from the fact that the death of the worker often resulted in little or no survivor benefits being paid to the spouse. When the worker suddenly died, spouses (typically wives) were surprised to find out that no pension provision had been made for them by the employer or their spouse.

Reacting to these and other problems, the federal government enacted the 1959 Welfare and Pension Plan Disclosure Act. However, this law was largely ineffective because it placed primary responsibility for policing the plans on the participants. As public awareness of the problems grew and pension horror stories appeared with increased frequency in the media, committees in Congress worked to develop better legislation.

The result was the Employee Retirement Income Security Act (ERISA). This law, passed in 1974, put into place a more comprehensive set of pension safeguards:

- Minimum standards for partial vesting were established (significantly reducing "years of service" requirements).
- The Social Security Administration became a tracking repository for required employer reports on the vested benefits of workers leaving firms.
- Funding and fiduciary standards were significantly strengthened.
- A plan termination insurance program, administered by the PBGC, was established.
- Stronger pension plan disclosure regulations were legislated.
- Modest provisions were introduced to encourage more survivors' benefits.

THE HAZARDS OF PENSION PLAN TERMINATIONS

It now seems like a very long time ago, but in 1963 a dramatic and important event occurred in American pension history. The nation was shocked when the Studebaker Corporation, a producer of automobiles, announced it was closing its operations in the United States and (as a result) could not meet its pension obligations. The company had established, 14 years before, a DB plan that ultimately covered about 11,000 employees. That meant that the company had made a commitment to its workers to pay them a specified amount when they retired (according to an agreed upon benefit calculation formula).

With DB plans, it is the company's responsibility to put aside sufficient funds to meet its pension obligations. When the Studebaker Corporation closed its South Bend, Indiana plant, there were assets worth $24 million

people have said, that it looks as though there's a shift of financial burden, or gain, from the working class, that loses a billion or two of pensions and health benefits, to the investing class, which make a billon or two of profit." Ross responded, "The real villains in the piece, if there are villains, are the old management pre-bankruptcy, who made commitments, promises to their workers they couldn't keep."[31]

(Where is Robin Hood when we need him?)

Another historic case that illustrates the hazards of coverage under DB plans is the Braniff Airlines shut down. In the spring of 1982, Braniff Airlines ceased doing business. Even before Braniff filed for bankruptcy, there were dramatic reductions in the number of employees working for the company. A few years before the shutdown there were about 15,000 employees working for Braniff (in the heyday of airlines). Just before filing for bankruptcy, there were only 9,500 employees left. Thus, a significant number of people were forced to leave Braniff, in most cases prior to the bankruptcy. What happened to the pension rights of these particular employees? And after Braniff filed for bankruptcy and terminated its pension plans, what happened to the workers who were still employed, were covered by the plan, and expected to receive benefits?

One thing is certain. Those people who had fewer than ten years of service working for Braniff Airlines—whether they had left before the bankruptcy or whether they were working at the point of bankruptcy filing—got nothing under the ERISA standards in force at the time. ERISA, at the time, required that employees had to have at least ten years of service (the most popular alternative of three vesting options available at the time) to be guaranteed receipt of a retirement benefit when they retired.

Other Braniff employees had some protection. Those workers who were retired and receiving pensions, and those with at least 10 years of service and not retired, were protected by the PBGC. This federally created corporation, which has the U.S. Secretary of Labor as its chairman of the board, was set up under ERISA to guarantee the continued payment of benefits to retired workers and the future payment of benefits to vested workers (limited in 2006 to $3,888 monthly for retirees age 65 or older). When a DB plan terminates without sufficient funds to meet these obligations, the PBGC takes over the plan and assumes responsibility for paying the benefits. Each company or union with a plan covered by ERISA must make contributions (insurance premiums) to the PBGC, at a rate determined by Congress, to cover the costs of providing this insurance protection.

A relatively recent example of the private pension troubles that can arise is what happened when UAL Corp., the parent company of United Airlines, filed for bankruptcy on December 9, 2002. Faced with the collapse of the airline, unionized employees of United agreed to enormous financial sacrifices (in terms of promised pay and benefits) to help the carrier shore up its finances. Workers' economic concessions after United filed for bankruptcy totaled nearly $13 billion.

Notwithstanding the concessions, United instituted a variety of cost-cutting actions that the unions charged broke faith with current employees and the company's retirees. For example, the company unilaterally decided to cut costs by reducing retiree health benefits for already-retired workers, including many individuals recently lured into retirement by company-offered early retirement incentives—workers who thought they would get the higher, precut benefits. Then United's management halted legally required contributions to employee pension plans, failing to make $72 million in contributions that were due on July 15, 2004. And, pursuant to an amended bankruptcy financing agreement it had negotiated with its creditors, United's management announced at one point that it would make no additional pension contributions before exiting from bankruptcy.

In December 2004, the PBGC tried to take control of the pilots' pension plan, triggering a legal battle with the pilots regarding the timing of the PBGC's action. In March 2005, the PBGC also moved to take over the pension fund for ground employees and mechanics, saying that the fund was almost $3 billion short of the amount needed to meet its obligations. All parties agreed that United was unable to meet its pension obligations. But all three involved parties (the employees, the company, and the PBGC) began legal maneuvering to achieve the best monetary outcome for themselves. The ground employees, for example, sought to delay the PBGC takeovers as long as possible—knowing full well that pensions would be cut for most workers when the PBGC took over.

On May 10, 2005, a bankruptcy judge approved United's request to terminate all its pension plans, and the PBGC took them over. As part of the court ruling, the PBGC hoped to receive up to approximately $1.5 billion in securities from United after the airline reorganized. However, for many employees the outlook was grim, since they were faced with benefits losses of nearly one billion dollars from the PBGC takeover (according to estimates announced by the PBGC).[32]

"I'm getting penalized in every way possible," former United pilot Howard Cohen told a *Denver Post* reporter. When he retired in 2002, this 63-year-old former 747 pilot began receiving a monthly pension of $10,000. Today he receives $2,700 monthly.[33]

The former United Airlines pension plan covered about 14,000 people. Of those, 6,700 are retired. Under the PBGC insurance provisions, these retirees receive only 43 percent of their promised benefits.[34]

TALES OF THE PBGC: WHAT TYPE OF MONSTER HAVE WE CREATED?

As we discussed above, Congress created the PBGC to protect workers if inadequately funded DB plans terminate. For example, the PBGC was there to step in when the poor economic conditions of the 1970s and 1980s caused plan terminations to rapidly increase. At the time, most terminating plans could meet their obligations; however, some could not.

Currently, however, the PBGC is responsible for the pensions of nearly a million workers and retirees who were covered by 3,277 terminated plans that were inadequately funded.[35] Termination of firms producing steel (and other metals), along with airlines, account for over 70 percent of the claims on PBGC funds. In 2002, the PBGC disbursed nearly $2.5 billion in monthly or lump sum benefit payments to retired plan participants.[36]

As we mentioned above, the PBGC gets its revenue from pension insurance premiums paid by companies and unions who sponsor covered plans. However, projected PBGC obligations to retirees have exceeded expected revenues of the organization for much of its existence. It was not until fiscal year 1996 that the PBGC had its first accumulated surplus, a happening that has not often been repeated. In fact, the PBGC's financial situation was so bad in early 2005 that the Secretary of Labor, Elaine Chao, declared, "the time to act is now. This system [the PBGC] is not sustainable. These are promises made, and promises made must be kept."[37]

In September of 2005, the PBGC stated in its annual report that the PBGC's long-term funding deficit stood at $23.1 billion.[38]

WHO WILL PAY THE COSTS?

Faced with a deteriorating PBGC fiscal situation, the Bush Administration in 2005 called for an increase in the premium that companies pay per participant. The Administration recommended, and Congress legislated, an increase from the current $19 per year to a new rate of $30 for each covered worker, with future premiums indexed to wage growth. Firms with financially troubled plans would continue to pay higher, risk-based premiums (discussed below).

The magnitude of this latest premium increase shocked many people, especially the companies that have to pay it. To understand the situation better, one must retrace the history of the pension insurance program. The struggle to find money to fund the PBGC obligations has a long history.

THE PBGC AND THE DUMPING PROBLEM

In 1983, the head of the PBGC went before Congress and testified that the agency would run out of funds unless Congress increased the premium on single-employer plans. The annual premium at the time was only $2.60 for each employee covered. The PBGC stated that due to underfunded terminating plans, PBGC liabilities were far higher than had ever been anticipated.

This statement surprised both the Congress and the businesses paying the premiums. This was the first time the agency had publicly revealed that it faced severe financial problems. A congressional committee looking into the situation concluded that "a major cause of the PBGC's problems was the ease with which economically viable companies could terminate underfunded plans and dump their pension liabilities on the termination insurance program."[39]

The possibility of rapidly escalating premiums caused many employers to call for changes in the reinsurance program. They correctly argued that companies with fully funded plans were, in effect, subsidizing unfunded plans as a result of legal loopholes allowing companies to dump their unfunded pension liabilities on the PBGC.

A major debate over these issues took place for several years, primarily in various committees of the Congress. In April 1986, legislation was finally passed that made it more difficult for employers to pass on unfunded plan liabilities to the PBGC. The key feature of the 1986 law was to distinguish between *standard* and *distress* terminations. When a standard termination occurs—where the employer is *not* in financial distress—employers must pay all benefit commitments under the plan. Only when a company has filed for bankruptcy, would clearly go out of business unless the plan were terminated, or where the cost has become unreasonably burdensome does the financial support of the PBGC come into play. Moreover, in such cases, the new law gave higher priority than before to PBGC claims in bankruptcy proceedings, thereby substantially increasing its claims on the distressed company's assets and reducing the practice of "dumping" unfunded liabilities onto the PBGC. The 1986 law also addressed the financial problems of the PBGC by increasing the premium for single-employer termination insurance.

HOW BAD CAN IT GET?

But the situation got worse, not better. No sooner had the new legislation passed in 1986 than the PBGC was confronted with distressed terminations of unprecedented proportions. PBGC's deficit nearly tripled, and its liabilities more than doubled. Reacting to a deteriorating situation, Congress acted in late 1987, again in 1990, and still again in 1994.

One big change resulting from these legislative actions was the creation of a "variable rate premium." As of January 1, 1991, an annual base rate of $19 per employee participant was levied on all plans. An additional charge of $9 per $1,000 of unfunded vested benefits was levied on plans not fully funded. This additional premium, however, was set to not exceed $53 per plan participant.

Unfortunately over the years the situation has continued to deteriorate. As we stated above, in September of 2005, the PBGC's long-term funding deficit stood at $23.1 billion, and the Congress continued its search for a reasonable solution. [A 2006 law was passed after this book was written.]

ERISA DID THE JOB, BUT ...

Historically, the principal focus of ERISA was to expand the supervision and regulation of private pension plans by the federal government and to create tax-exempt IRAs. But regulation costs money. In addition to the costs to taxpayers for the federal supervisory agencies and their staffs, considerable regulatory costs are imposed on the businesses with DB plans. These costs arise from the necessity of conforming to the law and providing information to the government in order for the regulators to carry out their various supervisory roles. Because of the complexity of the laws and regulations, businesses must often either develop staff and/or hire outside lawyers and consultants to provide them with the expertise necessary to ensure compliance with ERISA and other pension-related laws. As a result, pension management has become big business in the United States.

Understandably, employers have reacted negatively to the growing regulatory prohibitions and costs. A pension consultant to employers, Rebecca Miller, testifying at an Internal Revenue Service pension hearing, commented, "Every time the rules are changed, clients say, 'I'm going to junk this thing'."[40]

Over the years there has been an outpouring of complaints from pension consultants and employers before congressional committees about the high costs of reporting required information to the government and the costs of action needed to simply understanding the pension laws. Not surprisingly, some companies have terminated their plans because of the increased administrative burdens and costs. And new plans are almost never DB plans. Rather, DC plans are now the popular plan of employer choice.

Despite its limitations, the original 1974 ERISA legislation (and later amendments to it) went a long way to achieving its primary goal—making sure employees received promised pension benefits. Unfortunately, this achievement came at a significant price.

As far as employers were concerned, in addition to the added administrative costs, ERISA took away one of the most important ways of controlling their work force. While the availability of pension benefits could still be used as a recruitment tool, employers could no longer easily structure DB plans to restrict actual pension receipt to those workers who stayed with the company and who fit into their manpower needs.

Having lost this desirable pension tool, employers (as we discussed above) at the same time found that ERISA significantly drove up the costs of having a pension plan. First, there were the costs of understanding the laws. Second, as a result of the laws, more workers were actually getting benefits. Third, there was the substantial burden in added paperwork related to required reports required by the U.S. Treasury, the U.S. Department of Labor, and the PBGC. And fourth, there were the new costs of insurance premiums that had to be paid by companies in order to provide funding for the PBGC's plan termination insurance.

Early on, prominent pension actuary Paul H. Jackson "got it right." He predicted in 1977 that "the substantial impact of ERISA must, of course, result in a total reassessment [by employers] of the purpose and value of private pension plans.... Fewer new plans will be undertaken on a purely voluntary basis—the commitment is simply too all-pervasive."[41] The passage of ERISA, and the subsequent experience with its operation, was the beginning of the end for private DB plans covering large numbers of workers.

CHAPTER 6

The Pension Lottery: Personal Pension Accounts

The New York attorney general said in a lawsuit...that [H&R Block] steered clients, many of them low income, into individual retirement accounts that were "virtually guaranteed to lose money" because of low interest rates and high fees.
                                                          —*The New York Times*[1]

It must be concluded that privatization "privatizes" the only thing that should be shared: risk!
                                                          —Franco Modigliani[2]

Kathi Cooper graduated magna cum laude from the University of Texas with a degree in accounting and finance. She had worked for IBM for over 25 years. At age 52, Cooper was not too far away from retirement and was covered by a very good defined benefit (DB) pension (which she thought she had been promised by the company).

But then in 1994, and again in 1999, IBM changed her pension plan, covering her in both cases under a new kind of pension called a "cash balance" plan. When this happened the second time, Cooper sat down and calculated her new benefit. Much to her surprise, she discovered that the new plan significantly reduced the retirement benefits she would have to live on when she got older.

So one Sunday in mid-1999, at her Presbyterian church in the rural town of Moro Illinois, Kathi Cooper stood up during a part of the service when members of the congregation are encouraged to share their "joys or concerns." Cooper told the congregation that she had a concern. It was about the actions of her employer and the reduction in the pension benefit she had been promised. She said she was having trouble finding a lawyer who knew about pensions. All she could find in the Yellow Pages were lawyers who handled divorce, bankruptcy, and personal injury cases.

A week later when Cooper again came to church, a woman approached and handed her a piece of paper. On it was the name of a law firm and a phone number. The firm—Korein, Tillery—ended up representing Cooper as lead plaintiff among 140,000 IBM employees in a class-action lawsuit against IBM. So began a long legal battle.

THE PENSION "PROMISE"

What is an employer's responsibility with regard to economic security in old age and company-sponsored pensions? Not very much, according to Janice Gregory, senior vice president of the ERISA Industry Committee (a trade association for large employers with DB plans).

"Pensions are voluntary," says Gregory. "Some people may have expected to earn more benefits in the future under a certain plan formula, but *companies have a right to change their plans*, and this is made clear to employees" [emphasis added].[3] In fact, according to the law, companies may unilaterally freeze DB pensions for nonunionized employees with only 45 days notice. And employers can end or reduce their contributions to 401(k) plans at any time. For example, in December 2005 General Motors announced it would end its policy of matching 20 percent of the contributions made by salaried employees.

Regarding IBM, Congressman Bernard Sanders (D., Vermont) critically observed: "IBM had enough money to pay out a $260 million compensation package to former CEO Lou Gerstner, $260 million to one man, but they just could not keep their word to their long-term, dedicated employees. And, of course, it is not just IBM that we are talking about today. It is hundreds of companies that have done exactly the same thing. It is companies that have broken the law, discriminated against older American workers and slashed the pensions that those workers were promised."[4]

On August 1, 2003, the heads of blue-chip firms across the country were shocked to learn that a decision by Judge G. Patrick Murphy of the Southern District of Illinois had ruled against IBM in Kathi Cooper's case. Judge Murphy stated: "In 1999, IBM opted for a cash balance formula. The plans' actuaries projected that this would produce annual savings of almost $500 million by 2009. These savings would result from reductions of up to 47 percent in future benefits that would be earned by older IBM employees. The 1999 cash balance formula violates the literal terms of the Employee Retirement Income Security Act, that is, ERISA. IBM's own age discrimination analysis illustrates the problem."[5] IBM immediately announced it would appeal the decision.

In 2004, a settlement was reached. IBM agreed to pay $320 million in damages *even if IBM's appeal were successful.* And that is exactly what happened. In August 2006, an appeals court reversed the decision, finding no discrimination based on age. It agreed with plaintiff and the lower court that IBM's older workers were financially worse off under the new cash balance program but said that fact was irrelevant. There was no discrimination, said the appeals court, because workers with the same earnings and years of service, but of different ages, would get the same benefit *accrual.* That is, the court ignored the "promise" of benefits under the old plan.

The Cooper/IBM case is but one example of the continuing uncertainty American workers face regarding their ultimate pension benefits. In addition to the problems related to DB plans (which we discussed in the prior chapter), there are now a whole range of other problems arising from the introduction of new types of pension plans like IBM's cash balance plan. No doubt the most important development in recent years has been the dramatic shift by employers away from DB plans and the concurrent rise in new types of defined contribution (DC) plans.

NOW YOU SEE IT, NOW YOU DON'T

What Kathi Cooper and other IBM employees did not know in the 1990s was that the worst was yet to come. January 5, 2006, will probably go down in pension history as the day when it became clear to many people that DB pensions would suffer the same fate as the dinosaur. That day, IBM announced that it would freeze (starting in 2008) pension benefits from its DB plan for American employees. In its place, employees would be offered only a 401(k) plan.

IBM is a corporation known over the years for its generous and comprehensive employment provisions beyond salaries, treating its workers "as family," with all kinds of company perks. As important to most workers who took jobs at IBM was the company's promise of good pensions and medical coverage and great job security.

In part, IBM could do all this in the past because it was a pioneer and highly successful leader in the computer field; at one time IBM was the "blue chip" of blue-chip stocks. That is until the 1980s, when its competitors forced it into a period of struggle and decline.

Currently on an economic upswing, IBM announced in January 2006 that "the change to a 401(k) plan would give it competitive advantages both in attracting employees and containing labor costs."[6] Clearly a radically different attitude was emerging at the company.

IBM is not the only major company to announce such pension freezes. Others, for example, are Lockheed Martin, Verizon, and, Motorola. However, as *The New York Times* correspondent Mary Williams Walsh observed, "Once a standard-bearer for corporate America's compact with its workers, . . . [IBM's] pension freeze is the latest sign that today's workers are, to a much greater extent, on their own."[7]

THE FLIGHT FROM DB PLANS

It is not a coincidence that much of the support for shifting to DC plans comes from one group. This group is the same people who are warning us about baby boomers and other future elderly "breaking the bank" in the financing of the Social Security system. Many of these Merchants of Doom are representatives of mutual funds, insurance companies, banks, and brokerage houses. Can there be any doubt that one motive in trying to scare (they would say "educate") people about the retirement financing "crisis" is related to billions of dollars in fees—fees that the financial industry would get with any significant shifting of money from Social Security to personal financial accounts for retirement? The sellers of financial products, for example, would like to allow individuals to take some proportion of their Social Security payroll tax money and put it into personal investment accounts they would set up and manage, *for a fee*.

But financial institutions are not the only supporters of DC plans. As we see in the case of IBM, the increasing support for DC plans in the United States starts with employers. In the previous chapter we discussed the reasons for growing employer unhappiness with DB plans. Once corporations decided that these plans were not worth (from the company's self-interest point of view) the money they cost, they acted. Hundreds of companies, like IBM, began converting their DB plans to cheaper cash balance plans or freezing their DB plan coverage in favor of DC plans such as 401(k) plans. Not all have changed, however. A number of companies have kept their DB plans, providing additional benefits by adding on a DC plan—again typically a 401(k).

One explanation given to the public for these shifts is that employees, especially younger employees, prefer portable pensions. Yes, it may be true that these DC plans appeal to many younger workers, but they are certainly not popular with older workers and women. A study conducted by Jack VanDerhei for the Employee Benefit Research Institute shows how serious the problem is. The study found, overall, that "anytime a traditional pension plan was frozen and replaced with a typical 401(k) plan, some group of workers would lose part of the benefits they were expecting—and sometimes a big part."[8] The losers tended to be workers in late middle age and women of all ages!

While the corporate explanation is that these changes are taking place because younger employees prefer them, it is probable that this reason is a smokescreen for much more important reasons. The new plans are designed primarily to do two things: to lower employer pension costs and to shift the risks of investing pension money from the corporation to its employees. As a result of all these factors, it is now clear that DC plans are the plans of the *near* future.

THE 401(k) REVOLUTION

As noted in Chapter 5, under the Revenue Act of 1978, section 401(k), *employees* were permitted to make tax-deferred contributions to an employer-sponsored plan. The new section 401(k) was designed to encourage employers to create special DC plans that conformed to IRS requirements. And it did that beyond all expectations. At the end of 2003, there were 438,000 plans with aggregate assets of $1.9 trillion, and 42.4 million active participants.[9]

While many plans under section 401(a) today are profit-sharing or voluntary employee contribution plans with no employer contributions, the majority are 401(k) "thrift plans." In 410(k) thrift plans the company has the option of *matching* some proportion of the employee's contribution (which is the case for 75% of current participants).[10]

The annual dollar contributions that can be made by employees into 401(k) plans are limited by law. The contribution limit for "tax-deductible" contributions by individual employees is $15,000 (in 2006) and increases annually (in thousand dollar increments) based on changes in a government price index.[11] (Special contribution limits apply to certain employees who earn more than $90,000 a year, but workers who are age 50 or older can contribute an additional $5,000.)

A 401(k) plan is set up under the name of the employee just like a savings account in a bank; participation, however, is voluntary. The employee and employer contribute a percent of the employee's earnings into the account. But the money does not go to a bank. Rather, it goes to a financial management company—usually to mutual fund companies who invest the money, typically in some combination of stocks and bonds. At retirement (or at times of special need, such as a medical hardship) the employee can withdraw the money as an annuity or, what is more likely, in a lump sum—together with any investment earnings that have accumulated.

Participation in 401(k) plans has grown rapidly. But since participation is always voluntary, not all workers employed by businesses with such plans actually participate. Using data from the 2004 Survey of Consumer Finances, Boston College economists Alicia Munnell and Annika Sundén estimate that about one-fifth (21%) of eligible workers did not participate in 401(k) plans—down from 43 percent in 1988 and 35 percent in 1993.[12] Munnell and Sundén argue, however, that much of the percentage improvement in participation over the years "is illusory because it results from a decline in the share of workers who are eligible to participate."[13]

The Employee Benefit Research Institute estimates that the average 401(k) individual account balance in 2004 was around $57,000.[14] However, the distribution is skewed; looking at the median (half above and half below), the number drops to about \$20,000. Not surprisingly, account balances tend to increase with age. The balance for persons in their 20s was about \$32,000, while those in their 60s averaged \$136,000.

There are a number of reasons for the dramatic expansion of 401(k)s. First, as we argued in the last chapter, employers have turned against DB plans. The federal government, to make DB plans fairer and to insure that employees get the benefits they were promised, mandated administrative and benefit standards and introduced an elaborate regulatory system (mainly through the ERISA legislation). The result is that administration of DB plans is now much more complex and costly, while at the same time such plans have become less effective as tools in the management of the workforce.

In addition, employers know (often from bitter experience) that DB plans are difficult to administer. The *pension promise* under DB plans is certainly not as predictable and as easy to budget for as the employer pension *contributions promised* in DC plans. With DB plans, employers must make complex actuarial projections to predict future pension payouts and changing employment patterns, critical factors in assuring adequate pension funding. Also, employers have to deal with the risks arising from the fluctuations of financial markets—fluctuations that can dramatically change the funding status of the pension fund. Historically, plans that have been *overfunded* have often suddenly, with changing financial markets, become *underfunded*, requiring large, unexpected infusions of money from the sponsoring firms.

As we indicated above, another big reason for the rising popularity of 401(k) plans among employers is the fact that they are able to keep costs down; the costs are typically much less than DB plans. To fund a DB plan, companies pay on average around 8 percent of payroll into one central pension fund set up to meet future pension obligations; coverage is automatic for workers meeting eligibility requirements. In contrast, Alicia Munnell and Annika Sundén report that companies with a 401(k) plan generally only pay up to 3 percent of payroll and nothing if the employee chooses not to participate (remember Wal-Mart?).[15]

Finally, despite the greater risks and possible lower benefits, employers say that DC plans have been popular with employees in firms where they have been introduced. A major appeal is the "transparency" of the plans, given the fact that each employee has a personal account and periodically receives an account statement. In addition, when they change jobs, workers can take their pension with them; DC plans vest immediately and avoid the vesting and portability problems associated with most DB plans.

What supporters of DC plans often fail to mention is that a huge number of employees "cash out" their plans when changing jobs. In 2004, 45 percent of job-changers took out the pension money instead of rolling it over into an IRA or into their new employer's 401(k).[16] They did this even though they had to pay regular income taxes on the cashouts, plus a 10 percent penalty.[17]

DC PLANS AND THE LACK OF INFORMED CHOICE

"I would rather spend my time enjoying my income than bothering about investments."

"I know that [my mix of retirement investments] is utterly stupid."

"In retrospect, it would have been better to have been more in stocks when I was younger."

"I think very little about my retirement savings, because I know that thinking could make me poorer or more miserable or both."

These are *not* quotes from average people with a limited knowledge of economics and finance. Rather, they are statements by individuals who have received the Nobel Prize in economics![18] Almost half of the Nobel winners in economics interviewed by journalist Peter G. Gosselin indicated that they "failed to regularly manage their retirement savings."[19] And many admitted that they were probably wrong in having large amounts of their retirement funds in money market accounts or other low-interest investments.

Not surprisingly, survey data indicate that people who are not economists also have trouble making well-informed choices. Research shows that "people feel overwhelmed and confused by the amount of information available and the complexity of the choices they face."[20] In one British survey, 20 percent of individuals told survey interviewers that they made such decisions "without seeking any advice or information to help them make their decision."[21]

If your retirement money is in a DC plan, you are probably confronted by similar concerns. DC plans require individuals to make complex decisions regarding the investment of contributions. The risks and financial consequences of making bad decisions rest squarely on the individual. And once your money is invested, your job is far from over. Experts advise that the quality of retirement fund investment management varies considerably. This means that is important to periodically review performance and the mix of investments.

Contrast these recommendations with, for example, the actual experience of employees at Harvard University. Hard to believe, but about half of Harvard's 15,000 faculty and staff do not even specify (given the option) how their pension monies should be invested.[22] As a result, the money is put into the plan's default option, a *guaranteed low-return* money market account.

However, even before the issue of making investment choices, there is a choice regarding participation. Almost all DC plans are optional, and only a few people are proposing in the United States that participation be mandated (as is the case, for example, in Australia).

As we noted above, statistics show that 21 percent (2004) of employees eligible for participation in a 401(k) program do not participate. Moreover, it is the employees at lower ages and with lower earnings who are much less likely to participate.[23] According to a study by economists Munnell and Sundén, "procrastination and inertia emerge as important explanations both for lack of participation in 401(k) plans and for the fact that those who do participate rarely change their contributions."[24]

This inertia phenomenon is very significant for forecasting the success of DC plans. Large numbers of employees are unwilling or feel unable to make a decision as to whether participation is in their interests (despite the fact that employers are willing to contribute into their pension account). We should not be surprised, therefore, that there are serious problems related to the much more complicated decisions employees must make related to investing their DC pension money. In this regard, the Enron debacle provides an important lesson.

INVESTING IN "THE COMPANY"

The first rule of investing (the investment "golden rule") is: "Don't put all your eggs in one basket." The employees at Enron learned the hard way what can happen if you do not follow that rule and don't diversify. Many invested nearly all of their 401(k) balances in Enron stock, only to see the value of their holdings virtually disappear almost overnight when the company collapsed.

One of those Enron workers, Michael Lawson, told the *Washington Post*: "Me, I lost $20,000 to 30,000 in my 401(k) [when my Enron stock fell]. But a lot of other people lost considerably more." (Such as Andy Sharp and his wife Kristin Stahl, who, the *Washington Post* reports, estimated their loss to be close to $250,000.)[25]

Another Enron worker was 54-year-old Roy Rinard. He reacted to the loss of most of his retirement money in this way: "I never received any counseling as far as my investments. It would have benefited me to have gotten some advice. I'm a lineman. I'm not a stock broker. I had confidence in my company, and I paid dearly for it."[26]

WHAT FINANCIAL LITERACY?

Rinard's experience illustrates a major problem that arises with DC plans. This type of pension plan shifts most of the responsibility and risks of investing money for retirement to the individual worker. To make good decisions, individuals must be well informed and knowledgeable about financial matters. Markets and competitive forces do not work well when consumers lack the skills to manage their finances effectively. Discussing financial literacy, two Federal Reserve economists, Braunstein and Welch, observe that "Informed participants help create a more competitive, more efficient market."[27] Unfortunately this is not the case in the pension investment area. These two Federal Reserve economists reviewed a very large number of financial literacy programs currently underway. They concluded that there were a great many problems and that "many challenges remain in identifying the most effective and most efficient means of providing relevant information to educate consumers at appropriate points in their financial life cycle."[28] We think that's an understatement.

One of the decisions all employees have to make if participating in DC plans is the proportion of their money to be invested in various types of investments. The most common general choice is whether to invest in bonds that are supposedly safer compared with equities but typically have lower returns in the long run, or in equities which, though likely to return more in the long term, are also riskier.

The investment-mix decision is absolutely critical to the ultimate amount of benefits. However, a recent survey found that 37 percent of people saving for retirement say they are doing only a fair job of managing their retirement portfolios, and 7 percent say they are doing a poor job.[29] It is not difficult to understand these survey findings, given the fact that the U.S. Securities and Exchange Commission reports that *over 50 percent* of Americans do not even know the difference between a bond and an equity.[30] Clearly the financial educational job that confronts the nation is mammoth.

Many other studies over the years have also documented the limited financial knowledge of the typical investor.[31] An Investor Protection Trust survey, for example, found that less than one-fifth of investors surveyed were truly literate about financial matters specifically related to investing.[32] Most lacked basic knowledge about financial terms and about the way different investments work. Data from the 2004 Health and Retirement Study found that only 11 percent of those who stated that they were relatively familiar with money market funds knew that these funds were restricted to short term investments. And 80 percent of the surveyed individuals did not know that the best time to transfer money into bond funds is when interest rates are expected to decrease.[33]

The common response to these "informed choice issues" is to call for educating investors. But the practical problems with this remedy are enormous. As just one example, Boston University economist Zvi Bodie undertook a review of the help provided on the Internet to investors.[34] He found that every site he reviewed provided incorrect or logically flawed advice to investors wanting to follow a conservative, minimal risk strategy. According to Bodie, the educational materials and investment advice on the Internet are often dangerously misleading.

Thus, DC plans place major risk management burdens on financially unsophisticated employees; yet adequate education in financial affairs is difficult, if not impossible, to find. One of the major reasons given to justify mandating that workers participate in collective pension programs like Social Security is the short-sighted and ill-informed behavior of many individuals.

As some ask, "How can these same workers be counted on to make wise investment decisions?"[35]

IS PAYING FOR ADVICE A GOOD SOLUTION?

Even if financial education was more practical and effective, there are many people who do not want to spend a lot of time on investing activities. On this point, the experience of a company called Disciplined Capital Management (DCM) in Manlius, New York, is enlightening. As a pension-counseling company, DCM started by offering a traditional educational program for employed workers with 401(k) plans. The primary objective of the counseling was to promote a better understanding of investment options and risks. What the company quickly discovered, however, was that many people wanted someone else to do all the work! According to DCM principal, Craig Buckout, "We found many people went from wanting to be taught what to do, then progressed to wanting us to tell them what to do, and finally asked us to do it for them."[36] DCM is now a thriving business that "professionally manages" workers' 401(k) accounts. According to Buckout, they make "the investment decisions from the mutual fund options offered by the worker's 401(k) plan, monitoring, and rebalancing the account as necessary."[37]

Of course, all this professional help costs money. And while this approach relieves you of the day-to-day investment decisions, it certainly does not relieve you from the risks related to allowing "professionals" to take over and manage your money. YOU must still find competent, reliable, and trustworthy help—carefully investigating before contracting with any financial councilor or firm offering such services.

Unfortunately, that can be difficult. In 2006, for example, the U.S. Internal Revenue Service (IRS) took away the tax-exempt status from some of the largest "educational credit counseling services" in the country. The reason? According to the IRS Commissioner, Mark W. Everson, audits of these firms revealed that they existed mainly to prey on debt-ridden customers.[38] The IRS charged that they offered little if any counseling but, rather, were in business to sell people often inappropriate and costly "cookie cutter" debt management plans.

Everyone agrees that consumers should be making "informed" credit card and pension investment decisions. As we indicated above, however, most people lack even the most rudimentary financial knowledge to assume that responsibility. And, in our opinion, that reality is not going to change much in the future.

WHAT ABOUT THE ADEQUACY OF BENEFITS?

For those workers with pension coverage, the question of adequacy arises. It is difficult to talk about the adequacy of private pensions in the

United States, since there is such great variability in the benefits offered from business to business. There are "good" plans with generous benefits, many with inadequate benefits, and others that are in-between. One study found that in the 1990s a little over 60 percent of persons receiving Social Security *and* an employer-sponsored pension received reasonably adequate total pension income. But half of those receiving only Social Security did not.[39]

Advocates of DC plans often claim that in the future individuals with such plans will get attractive benefits. Various researchers, calculating hypothetical benefits *using simulation modeling*, have shown that individuals covered continuously, for example by a 401(k), "can accumulate significant retirement wealth, perhaps even more than they would have received from a traditional DB plan."[40]

Real-life experience with DC plans, however, indicates that the actual income long-term employees receive is often much lower than hypothetical simulation projections. There is a long list of reasons why benefits are lower, the main ones being:

- High fees charged by some financial managers have a significant negative impact on final payout.
- When individuals leave the company prior to retirement, many do not rollover pension accumulations but instead cash them out.
- Employers sometimes cut back on their matching contributions, especially during recessions.
- Individuals frequently follow an investment strategy that is too conservative.
- Ignoring the advice of most experts, many individuals do not diversify their investment holdings, including individuals who invest large amounts in their company's stock (often encouraged, or required to, by employers).
- At retirement, most individuals take lump sums instead of annuities, sometimes quickly spending the money.

THE HIGH COSTS OF DC PLANS

One of the most complex and controversial issues related to comparing DC plans with other pension alternatives is administrative and investing costs. As we have indicated previously, one of the major reasons why private companies moved away from DB plans was rising employer costs, in part a result of regulatory requirements necessary to guard against fraud and irresponsible administration of the plans. But as DC plans grow in importance, it is inevitable that they too must be regulated and that many people will have to be hired to exercise appropriate oversight to make sure workers get the benefits they deserve.

Of course, regulatory oversight is just one major source of costs. Money has to be collected, processed, and accurately allocated to individual accounts. Financial managers must search out safe investment opportunities and develop financial portfolios with the money. Eligibility for payments out of the funds must be verified and accurate payments made.

Individuals are typically given many options with regard to the type of funds their money might be invested in. For example, they usually must decide between low-risk versus growth-oriented investment options. Should an international component be included in the portfolio? What about diversification by investing in real estate? To what extent should special bonds be purchased that explicitly protect funds against inflation? The list of options goes on and on.

In dealing with these questions, another big cost component is created—marketing and sales costs related to companies (and their sales forces) wooing, informing, and selling various products to potential clients that respond to these "investment strategy" questions. In addition, often overlooked in the discussion of costs are the costs related to educating employees with regard to the financial decisions they will have to make.

The Congressional Budget Office has calculated the administrative costs that are associated with various financial products.[41] They estimate that financial management costs can result in a reduction of 21–30 percent in the assets available to pay benefits at retirement. That is one-quarter to one-third of the cost!

We are not just talking about DC plans. Currently about half of participants in DB plans take their pension as a lump sum at retirement. Hopefully they will invest most of the money. But at that point, the same issues we raised for DC plans become relevant. Workers with DB plans who take lump sums must "manage" the received funds to ensure that retirement goals are achieved. This immediately raises issues of financial management costs, investment skills, and so forth.

When advocates talk about the high rates of return that investors can get from private plans (perhaps higher than Social Security), they often do not give numbers that take account of these administrative costs. But as is made clear in the Congressional Budget Office study, these costs can take a huge bite out of your investment fund returns.

BEWARE! BUYING INSURANCE; INVESTING IN PENSIONS

As we discussed in Chapter 4, pensions are a special kind of insurance to deal with problem events in our lives—disability, serious illness, premature death, and retirement monetary needs. It has been difficult, however, for the typical American to decide how best to create wealth to supplement the modest benefits coming from Social Security. Adding to this challenge are the many problems over the years related to private businesses that sell investment and insurance policies, and the private employers that provide pension opportunities.

Buying insurance and obtaining pension coverage are not like buying steak in the supermarket or a tee shirt at the mall. Rather, it involves decisions requiring a lot of general knowledge about financial and investment issues and a significant amount of specific knowledge about complex financial products.

Also important is that buyers have relatively easy access to information about alternatives in the market. Unfortunately, in buying various kinds of insurance, salespeople (whose livelihood usually depends on commissions from sales) have a very strong incentive to keep the buyer away from other sellers and to "pitch the sale" by providing highly selective information.

The general problem of individuals buying protection (related to death, disability, long-term care, or retirement) is illustrated by a company called First Command Financial Services. First Command is an international financial services firm based in Fort Worth, Texas. It specializes in providing financial services (especially mutual funds and life insurance) to military families. On December 15, 2004, the Securities and Exchange Commission (SEC) alleged that military personnel were being misled by the firm and that those affected were entitled to a refund. First Command neither admitted nor denied the accusations of misleading investors but agreed to pay a $12 million settlement to military families. The SEC said the firm exaggerated its financial success rates, covered up high fees on long-term contractual plans, and neglected to tell customers that most of their early investments went to commissions.

An editorial in *The New York Times*, in reaction to this development, commented: "When unscrupulous people go after the wallets of underpaid soldiers, it's always offensive, but in a time of war, it stirs special outrage. . . . At least since the Vietnam War, and with increasing intensity since the Iraq war began, insurance salesmen have been fleecing American soldiers, with the tacit—if not explicit—approval of some lawmakers and Pentagon officials."[42]

First Command is successful in its selling practices partly because many of its sales agents are former military personnel. First Command has more than 1,000 sales agents, many retired officers, in nearly 200 branch offices located near military bases around the United States and in foreign countries.

The problems related to selling financial packages to the military go far beyond First Command, which is one among many companies in this business. After a six-month investigation of insurance selling to military personnel, *The New York Time*s editorial staff reacted angrily to the widespread misselling of insurance and investment opportunities to soldiers:

> The abuses center on the sale of complex high-commission, insurance-based investments to recruits. Many of the sales occur on the [military]

bases and in the barracks—a direct violation of Defense Department rules. The process is often greased—and tainted—by the presence of retired military officers who have become sale agents.... Many of the soldiers do not need any more insurance than they receive through the military for a nominal cost. Those who do would probably be better off with something other than the typical...coverage offered by these hucksters for $100 or more a month.[43]

Selling unneeded insurance to soldiers is just one example of the problems that have arisen over the years. Unfortunately, the history of private insurance and pensions in the United States is full of stories about self-serving providers and misled buyers. In the world of insurance and pensions, competitive markets often do not work very well. It's important to remind ourselves of some of the horrible things that have happened.

INCOMPETENT OR ILLEGAL BEHAVIOR

In 1994, the investments of 10 million (yes, million) mutual fund shareholders in Russia's MMM Co. were wiped out almost overnight.[44] A *unique* occurrence in an unstable, unpredictable country? Not if you consider that over the years, millions of Americans have also lost a huge amount of money as a result of incompetent or illegal behavior by purveyors of investment and retirement products. The examples of incompetent or illegal behavior are virtually unlimited. Here are a few:

Example #1. Out of the little rural town of Fox in the state of Alaska, Raejean Bonham (with no financial training or credentials) set up in 1998 what looked like an appealing investment opportunity (which turned out, however, to be a classic Ponzi scheme). Bonham promised people huge and quick profits (a 50% return!)—paying gains to the first group of investors using the money from those in the second round, who were paid by the third (and so forth). In only two months, Bonham enticed 1,210 investors in 42 states to send her $10–15 million.[45]

Example #2. In January 1987, Thomas Keating, head of Lincoln Savings and Loan in California began selling bonds of the S&L's parent company, American Continental Corporation. Investors (including many older persons) were told these bonds were just as safe as a federally insured certificate of deposit. But, as it turned out, this assertion was totally false.

In April 1989, federal regulators seized control of Lincoln S&L when it was discovered that the principle activity of Lincoln was *not* loaning money for low risk residential mortgages. Instead, Lincoln was selling special bonds to raise money for speculative real estate investments. Nearly 67 percent of Lincoln's assets were high-risk land ventures and commercial development projects. Lincoln closed its doors, as did many other savings and loans across the United States, when the real estate bubble burst.

Example #3. James Darr headed the limited partnership division of Bache & Co. (later to become Prudential-Bache Securities) from 1979 to 1988. Over that period, more than 100,000 investors poured billions of dollars into a series of limited partnerships set up by Darr and his associates. Investors were assured that these were perfectly safe, low-risk investments. Again this was a totally false representation of reality.[46] When the partnerships ultimately collapsed, most investors got back just a few pennies on every dollar invested.

Example #4. On December 2, 2001, the Enron Corporation filed for Chapter 11 bankruptcy protection. A number of company executives gave wrong information about the company's economic health to stockholders and employees up till the last moment. Enron had a 401(k) retirement plan for its employees, with Enron stock as the major asset held in these accounts. Just prior to the Chapter 11 filing, Enron stock dropped in value, worker accounts were temporarily frozen by management, and in general, workers found it difficult to shift their assets in a timely manner into other investments. The company's bankruptcy, of course, dramatically reduced the value of these employee retirement accounts. A share of Enron, which in January 2001 had traded for more than $80, was worth less than 70 cents a year after Chapter 11 bankruptcy was filed.

Example #5. And yet another illustration is what happened at WorldCom Inc. In 2002, with the financial world still reeling from the collapse of Enron and also (because of that scandal) the collapse of Enron's former auditor (the Arthur Andersen accounting firm), a new scandal arose. Allegations were publicly announced of massive fraud at another American corporation, this time the huge, global telecom firm called WorldCom. Investigations eventually uncovered what was described as the biggest accounting fraud in American history.

There were many consequences of this fraud. Once again, the decline of WorldCom had a huge impact on the retirement situation of WorldCom workers. WorldCom's only retirement plan was a 401(k), covering 103,000 workers and retirees. Interviews with many of these employees suggested that all or substantially all of retirees' retirement money in the 401(k)s was invested in WorldCom stock.[47] In 1999, the company's employees held WorldCom stock worth about one billion dollars. In 2003, that stock was worth less than $20 million—down 98 percent.[48]

Again, employees were shocked by what happened. "When my colleagues asked me why I put so much money in WorldCom, I told them: 'Why wouldn't I invest in the company I based my career on?'" said Cara Alcantar.

Wrong answer. Alcantar's decision violates the first basic tenet of investing: diversify and spread your risks.

Example #6. In 2003, 16 financial firms were implicated in a mutual fund trading scandal related to "late trading" and "market timing" that adversely affected clients' investments. By the end of 2003, three mutual fund company chief executives were forced to resign. Nearly a dozen other fund company executives were fired or forced to resign. More than 15 brokers were fired for allowing improper trading in mutual funds. Retirement plan services company Security Trust was forced to shut down.[49]

These six American scandals are good examples of the dangers individuals face when they try to prepare for retirement through personal initiatives. But we want to emphasize the fact that there have been many, many others. Financial industry insider John Bogle (founder of the well-respected Vanguard mutual funds) describes the situation as he sees it in his recent book, *The Battle for the Soul of Capitalism*.[50] This is not a case of "a few bad apples," he argues: "I believe that the barrel itself—the very structure that holds all those apples—is bad."

There is no way to escape it. All individuals are faced with a variety of risks related to the honesty and competence of employers and people in the financial and, of course, other industries. These risks include companies going out of business or dumping their retirement plans; companies inadequately funding plans and/or manipulating actuarial/accounting reports to hide problems; the promotion of "get rich quick" schemes by salespersons; excessive fees and commissions; brokers and financial planners that are incompetent; and illegal acts of investment and trading (such as "late trading" and "market timing").

Thus, the risks associated with incompetence and fraud are very important in evaluating both private and public pension plan investments.

INTERNATIONAL PENSION REFORM

Internationally, an important experiment in pension reform is taking place. Beginning with Italy (1995) and Sweden (1998), there are now six countries with national public pension programs that are called "notional defined contribution plans" (NDCs). These NDC plans blend the DB and DC approaches. Like DC plans, NDC benefits are tied to employee and employer contributions, which are "credited" to individual account records. Unlike DC plans, however, *no contributions are actually deposited in individual accounts*. Instead, retirement benefits are paid primarily using pay-as-you-go financing. An indexing procedure based on rising average national wages is used to periodically increase the balances ("returns") recorded in the personal accounts. At retirement, annuitized benefits are calculated based on the account balances (adjusting for changes in average life expectancy over time).

This new approach was created by these countries as a way to cope with rising pension costs. As Boston College sociologist John Williamson points out, the NDC approach "offers a way to shift from the defined benefit model to a less generous defined contribution model without the diversion of payroll tax revenues into funded individual accounts."[51] NDC plans provide an opportunity to stabilize contribution rates over a long period of time. But, as with regular DC plans, the size of a person's account determines generally what they get back.

"Politically, the approach assists countries in the benefit retrenchment process—cloaking cutbacks with mechanistic program provisions related to notional credits, indexing procedures, life expectancy adjustments, and transitional cost relating to prior programs."[52] In fact, the governments hope that the NDC approach will actually increase political support for their national pensions—by giving people a sense of ownership and a feeling of greater individual equity.

Of course, NDC pensions are not entirely new to the United States. As we discussed earlier in this chapter, hundreds of private companies in recent years have replaced their DB plans with somewhat similar "cash balance" plans.

LEARNING FROM CHILE AND THE UK

The United States in recent years has been debating a radical change in Social Security that would convert some (eventually, perhaps all) of the program into mandatory private personal accounts. There is now enough experience from other countries to give us some insights into what is likely to happen if we introduce such a change. A significant number of countries have already gone down the privatization path, and the lesson to be learned is "beware."

One of these countries is Chile, which many advocates of privatization have pointed to over the years as a shining example of a successful national privatized DC system. Sponsored by conservative think tanks like the Cato Institute, Jose Piñera, a former labor minister in Chile who was in charge of the reform, has toured the United States praising his country's approach. His message: "We [in Chile] have become a nation of owners. We've changed the concept of retirement. I'm a firm believer that this can be done in the United States."[53] And according to President George W. Bush, "It [the Chilean system] is a great example" from which we in the United States can "take some lessons."[54]

Yes, there are lessons to be learned from the countries that have privatized Social Security, providing us with a vision for our possible future. Unfortunately the experience of these nations has been terrible. Let's start with the experience in Chile.

CHILE: BEGINNING OF A NEW APPROACH TO PUBLIC PENSIONS

The flight from Social Security to DC plans started in South America with the actions of a military despot, General Augusto Pinochet of Chile. As observed by Robert Myers, former chief actuary for the Social Security system in the United States, "Chile [in 1981] fired a shot that was heard around the entire social security world when it privatized its long-established 'traditional' social insurance program."[55] Facing extremely serious financial issues related to promised Social Security benefits, Pinochet implemented radical pension reform. Chile's Social Security program was replaced with a new *public* system the world had never seen before—a national mandatory savings scheme *administered primarily by the private sector*. All Chilean wage and salary workers were required by law to participate (except for the military and a few other exceptions).

Then, and currently, most Chilean workers are required to put 10 percent of their wages into a privately administered retirement account, one selected by the worker from an officially approved and regulated group of financial management companies. Once a worker chooses a financial management firm, the value of the worker's pension money is kept in a separately designated account. Workers, however, are allowed to move their retirement funds from one investment manager to another if they are dissatisfied with the current company's performance.

At retirement, workers can choose to receive a price-indexed life annuity based on the accumulated funds in their account or can opt to make "scheduled withdrawals" from the fund. Also mandated as part of the overall scheme are survivor term-life insurance and a disability protection program, both funded by additional worker payments.

When it was established, the Chilean program was unique globally, with its *private* sector fund management and competition among various investment companies. Competition was supposed to keep the administrative costs down. But with private firms competing for very large amounts of retirement funds, there was always the risk that one or more of the financial management companies would try to attract business by using misleading advertising or other inappropriate marketing regarding future returns. Nor could it be certain that some companies would not, despite the best of intentions, mismanage the monies entrusted to them.

To reduce these and other risks the Chilean government set up watchdog government agencies with major supervisory and regulatory responsibility. Their purpose was to decrease the problems arising from firms making extraordinarily poor investment decisions (and consequently producing very low benefits for its clients). The regulators were also charged with preventing firms from engaging in illegal marketing or investment activities.

But if regulation fails, the government stands ready to assume the role of "payer of last resort"—guaranteeing that people under the Chilean system will received specified "minimum pensions" regardless of private fund performance. That is, when at retirement the accumulated funds in a worker's personal account does not yield a benefit that is 85 percent of the Chilean minimum wage, the government promises to make up the difference. Also, the government has agreed to step in when necessary to deal with the problems arising for current and future pension recipients should an investment management firm become bankrupt.

LESSONS LEARNED FROM CHILE

It is over two decades since Chile privatized its public old age pension system. In operation for so many years, its success can now be evaluated. And the assessment, according to Chilean political leaders themselves, is very negative.

In the debates leading up to the 2006 presidential election in Chile, both candidates, Michelle Bachelet and Sebastian Piñera, agreed that their country's pension system had very serious problems and needed immediate repair. Ms. Bachelet, who eventually won the election, characterized the system as being "in crisis."[56]

Sociologist John Williamson has recently reviewed the Chilean progress to date. One major problem he points to is inadequate benefits:

> In the Chilean economy, there are many part-time or seasonal workers and many who work on short-term contracts or work in the informal sector. The bad news is that these workers have generally not done well. Many workers, particularly women and others with low wages, are unable to accumulate enough funds to provide a pension greater than the level of the guaranteed minimum pension. Additionally, many of these workers are unable to accumulate the 240 months of contributions needed to become eligible for the government-subsidized guaranteed minimum pension. What happens to them? When they retire they spend down the assets in their individual accounts over a period of several months or a few years, and then with luck they get a very modest means-tested pension called the assistance pension. Since there is a cap on the number of assistance pensions, many end up dependent on their families for support.[57]

In 2005, the World Bank, at one time an enthusiastic promoter of the Chilean approach, reviewed the situation and issued a highly critical report. Perhaps the most important conclusion of the World Bank was that while most workers in Chile are supposed to be covered by the new pension program, in reality more than half of them in any particular year do not participate in the plan. Moreover, the World Bank pointed to special survey data indicating that those workers who do participate often show reluctance to do so. What the survey found is that workers seem to perceive the Chilean DC accounts as relatively risky investments for retirement and hence view negatively the private coverage provided by them.

Even if covered, many Chilean workers make a deliberate decision to stop contributing to the pension system after completing the minimum contribution required by law—shifting their savings activities to other options. In fact, survey research shows that *many workers still prefer government schemes that pool resources to reduce the risks of poverty.*[58] Thus, Andras Uthoff, director of the UN's social division in Latin America, concludes: "The bottom line is that this system does not work with...[the current Chilean] labor market."[59]

Another problem is Chile's pension industry structure; it has turned into an oligopoly, rather than an industry with many companies engaged in vigorous competition. At the peak, there were 22 private companies competing for worker business and the management of money in individual worker accounts. But gradually, various companies have dropped out of the market, leaving only six large firms in 2006. In theory, competition is supposed to keep prices and profits down. However, in Chile the reality has been exactly the opposite—extraordinarily high charges, not low administrative costs. (This has been true, to date, in all other countries using the privatization approach.)

In fact, during the early years of Chile's pension program, it was common for *about half of the money* contributed by Chilean workers to be lost to various fees and other charges! Fortunately, these costs have gone down over the years, but still the fees associated with running the private part of the system have exceeded 10 percent of total contributions in recent years.[60]

Clearly, the Chilean privatized approach is not cheap for covered workers. But it is also not cheap for the government. Even with the transfer of most responsibility to the private sector, the government still spends about five percent of the country's gross domestic product on (1) pensions for the poor, (2) special retirement benefits for the military (who are exempted from participation in the private system), and (3) expenses related to transitional costs arising from switching from the old system to the new one.[61]

Over the years, 12 Latin American countries and some countries in Eastern Europe have adopted the Chilean approach. In these countries, as with Chile, administrative costs are running very high.[62]

The most important point to remember is that when proponents argue that private accounts can invest more wisely and provide higher returns, they almost never take into account the fees that will be charged. And they do not adjust the numbers for the greater risk that individuals have to take to increase the probability of higher returns. If, as in the case of Chile, risk is controlled, there is again a cost to do this, resulting in a lower return.

What ultimately matters, of course, is the degree of retirement income adequacy that the system produces. Here too the prospects are discouraging. One recent study suggests that over half of workers in the Chilean system "might not get a decent retirement income."[63] As a result, many people will be turning to the government to get help.

THE BRITISH EXPERIENCE

Two major *industrialized* countries have also privatized their national pension systems—the United Kingdom and Australia. Australia's experience is relatively short, and the system is still evolving.[64] However, Britain's privatized system has been in operation since 1986.

That nation's economic and political characteristics may make it a more relevant frame of reference than Chile for anticipating what privatization might lead to in the United States. Even as advocates for privatization in the United States have touted Chile's experience, they have pointed to Britain as another shining example of privatization that works. However, as in the case of Chile, there is a big gap between promises made and the reality. A comprehensive review of the British privatization approach by a British blue ribbon commission appointed by the government concluded in 2005 that the British pension system was clearly not working well and required immediate and major change. Shortly thereafter (in May 2006), the Labor government announced its agreement with the conclusions of the commission. Moreover, it surprised the nation by proposing to completely abolish the existing DC pension approach in favor of strengthening public pensions and creating a new savings incentive scheme.

The Pensions Commission (2002–2005) reviewed the United Kingdom's entire public/private pension system. Their charge was to assess the present system's effectiveness and to make recommendations for change. In its final report, the Commission concluded that the current system was "extremely complex, in some segments cost-inefficient, and for many people [did] not provide clear and comprehensible incentives to save. It will produce a highly unequal distribution of income, and it will leave many individuals with pensions they will consider inadequate."[65]

The *Economist* magazine, a long-time advocate of the DC approach, was forced to acknowledge the failure and the need for change in Britain. "By spelling out the choices with bleak clarity," wrote the *Economist*, "The commission prepared the ground for the sweeping changes that it recommended . . . [Labor presented] a sensible pensions plan this week because they opened up policy-making to independent scrutiny and advice."[66]

Let us look more closely at the British approach and its history, which have generated the commission's conclusions and major government action. The commission report was evaluating the results of a pension approach that began in 1986 with legislation developed by a Conservative government under the leadership of Prime Minister Margaret Thatcher. This legislation radically changed the British pension system. A "Personal Pension" option (sounds familiar?) was added to the existing schemes—the flat-rate state pension, the earnings-related state supplemental pension, and "contracted out" schemes administered by private employers.

Before the Thatcher reforms, workers could opt out of the public earnings-related scheme (but only if covered by an employer-sponsored scheme as good or better). Thatcher expanded the contracting out to give workers a Personal Pension option (totally unrelated to any employer plan).

The Personal Pension option allows workers to set up their own DC plan, with a portion of payroll taxes allocated to the plan—the individual retaining some investment control, primarily by choosing among eligible financial managers. To this mix, the Labor government then added in 2001 another DC pension option called the "Stakeholder Pensions." Stakeholder Pensions are DC plans designed to provide private pensions at low cost to *lower earnings* workers who do not have other *private* pension coverage.

On October 12, 2004, the Pensions Commission published its first report on interactions and the success of this mix of public and private plans, which the commission's chairman characterized as "the most complex pension system in the world." The commission raised major questions regarding the inefficiencies that had arisen because of the new Personal Pensions. It reported that more than one third of all Personal Pension contracts had lapsed after four years (that is, either no new contributions were made or the funds were transferred to another provider). Moreover, they reported that the percentage of lapsed plans had been increasing over time.

The commission also raised concerns about administrative costs. Stakeholder Pensions were developed in part as a reaction to the very high administrative costs associated with Personal Pensions; the fees that can be charged for Stakeholder Pensions are strictly limited. However, even with this statutory ceiling placed on administrative charges, participants can lose up to one-fifth their pension accumulations due to administrative costs.

Over the years, except for Stakeholder Pensions, British financial managers have been able to charge whatever they wanted to recoup expenses and make profits. It was hoped, however, that competitive market forces would eventually push charges down. In fact, charges have remained high, although they have varied enormously from company to company. Unfortunately, over the years it was impossible for most individuals to compare the costs of various competing plans; this is because charges have been imposed in a bewildering variety of ways—often, according to government authorities, disguised or presented in a misleading fashion.

It was because of the high Personal Pension costs that the Stakeholder Pension was introduced by the Labor government when it came into power. The fees and charges for this new type of pension were limited by law to about 1 percent. In response, financial institutions complained that with these limits there was insufficient money to inform people of the product (that is, they could not market the product effectively). Thus, the take-up rate of Stakeholder pensions has been disappointedly low, presumably in large part because of the lack of product marketing by financial firms.[67]

In general, *ineptness, fraud, and disinformation have dominated the history of British DC plans.* Perhaps the biggest shock to the nation came with the 1993 revelation that financial institutions were using unethical and illegal procedures to encourage thousands of workers to opt out of their employer-administered plans into the Personal Pension option. The government was horrified to discover that a very large number of salespersons had performed inadequate analyses of clients' situations and provided biased information—virtually guaranteeing bad consumer decisions.

In reaction to this scandal, the British Securities and Investments Board mandated that all investment managers review their records, try to identify cases of mis-selling, and make restitution. The Board also promulgated additional standards for giving advice and new rules for providing pension information. Unfortunately, these actions did not totally stop the scandalous practices.[68]

Everyone in the United Kingdom agrees that one big pension problem in Britain is the complexity created by the large number of pensions. A variety of difficult to understand provisions and rules accompany all five pension programs. The mis-selling scandal is just one result of this complex reality. Experience over the years has shown that many individuals have turned, sometimes in desperation, to "professionals" to help them deal with the complex task of retirement planning and choosing from among pension options. But they are finding it difficult to get good advice.

The Pensions Commission, in a dramatic negative judgment of past pension policy, summed up the situation as follows: "If contracting out [into Personal Pensions] did not exist, it would not be invented now."[69]

A FAILED SYSTEM MUST CHANGE

Based on the work of the Pensions Commission, the Labor government in 2006 unveiled a dramatic pension reform proposal.[70] In calling for radical pension change, the Labor government argued that the current system of DC plans was too complicated, poorly understood by the public, a disincentive to saving, very expensive in terms of investment and management fees, and a large regulatory burden on the government. Moreover, the government found that as time went by, Personal Pensions were becoming less popular. Increasing numbers of workers with Personal Pensions were opting to go back to coverage under the *public* pension scheme, and fewer people than expected were taking up the newer Stakeholders Pensions.

In place of the old system, the Labor government proposed that higher benefits be provided in three ways: (1) beefing up the two existing *public* plans, (2) dealing with problems plaguing employer-sponsored DB plans, and (3) creating a new savings plan option. The new savings plans would begin in 2012. They would be low-cost and portable pension savings accounts for employees earning up to £33,000 (around $60,000) a year. Contributions into the plan would be up to 4 percent of the employee's wage. In addition, employers would also add, at a minimum, another 3 percent, and the government would add 1 percent in tax relief. To encourage participation, workers would be enrolled automatically in the savings scheme unless they made a conscious decision to opt out.

The Labor government pension reform proposal is the most dramatic action taken since the Thatcher government privatization efforts and represents a dramatic reversal in policy. Once again, however, the new savings accounts will confront workers with decisions about how their money should be invested.

Who the investment managers would be was left as an issue for future discussion (i.e., a factor still to be determined when the government first announced its proposal). The Labor government posed two possible options—administration of the savings funds by a governmental organization, as recommended by the Pensions Commission; alternatively, participants could be given the choice among a variety of private investment companies (similar to what now happens in the case of Personal Pensions). Regardless of which is chosen, all the issues and problems we discussed above about informed choice, administrative costs (and so forth) immediately arise again.

The British experience highlights many of the problems the United States may encounter as reliance on DC plans grows—as well as possible problems if Social Security is privatized into personal accounts. Most plans that have been proposed for the United States, however, have provisions that try to deal with some of the potential problems.

YOU'RE ON YOUR OWN

We began this chapter talking about pension developments at IBM. Perhaps the most important development was the company's announcement in early 2006 that it was freezing its DB plan for American workers and offering them only a 401(k) plan in the future. The company gave as one of its main reason for the move a desire to make pension costs more predictable so that it can compete more effectively. Moreover, IBM estimated that the shift would cut its pension costs by about $3 billion over the next few years.[71]

As we indicated before, IBM is only one of many companies that have decided to radically shift their pension offerings to workers. Clearly a major pension policy change is occurring throughout American industry. "The death knell for the traditional company pension [a DB plan] has been tolling for some time now," writes Mary Williams Walsh of *The New York Times*.[72] In its place is to be a DC pension. The *Times* starkly expressed the problem with this trend in an editorial: "Even a good 401(k) doesn't offer the safety of most old-fashioned pensions, which pay out a guaranteed set of benefits to retirees. A safe retirement based on a 401(k) account requires decades of *discipline*, something many people don't have" [emphasis added].[73]

The New York Times editorial goes on to illustrate one of the basic problems that arise. The newspaper cites a recent report by Hewitt Associates, stating that when individuals are allowed to decide for themselves, 45 percent of American workers cash out their retirement plans when leaving a company, rather than "rolling it over" into a new one to keep the money accumulating and available for retirement. What the *Times* fails to point out, however, is that most of the "old-fashioned" DB pensions have also been changing. For example, historically, DB pension used annuities to pay pensions till death; now, like DC plans, many of the pensions are paid out in lump sums.

But even if workers keep money in plans for retirement, we have pointed out that they will be faced with the difficult realities of DC plans. Workers will be required to make complex decisions and assume all the financial risks associated with such plans. To deal with these risks will be a challenge, demanding more than just discipline. Few people would argue the fact that it will also require a great deal of knowledge, financial skill, and, ultimately, probably a lot of luck.

Welcome to the new world of the "pension lottery."

· · · · · · · · · ·

CHAPTER 7

To Work or Not to Work: That Is the Question

I put thirty-four years into this firm, Howard, and now I can't pay my insurance! You can't eat the orange and throw the peel away—a man is not a piece of fruit.

—Willy Loman in Arthur Miller's *Death of a Salesman*

No longer is it just Disney toys and Nike shoes made in Haiti and Indonesia, it's software engineering, accounting, and product development [jobs] being "outsourced" to India, the Philippines, Russia, and China.

—Stacey A. Teicher[1]

Increasingly, the "answer" given to population aging and rising pension costs is encouraging or penalizing older people so that they work longer. Many people argue that government and employers must make sure policies and practices do not encourage people to leave the workforce "prematurely." And it is taken for granted that the age of eligibility for public and private pensions must increase. And employers are expected to hire additional older workers.

Such prescriptions, however, contrast sharply with past declining retirement ages and past and current employer practices of getting rid of older workers as early as possible. Workers were liberated in the twentieth century from long years of employment—often years of drudgery. But now the boomers are being told that policies encouraging retirement at an early age must change. Instead, "old folks" should continue working (or go back to work).

The Economist magazine editorializes that "it is up to [future] individuals to make the most essential change of all: to accept that early retirement was an historical aberration and to prepare for longer working lives. Their priority must be to remain employable. This will mean a greater willingness to invest in themselves, ensuring that they keep their expertise and skills up to scratch. It will also often mean accepting lower wages if their productivity does decline."[2]

Is this "the solution" to the growing costs of Social Security and the declining role of pensions? Clearly, to answer this question we need to know more about the origins of unemployment, the reasons why retirement ages have dropped dramatically, and the views of employers regarding the employment of older workers.

This chapter looks closely at employment issues related to older workers. What accounts historically for the dramatic downward shift that has occurred in retirement ages? Must we now do things differently, expecting older workers to remain longer in the paid labor force? If so, what policies must be changed to make that happen? Why is it likely in our opinion, despite worries about an aging population, that policymakers will be unable to "turn back the clock" to a time when more older people were working?

First, however, we need to alert the reader to an important distinction in terminology. Throughout most of the book when we talk about the aged or older persons, we are generally referring to people in their sixties or older (usually age 65 or above). In addressing the issues discussed in this chapter, however, we are usually focusing on workers who have reached middle age and those approaching retirement age (generally, the 45–64 age group). That is, we are talking about the behavior of baby boomers and older workers in general prior to their retirement years.

IT'S THE MARKET AND UNEMPLOYMENT, STUPID!

Under communism in the former Soviet Union and in Mao's China, there was no unemployment: everyone old enough was assigned a job. But the Soviet and Chinese central planning process that ran those countries was not able to bureaucratically shift large numbers of workers into the jobs most needed by the economy. The result was superb job security but a huge waste of available labor. That meant there was much less economic growth, less output, and a generally lower standard of living.

The opposite occurs, however, in the United States and other countries dominated by the competition of "market oriented economies." There is much less waste of labor but high job *insecurity*. And some think that insecurity is increasing as a result of globalization and what seems to be a growing job flight to other countries.

Historically, however, the loss of jobs to firms overseas is nothing new. But "what started as a necessary response to the intrusion of foreign manufacturers into the American market place got out of hand," writes journalist Louis Uchitelle. "By the late 1990s, getting rid of workers had become normal practice, ingrained behavior, just as job security had been 25 years earlier."[3] Uchitelle's conclusion is controversial, but most experts would agree that the labor force *is* currently undergoing dramatic changes.

Men and women in the American industrial labor force have always been subject to great insecurity on the job. That is why in the 1930s the nation created a national unemployment insurance program to help workers and their families deal with unexpected job loss. But these unemployment insurance benefits are only available for a limited time period; it is assumed that workers will get other work. Moreover, even in recessions, because of various eligibility requirements a lot of people do not have unemployment insurance coverage. On average only about a third of unemployed workers are covered by unemployment insurance. The percent varies, going higher during economic downturns.

Job insecurity is also one important reason why the United States developed public and private pension programs. As we discussed earlier (and will discuss further in this chapter), pensions have become a major way of dealing with unemployment problems. In the process, however, they have created other problems.

Policy in market economies stresses that workers should be encouraged to shift to the jobs where their labor is most needed—even if that means moving (often with hardship) to another part of the country and/or completely changing job skills. But workers, especially older workers, often find it impossible to meet the demands of the available jobs. Or, they are reluctant to take the new jobs under what they consider unacceptable terms (inadequate wages, commuting demands, and so forth). They may also lack geographical mobility or the required skills, finding themselves unable to remedy their skill-deficit situation. Finally, when jobs are moved or created that are outside the country, domestic workers (no matter what they do) face the reality that they do not have access to some employment opportunities.

Karl Marx wrote in his attack on capitalism that the key to understanding unemployment was the capitalists' need for a "reserve army" of unemployed workers to keep wages low and profits high. Given America's labor history, Marx's view is not to be dismissed out of hand, especially in light of Alan Greenspan's long tenure (1987–2006) as head of the Federal Reserve Board of Governors. Over that period, Greenspan (described by some as an "inflation hawk")[4] frequently warned of a need to head off severe inflation, an inflation that he thought was lurking just around the next economic corner—but one that never appeared. As Greenspan stated, "if you wait to see the eyes of inflation, then it's too late."[5] The Federal Reserve, fearing an "excessive" reduction in unemployment, has deliberately dampened job growth over the years with actions that have been characterized by critics as Greenspan's "preemptive strike" on inflation.

The result? Larger numbers of workers (including older workers) remained without jobs.

EFFICIENT MARKETS MEAN CONSTANT JOB OBSOLESCENCE

It is important to understand the basic origins of unemployment and how they relate to old age. To do this, we focus in this section on one important source of job loss and one particular industry example, the textile industry. It is very instructive to look back in America's history to the key role that cotton textiles have played in our economic development and to understand the impact they have had on our ever-changing labor force.

Eli Whitney was a mechanical engineer and inventor. In 1793, it took Whitney just 10 days to put together the first cotton gin, a machine to separate cotton fibers from the seed. His invention revolutionized the production of cotton.

Before this invention, it took one person almost a whole day to remove the seeds from one pound of cotton. With Whitney's cotton gin, a worker could produce not one but fifty pounds of cotton each day—a spectacular rise in productivity. As a consequence, American cotton became much more competitive on world markets, and, at the same time, most of the human jobs created to separate cotton suddenly *disappeared*.

In the colonial days, the bulk of America's cotton production went to England to be turned into textiles. England was the first country to industrialize, and cotton played a major role in that industrialization process. Textile factories were built across the English countryside, and huge numbers of new jobs were *created*.

But most of those jobs were not to last. In a relatively short period of time, these jobs, like the ones before the cotton gin, "disappeared." If you visit parts of England today you can still see the mounds and ruins of the old textile factories scattered across the countryside. What happened?

England ultimately lost out to the new technology and competitiveness of textile mills built in the northeastern United States. This new American industry *created* many jobs and triggered an industrial expansion in what was up till then a basically agrarian economy. Many New England communities—such as Manchester, New Hampshire, Pawtucket, Rhode Island, and Lowell Massachusetts—prospered with the appearance of the new mills and jobs. If you travel around New England today, you will find many of these factories still standing—often empty, however, and certainly not producing textiles.

That's because the good economic times in New England did not last either. Almost all of the New England mills eventually lost out in the twentieth century to newer mills in the American South—mills with newer equipment and cheaper labor. The result was huge numbers of displaced workers in the northeast.

And, of course, more recently the South has been steadily losing textile jobs to the point that few are left. Where did the jobs go this time? To mills in India, China, and various other developing countries.

Here then is the dilemma. Economic efficiency (that is, the allocation of economic resources to maximize production and consumer satisfaction) means that jobs are constantly becoming obsolete—as well as the workers that were trained to fill those jobs. *Technological changes* (embodied in new machines and innovative production organizations) typically create the need for workers with different skills. In addition, the *shifting preferences* of consumers as a result of new products and *shifting relative product prices* increase the demand for workers in the more popular industries. Moreover, differences in wage levels, natural resources, infrastructure, and other factors change the competitive advantage of different individuals, regions, or countries (what economists call "comparative advantage") and result in changing labor demands in various regions and countries. Taken together, these three sources of economic change—technology, consumer preference, and comparative advantage—mean that no job is really secure. It is estimated, for example, that for the 16-year period from 1973 to 1988, about one in five American manufacturing jobs was either destroyed or created each year—with about one in ten jobs disappearing and a slightly fewer number of jobs being created.[6]

For example, remember that TV commercial with the Maytag repairman who just sat around with so little work to do (because Maytag products were built so well)? Well, he won't be waiting around anymore in Newton, Iowa or Herrill, Illinois or Searcy, Arkansas. With the 2006 acquisition of Maytag by its historic competitor, Whirlpool, came the announcement that Maytag facilities in these three towns would close, putting 4,500 employees out of work. Maytag was the "second name" for the town of Newton; the company was founded there in 1893 and ever since had dominated the town's economic, political, and cultural life. But only a few of the workers in Newton and the other towns were offered other jobs, and then only if they were willing to leave their community and move to states with Whirlpool facilities (plants in Ohio, Oklahoma, or Mississippi).

The key point is this. *When you take a job, you take on a great risk. No worker can predict what will happen in the labor force during his or her lifetime.* Nor can workers easily shield themselves and their families from the insecurities generated by constantly changing production patterns and processes. When factories and machines become obsolete, we discard them and cast them aside. But what should we do with humans who become obsolete?

CONFUSING POLICIES REGARDING WORK IN LATER LIFE

No other age group is more threatened by the turbulent ups and downs of the job market than older workers. Unfortunately, great national confusion exists over what public policy should be toward workers who get old. What economic roles are appropriate for individuals in later life? Over the years, at one extreme were policies that *required older people to work*. At the other extreme were policies that encouraged them to stop working and policies that actually *prohibited them from working*. Policies promoting both extremes have existed throughout American history.[7]

Requiring people to work has held a prominent place in American "welfare policies" from the very beginnings of the nation. Encouragements for older workers to stay on the job are the Age Discrimination in Employment Act (1967), liberalization of the Social Security earnings test, and the expansion of partial retirement options.

At the other extreme, before the 1967 age discrimination legislation, individuals were forced out of the labor force by mandatory retirement rules (discussed below) that were common throughout American industries. Also, early retirement buyouts and pensions offered by employers have had a huge impact in reducing labor force participation by older workers.

There seems to be increasing agreement today that older workers who are not yet frail are a potentially valuable resource. *But America's ambiguity toward the labor force participation of older persons is not likely to be resolved—ever!* As in many policy areas, it is in large part the product of conflicts in values and goals that are themselves difficult to resolve. But also, in a fundamental way it is a matter of "income vs. leisure" choices as to how we want to divide up the nation's growth. Do we want more income to purchase goods and services we will consume? Or do we want more time out of the labor force to participate in various other forms of life activities (such as recreation)? Let's look more closely at the nature of this choice.

"THE OVERWORKED AMERICAN"?

According to Cyril Northcote Parkinson, the first law of work (known as Parkinson's Law) is that "work expands to fill the time available for its completion." But an equally important issue is how we allocate our time among all the different kinds of work and between work and nonwork (commonly called leisure). Every individual during his or her lifetime makes important choices. Each of us chooses and allocates our time among participation in:

- the paid labor force,
- indoor and outdoor housework,
- personal care,
- volunteer work, and
- religious, recreational, and civic engagement activities.

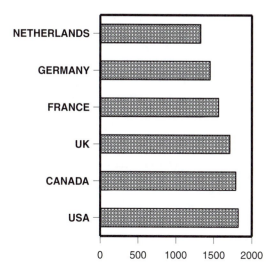

Figure 7.1. Average annual hours worked, 2001.
Source: OECD labor market statistics.

Looking at the list, you probably would not be surprised to learn that survey data show that time-wise Americans actually do more unpaid than paid work.[8]

The division of our time among these options is referred to by economists as the "work-leisure choice."[9] Differences in work-leisure choices occur not only among individuals, but there is also great variation among nations. Figure 7.1 shows the average annual hours worked in six industrialized countries. The United States ranks highest as far as hours worked are concerned—a result of the steady increases in the average number of hours people have worked over the last three decades. Yes, we said "increases" in the hours people work on average in the United States.[10]

The most comprehensive study done to date on trends in work versus leisure has been carried out by Boston College economist Juliet Schor. She argues in her book, *The Overworked American*, that Americans are trapped in an "insidious cycle of work-and-spend"—that is, habitually choosing to work (for more income) so that they can "enjoy" increasing amounts of consumption and keep up with the spending of their friends and neighbors.[11] But as Americans consume more (bigger houses, more and fancier automobiles, an almost infinite variety of electronic wonders, and so forth), they tell us that they are no happier (or less happy) than generations before them that got by on much less.[12]

There are two major problems arising from this never-ending spiral of work and consumption. First, many Americans are literally working themselves to death (hypertension, depression, sleep disorders, exhaustion, gastric, and heart problems). Second, they are starved for time to do the things they say are very important in their lives: more time with a spouse, children, and relatives; enjoying and keeping up a home; finding enough time for hobbies and recreation; and so forth.

This work/leisure reality is somewhat surprising. Over the years many commentators have predicted that there would be a huge increase in leisure (in fact, a kind of forced leisure) as a result of robotics and other automation, general productivity growth, and consumer goods satiation.[13] These prognosticators predicted (incorrectly) a looming crisis of excess leisure time. Instead, most people today still have too little time—that is, until they reach the retirement years. (Even then, many find that time remains a scarce commodity.)

PROMOTING RETIREMENT

Why is it that most of our increased leisure in recent decades has been bunched at the end of the life cycle? To understand this phenomenon we need to look at the attitudes of employees and employers. Employers see it in their self-interest to encourage or require long hours while people are young, and to get rid of workers when they become old.

Regarding younger workers, it is often seen as cost effective to expand overtime, rather than hiring new workers. In times of economic stress, workers are often threatened with job loss unless they are willing to work longer hours without additional pay; this is especially true for salaried workers. Once a company invests heavily in capital equipment, there is a strong financial incentive to use it as intensively as possible, hiring workers for long work shifts. And finally, it is advantageous to spread the costs of fringe benefits over fewer workers who work longer hours, rather than hiring more workers to attain a given level of output.

Juliet Schor argues that these "key incentive structures of capitalist [market] economies contain biases toward long working hours. As a result of these incentives, the development of capitalism led to the growth of . . . 'long hour jobs.' The eventual recovery of leisure came about because trade unions and social reformers waged a protracted struggle for shorter hours. Some time between the Depression and the end of the Second World War, that struggle collapsed."[14]

But workers are not treated the same at all ages. Employer attitudes and policies have been very different towards *older* workers. Instead of promoting longer hours, employers have promoted "retirement." Over the years, older workers have been seen by most employers as lacking physical vigor, being "tradition bound," less willing to adjust to technological change, less appropriate for retraining, less productive, and more costly. When employers run into trouble and need to reduce the number of employees, old workers are usually the first to be encouraged to go. The result (as we discuss below) has been the development of an elaborate set of mechanisms and policies to get them out of the labor force.

WHY RETIREMENT?

One thing is very clear. "Retirement is a phenomenon of modern industrial society.... The older people of previous societies were not retired persons; there was no retirement role."[15]

A number of developments, however, changed things. Even before public and private pensions were widely established, large numbers of older persons were not in the labor force. You might be surprised to learn that as early as 1900 almost one-third of all men age 65 and over were "retired." During this period, men were not working largely because of health problems.

Unable to work, how did these people survive economically? As we discussed in Chapter 3, prior to the institution of pension systems older persons not in the labor force had to rely on their own (often meager) resources, help from relatives, or public and private charity.

Over the years, however, recognition spread that complete reliance on these sources of old age support was unsatisfactory. Few people could save enough; parents disliked receiving "charity" from their children; and charity from outside sources was viewed as demeaning and inadequate. Thus, to begin with, public pensions were, in part, a reaction to the need for more rational support mechanisms to assist older persons unable to work.

But other factors have also played a role. Industrialization in America created new problems for workers. In contrast to life on the farm where, if desired or necessary, people could almost always continue work at reduced levels, nonagricultural industries were characterized by work where older workers could not scale-back time spent on the job.

Industrial workers were faced with large amounts of job insecurity. Recurrent recessions and depressions and shifts in employment opportunities created competition for the old and new jobs. Job obsolescence was a constant threat, as technology continued to change rapidly. Age discrimination in employment was rampant. Thus, another motivation for establishing pensions and the accompanying retirement was to facilitate and often encourage older workers to leave the work force—creating jobs, it was assumed, for younger workers.

Probably most important of all, however, was the fact that throughout our history industrial growth—fueled by rapid technological change—has resulted in vast increases in economic output. Economic growth provides an expanding option for greater leisure, together with a simultaneous increase in living standards. That is, the rapid economic growth of the nineteenth and twentieth century made it possible to more easily support older people who could not (or did not want to) work or whose employers did not wish them to work. In other words, retirement became more economically feasible.

To summarize, then, we see the "institutionalization of retirement" arising as a result of and a reaction to

- the needs of large numbers of elderly who were unable to work,
- industrialization changing employment opportunities for both the young and the old, and
- an expanding national economic potential over the long run that opened up opportunities for more leisure.

But that is not the whole explanation. Complementing these changes was the rise of pensions. Pension programs were developed that "provided compensation based upon years of service rather than upon need per se." These pensions were to emerge and be perceived "as an 'earned right' and were to become instrumental in defining a retirement status as appropriate for the older worker."[16] Today, given the ages when most workers retire—from ages in their late 50s and early 60s—we find that a major portion of life is spent in this special period. In fact, the retirement period now lasts longer for most workers than the period from birth until the year when they take their first full-time job.

UNEMPLOYMENT AND PENSIONS

It was 2006. The biggest automaker for decades, General Motors (GM), was in trouble—like a prizefighter in the ring, injured and "on the ropes." GM reported a 2005 calendar year loss of $3.4 billion (or a whopping $8.6 billion if "special items" were included in the calculation). GM Chairman and Chief Executive officer, Rick Wagoner, reported that "2005 was one of the most difficult years in GM's history, driven by poor performance in North America, ... [due in part to] our huge [employee benefits] legacy cost burden, and our inability to adjust structural costs in line with falling revenue.... In order to improve financial results in 2006 and 2007, we are moving quickly to implement several important actions that will address these weaknesses in North America."[17]

On March 22, 2006, GM (with union leaders' agreement) began to implement one of those "important actions" Wagoner had promised. GM announced that it would offer buyouts and early retirement packages *to every member* of its 113,000 unionized workers. The lump sums offered varied by years of service, ranging from $35,000 to $140,000. (A few days before, Ford Motor Company had announced a somewhat similar early retirement program.)[18]

The incentives worked. Three months later, GM reported that 47,600 union workers of GM and Delphi (its affiliated major parts supplier) had accepted early retirement or buyout offers.[19]

The GM action reminds us that those who say we must work longer in old age are ignoring history. *From almost the beginning of the industrial revolution until now, pension payments of various kinds (and retirement policies in general) have been a primary mechanism used to reduce the size and composition of companies' work forces.* Just like GM and Ford, over the years various employers, unions, governments, and workers—reacting to cyclical and structural employment problems arising in market-oriented economies—have supported a steady progression of lower pension eligibility ages.

Early in America's history, public and private pensions became the dominant path to early retirement—what some have called the "buffer years."[20] The buffer years are the years that employers and workers use to deal with the trials and tribulations of changing manpower needs and a manpower history in the United States filled with the problems of chronic unemployment. Like the case of GM and Ford, early retirement pensions have been used (usually successfully) to encourage workers to leave jobs and often to leave the labor force entirely.

Why have these pension policies been so successful in changing the participation rates of workers? Research indicates clearly that older worker retirement decisions are strongly influenced by the availability of pensions. MIT economist Peter Diamond, for example, points to research showing that over the years "the rules governing access to retirement pensions and the rules relating to the size of monthly retirement benefits to the age at which they start . . . play an important role in determining retirement behavior."[21] That is, to put the matter more bluntly, our experience to date is that if workers are given the opportunity to stop working with a reasonable pension, *many will seize it.*[22]

Federal government surveys in 1990 and 1994, for example, asked older workers who had recently left the labor force why they left.[23] Only a very small percent (14%) said that they left involuntarily.

That's right. Research has found that most workers retire as soon as they think it is financially feasible and, once retired, they usually adjust well to their new situation. The notion that most people are forced to retire and suffer in retirement from boredom and psychological distress is a myth.[24]

As a result of the new pension programs, together with workers' attitudes toward work, we have seen a dramatic change in work patterns when workers get older and the evolution of what many call a "retirement revolution."

THE "RETIREMENT REVOLUTION"

Any list of the most significant developments of the twentieth century would include the dramatic decline of male older worker participation rates over the century and the significant rise in leisure during retirement that went with it. Almost a half century ago, Eugene Friedmann and Robert Havighurst, pioneers in the field of social gerontology (i.e., study of aging), described retirement this way: "Retirement is not a rich man's luxury or an ill man's misfortune. It is increasingly the common lot of all kinds of people. Some find it a blessing; others, a curse. But it comes anyway, whether blessing or curse, and it comes often in an arbitrary manner, at a set age, without direct reference to the productivity or the interest of the individual in his work."[25]

Yes, retirement was avoided over the years by what Friedmann and Havighurst call "men of action" (statesmen, many self-employed farmers, and various professionals). The choice of these individuals to continue working does not accurately reflect, however, the more general historic transformation in work patterns that occurred during the twentieth century. Society encouraged older workers to retire, and most people welcomed retirement with open arms. Instead of avoiding retirement, workers have retired as soon as they thought it was economically feasible. As one observer described the situation, "everyone is in favor of keeping older people in the labor force except the unions, government, business, and older people."[26] That observation astutely summarizes the paradox of retirement policies in the United States. Everyone talks about permitting and even encouraging older people to work, but until recently, fewer and fewer did. In fact, public and private actions, as compared to words, have been instrumental over the years in biasing the work-retirement choice toward retirement.

What about the boomers? A Congressional Budget Office study found that many "are not waiting until age 62 or 65 to stop working. Over 4 million already have left the labor force either because they are disabled or because they have retired. If they follow in the footsteps of workers now in their early 60s, perhaps one-third of the men and nearly half of the women will be out of the labor force before their 62nd birthday."[27]

Participation Rates: Some Statistics. The labor force participation rate for *men over the age of* 64 dropped from 46 percent in 1950 to only 16 percent in 1998.[28] (In 2005, the rate was 15%.) Moreover, what was truly amazing is that by 1985 nearly one-third of all men *ages 55–64* were totally out of the labor force, and about one-quarter were out between the *ages 55–59.*[29]

Around 1985, however, something seemed to change. Participation rates for older men began to slowly rise. For example, the rate for men *ages 60–64* rose from 34 percent in 1985 to about 38 percent in 2002.[30] (We discuss the possible reasons for this upturn below.)

In contrast, the proportion of females in the labor force has risen sharply in almost *all age groups*, with an overall increase in total female participation in the labor force (*ages 16 and over*), from 26 percent in 1940 to 58 percent in 1990. The labor force participation rate for older women *ages 55–64* has also risen rapidly, from 27 percent in 1950–57 percent in 2003. But, as with men, participation rates have declined at the later ages. For example, the participation rate for women age 65 *and older* was only 11 percent in 2003.

Part-Time Work. The number of hours people work varies greatly. Part-time work is most common among the very young, women workers, and the elderly of both sexes. The U.S. Bureau of Labor Statistics reports that about half of workers age 65 and older in 2001 were working in part-time jobs. Much of this part-time work was concentrated in the service and retail trade industries where wages tend to be low.[31]

Some older persons work out of necessity; others do so by preference. A survey by AARP of 2,001 workers aged 50 to 70 asked about work intentions in retirement. Respondents were forced to select only *one* major factor in their decision to work. The responses made it clear "that *the need for money* [was] the primary motivator."[32] Many older people today need to supplement what they feel is inadequate retirement income with earnings from a job. Others are forced by health limitations to cut back on the hours they work. And some who have become unemployed are forced to take part-time work as a stopgap measure.

Also there are some employed workers who clearly prefer a gradual withdrawal from work to an abrupt stop; they seek a "phased retirement." They want more leisure later in life but still value highly the various monetary and social benefits arising from some amount of labor force attachment.

For those who want it, phased retirement is not always an easy objective to achieve. There are many more workers who would like to work part-time than actually do. The big problem is that few employers currently make formal provision for their full-time workers to shift to part-time work. The 2003 Cornell Study of Phased Retirement found that 73 percent of surveyed establishments would permit an older employee to reduce hours before official retirement, but few reported that this was part of a formal written policy.[33] And many were openly hostile to the idea. For example, one employee who asked for phased retirement was told, "If you want to do it, you'll have to find someone else to take up the slack."

One can look for part-time work elsewhere, but again, satisfactory jobs are not readily available, especially given age discrimination (discussed below). Thus, most older workers face rather limited choices. Rand economist Michael Hurd provides a good summary of the situation: The reality is that "someone approaching retirement who wants to retire gradually from a career-type job will have to change jobs, losing job-related skills, and [will have] to compete for low-paying, easy-entry jobs. Faced with that option most retire completely."[34]

However, it is interesting to note that the United States has higher rates of participation than most other industrial countries. As the international comparison in Figure 7.2 shows the labor force participation of older male

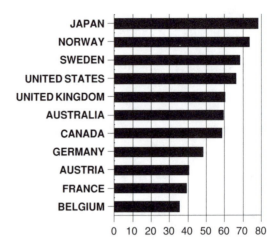

Figure 7.2. Percent men employed, aged 55 to 64 (2000). *Source:* OECD. *Economic Outlook*, No. 72 (2000).

workers in the United States (aged 55–64) is relatively high by international standards.

Participation Rates: Down or Up? As we indicated above, more recently there has been a rise in the participation rates of older workers. Various reasons have been given for this change: abolition of mandatory retirement, the shift from defined benefit to defined contribution plans, improvements in health at older ages, and/or elimination of certain Social Security rules that acted as work disincentives. For example, the Social Security "retirement earnings test," which reduces benefits if one earns over an exempt amount, now applies only to people below the "normal retirement age" (which ranges from age 65 to 67, depending on one's year of birth).

Macroeconomic events have no doubt also been a factor. Some economists have pointed out that the "strong American economy at the end of the twentieth century temporarily delayed the inevitable continuation of the old trends toward earlier and earlier retirement among American men."[35] Fewer are encouraged or forced to leave employment; more continue to look for work; and fewer are likely to "give up."

Operating in the opposite direction is the changing "ability" to retire. For example, the 2000–2003 economic recession had a big negative influence on worker confidence. The increase in unemployment during this recession followed an unprecedented peacetime decade of economic growth and prosperity. Accompanying the downturn was also a sharp drop in stock prices, hurting millions of workers who had retirement funds in individual investment accounts such as IRAs and 401(K)s. Many workers nearing retirement saw what they thought was a big retirement nest egg suddenly shrink or disappear, causing them to delay their retirement plans. A 2002 survey by AARP of investors aged 50–70 found that of those who had lost money in stocks and had not yet retired, 21 percent reported that they had postponed retirement as a result of their losses.[36]

No doubt all these developments (and others) have caused many workers to rethink their retirement plans. But will the decline in the number of workers *not* retiring early continue? Many policy analysts think so. But, as we discuss below, given historic trends toward earlier retirement ages, given worker preferences not to work, and given employer skepticism regarding the productivity of older workers, it would be premature to conclude that the long-term decline in retirement ages has stopped permanently (or perhaps reversed).

Yet, there is a new factor in the mix! There are now increasing numbers of policymakers arguing that, whether we like it or not, the economics of "population aging" *requires* (that is, necessitates) that people work longer in the future.

"LET'S PUT THE OLD FOLKS BACK TO WORK"

Yes, there are some in the United States who have a very clear notion what our reaction to the past changes in labor force participation should be. Given sharply increasing pension costs and the fact that the proportion of younger workers is declining, they argue that older persons should work longer. They point out that most individuals are still relatively healthy and living longer. Moreover, given forecasts of manpower shortages, they predict that older workers who are willing to stay in the work force longer will find it easier to find work.

These two seemingly obvious conclusions about the future, however, turn out to be suspect. It does not necessarily follow from what we know about past work/hiring practices and current attitudes that more "elder work" is the answer. The fact is that most employers may not need, or be inclined to hire, older workers. Moreover, older people may not want the new jobs, even if they are offered. Finally, it is not at all certain that the predictions of labor shortages are correct. Let us look more closely at each of these issues.

Raising the Social Security Retirement Age? First, is it feasible politically to keep the boomers working longer? It is not likely that we can moderate business cycles and keep unemployment low over the long run. Nor will we be able to stop the continuous job destruction that results from shifting manpower needs—given changes in domestic and international markets. Therefore, it would not be surprising if the strong antiwork attitudes of employers, unions, politicians, and workers toward older workers continue.

73 percent of workers aged from 51 to 61 said that they would lik
continue paid work following retirement.... Yet, actual employment ra
among older Americans are far lower than one might expect from [su
survey responses."[41] Why?

An early Harris survey focused on "the myth and reality of aging i
America." One of the most widely publicized findings from that survey wa
that a very large number of older persons wanted employment. Not reported
were the reasons why they were not working.[42] For only a small minority
(15%) was the unavailability of jobs the main reason. When asked, "What
keep's you from working?"—the other answers were:

- Poor health (57%)
- "Too old" (28%)
- No work available; a lack of job opportunities (15%)
- Lack of transportation (10%)
- Other reasons (8%)
- Would lose pension benefits or pay too much in taxes if worked (4%)

In 2003, the U.S. Bureau of Labor Statistics similarly asked workers who
expressed an interest in working why they were not looking. About one-
third reported that they were too discouraged about job prospects. Others
cited ill health (10%), family responsibilities (8 %), and a variety of other
reasons (for example, transportation problems).[43]

Changing Employer Attitudes? Another factor influencing decisions
about working is employer inflexibility. Up till now, most employers have
kept work rules, job descriptions, and "job ladders" very rigid; there has
been little interest among most employers to make the necessary changes
that would make it easier to match older workers with existing employment
opportunities.

Some say, however, that employer attitudes will soon change. Given the
slower rate at which young people will enter the labor force in coming years,
they argue that businesses will be *forced* to rethink how they will get the
labor necessary for producing their products and services.

One can already find a few examples of such change occurring and the
introduction of innovative employer practices. For example, recently Toyota
adapted its automobile assembly workstations to accommodate older workers, and BMW has recently set up a factory in Leipzig, Germany, which is
designed expressly for the employment of people over age 45.[44]

But watch out. You will constantly read that faced with the changing labor
force reality, workers and employers *have* to change. However, it seems to
us that this may be wishful thinking. The outcome is not as predictable as
some would suggest, at least not in the near term.

To begin with, as Peter Cappelli of the Wharton School of Management points out, during the next couple of decades "not only will the [American] population continue to grow, but so will the labor force. The Bureau of Labor Statistics estimates, for example, that the labor force will grow from 153 million in 2000 to 159 million in 2010. The assertion that the labor force will be smaller in the years ahead is simply wrong."[45]

Employers Have Many Options. Moreover, hiring additional older workers is not the only option available to employers who need more labor. Firms can respond to demographic changes in the availability of labor in a number of ways; recruiting and hiring different types of workers (such as older workers) is only one of many ways. For example, throughout the history of industrialized nations, many firms have invested heavily in more physical capital—building or buying machines that substitute for people. Alternatively, as we discuss later, employers can encourage government liberalization of immigration policies favoring applicants with needed skills (or, as is common, use undocumented workers). Or, alternately, they can encourage more women with children to stay in the labor force by, for example, offering better day care options.

The Global Labor Force. An additional employer alternative to employing older workers is shifting jobs to developing countries that have large labor surpluses and pay much cheaper wages ("off-shoring"). On June 6, 2006, the chairman and chief executive of IBM addressed 10,000 company employees. The employees were told how critical their contributions were to the corporation's success and were praised for their good work. What is surprising is that the meeting was held on the expansive grounds of a magnificent palace—once the home of a princely maharajah in Bangalore, India. While the company was laying off thousands of employees in the United States and Europe, its Indian labor force was growing rapidly (from 9,000 in early 2004 to 43,000 employees in 2006).[46]

The outsourcing is not always abroad. The United Airlines mechanics we mentioned above lost their jobs when United Airlines outsourced the mechanics' work to contractors in Alabama and North Carolina who employed nonunion workers and in most cases paid lower wages. As Louis Uchitelle points out, "in an earlier era, the two sides [the union and management] would have tried to settle their differences through negotiation.... The outsourcing of maintenance did not exist before the 1980s.... But now layoffs and outsourcing had become an easy and acceptable option."[47]

Not just the number but also the variety of jobs being exported is increasing. For example, in 2004 the Boeing Company (one of the biggest plane makers in the world) off-shored many engineering jobs to a new work center it created in Moscow (yes, Moscow!). According to *The Economist*, "the idea of the sort of work susceptible to out-sourcing seems to expand every month"—banking, insurance, law, and pharmaceutical trials (to name some new areas of very rapid growth).[48]

These are not just blue-collar jobs. The Forrester Company, a prominent business research firm, estimates that over the coming decade, 3.3 million *white-collar jobs* in the United States will be exported by the year 2015.[49] Another study by economists at the University of California, Berkeley, estimated that overall even more jobs might be at risk, as high as 14 million.[50]

Thomas Friedman, *New York Times* journalist, argues in his book *The World Is Flat* that the changes occurring are of extraordinary proportions:

> Capitalists can [now] sit back, buy up any innovation, and then hire the best, cheapest labor input from anywhere in the world to research it, develop it, produce it, and distribute it. . . . What is going on today, on the flat earth, is such a difference of degree that it amounts to a difference in kind. Companies have never had more freedom, and less friction, in the way of assigning research, low-end manufacturing, and high-end manufacturing anywhere in the world. What this will mean for the long-term relationship between companies and the country in which they are headquartered is simply unclear.[51]

A New Opportunity? Thus, given the options available to many businesses, the older demographic profile evolving in industrialized countries does not necessarily mean there will be serious labor shortages in the future.[52] Nor does it mean that all older workers will find that it is much easier to obtain suitable reemployment after losing or shifting jobs. (Of course, there will certainly be spot shortages in different areas.)

Hopefully, however, the new demographics do provide an opportunity to devise and promote better policies and programs for a more efficient use of potential labor force participants. Raising the size and productivity of the labor force through manpower policies is seen by some policymakers as a major alternative to current calls by some for cutbacks in retirement benefits for the old.

Thus, the biggest retirement issue of this century is likely to be whether both workers and employers see the need and are willing to modify the "retirement right." Will work and retirement options be changed or replaced to include what each group sees as viable work opportunities in later life, options that would complement the retirement life everyone now expects and almost all would like to enjoy later in life?

FIRST, LET'S GET IT STRAIGHT: WHY DO OLDER WORKERS NOT WORK?

As we explained at the beginning of this chapter, job loss is to be expected. In the modern economy, most workers do not hold just one major job throughout their career. In fact, American workers, on average, have had ten jobs by the time they reach old age.[53]

What we find, however, is that as we grow older, apart from our attitudes, searching for a job does become harder. A variety of special problems face middle-aged and older workers seeking to remain in the labor force: (1) age discrimination, (2) job obsolescence, (3) changing job-performance capabilities, and (4) employer-sponsored early retirement incentives.

In addition, older workers, while often protected by seniority against job loss, generally find themselves as vulnerable as younger workers to plant shutdowns and the many dislocations arising from mergers and government spending cutbacks. These problems create immediate difficulties for workers and their families. However, they often also have an economic impact on the family situation during the retirement years. Long-term unemployment, for example, often wipes out savings and/or can make the act of saving for retirement difficult, if not impossible. Moreover, a major cost of long periods of unemployment is a significant reduction in future public and private pension benefits.

These special employment problems associated with age are part of a larger set of factors influencing individuals in their decisions to work or not to work. In this regard, economists have done a lot of research to identify the important factors influencing labor force participation and choices made between work and leisure. Unfortunately, there is still a lot we do not understand. Brookings economist Gary Burtless has reviewed the research and concludes:

> Economists cannot claim to have offered a persuasive explanation for the trend toward earlier retirement with the terms of their basic model. In a trivial sense, of course, the economic model can "explain" earlier retirement. Some combination of changes in wage rates, inherited wealth, pension plan incentives, the population distribution of health, physical and mental requirement for standard occupations, and individual preferences also certainly accounts for lower participation rates of older men. However, this is a little like explaining the operation of a television set by saying that some combination of metal, plastic, electricity, and electromagnetic signal produces a moving picture on a piece of glass.[54]

In addition to personal factors specific to particular individuals, it is important to recognize the *institutional* pressures and constraints placed on individuals in their determination of taking a job and *when* to retire. We begin with a discussion of age discrimination.

Age Discrimination. Roger Reeves was a supervisor at a toilet seat manufacturing company in Mississippi. At the age of 57 he was fired, after 40 years of service. His sacking occurred a few months after the director of manufacturing allegedly told Reeves that he was "too damn old to do the job" and that he was so old that he "must have come over on the Mayflower."

Reeves took his former employer to court and won a favorable decision, but not before the case went all the way to the U.S. Supreme Court. This case is but one example of occurrences that raise concern about the extent of age bias in private and public employment policy. That is, it is likely that employers often make hiring and firing decisions based on inaccurate and stigmatizing stereotypes of older workers.

The nation was first made aware of the extent and nature of discrimination toward older workers in 1965 through a shocking report issued by the U.S. Department of Labor.[55] This report documented that, at the time, more than 50 percent of all available job openings were closed to applicants over age 55 because of employers' policies *not* to hire any person over that age! Moreover, about 25 percent of the job openings were closed to applicants over age 45.

Since its passage in 1967, the federal Age Discrimination in Employment Act (ADEA) has attempted to protect individuals from age discrimination in hiring, discharge, compensation, and other terms of employment. This law originally covered (with some exceptions) persons between the ages of 40 and 65. It was amended in 1978 to include workers up through age 69 and again in 1986 to prohibit mandatory retirement at any age.

As a result of the ADEA legislation, the more blatant acts of discrimination—such as forced retirements and newspaper ads restricting jobs to younger persons—have virtually disappeared. However, much of the discrimination has simply gone "underground." Thus, it is difficult to determine the total extent to which discrimination has in fact lessened. There is little reliable evidence that exists to answer the question. Many researchers, though, point to the much longer duration of unemployment for older men who lose their jobs as a crude indicator that the problem exists. For example, the U.S. Department of Labor reports that for 2005, the average duration of unemployment was 16–18 weeks for workers aged 20–34 but 24 weeks for those aged 45–64.[56]

Another indicator of problems is the number of workers who formally file age discrimination charges with state agencies or the federal Equal Employment Opportunity Commission (EEOC). The EEOC reports that rather than declining over time, the number of complaints has been fairly steady over the past decade—fluctuating between fifteen and twenty thousand complaints each year.

There are a number of research studies that document the high prevalence of skeptical employer attitudes and stereotypes that discount the productivity and competence of older workers.[57] In 1993, the Fair Employment Council of Greater Washington conducted a job hiring experiment. They mailed the job resumes of equally qualified older and younger job seekers to almost two thousand companies and employment agencies across the country. "The applicants were in fact 'testers'—fictitious job-seekers who applied for these jobs for the sole purpose of testing for bias."[58] The overall response rate of companies to receiving a resume in the mail was very low (for both younger and older workers), and 90 percent of the replies were negative (to both ages). Only 79 companies out of 1,860 showed any interest. In 27 percent of these cases, however, the older applicants *were treated less favorably* with a clear indication of age bias.

A more recent but similar study mailed 4,000 letters with resumes to firms in Boston and St. Petersburg.[59] "A younger worker in either state was more than 40 percent more likely to be called ... for an interview than an older worker, where older is defined as age 50 or older."

Discrimination these days is not always as blatant as in the case of Roger Reeves when he was fired from his job as a supervisor at a toilet seat manufacturing company. But even in this case, proving discrimination was not easy. The company claimed that Reeves was fired not because of age but because he had kept shoddy attendance records for the staff he supervised. Reeves' complaint eventually resulted in a trial, with a jury ruling in his favor. An appeals court then reversed the jury's decision.

On June 12, 2000, the U.S. Supreme Court, on appeal, reversed the decision again and ruled that it is not necessary—as some appeals courts had held—for an employee to provide specific evidence pinpointing discrimination as the real reason for being fired. The Court argued that it might be enough just to show *some* evidence of age bias and to present evidence that casts doubt on the employer's given reason for a dismissal. The Supreme Court's ruling was very significant, since juries (when given significant discretion by the law) are more likely to be more sympathetic than judges in discrimination cases.

AARP supported Reeves' case. The AARP lawyers argued in their brief that if the evidence in this case were ruled insufficient, it would have set the standard of proof for age bias so high that few, if any, victims would ever be able to prove their claims. The favorable Supreme Court decision now makes it easier for older workers who claim age discrimination to get a jury trial and ups the odds they will win their case.

In general, however, the evidence to date (admittedly scattered) indicates that while existing laws against age discrimination have helped older workers *remain employed*, it has done little to help them become reemployed once they lose a job in the later years. In fact, some have argued that the primary impact of age discrimination laws may be to reduce the hiring of older workers. Richard Posner at the University of Chicago School of Law argues, for example, that fewer older workers are hired (1) because of the higher costs employers face in the hiring of older workers as a result of their new legal rights under the ADEA and (2) because of the fact that the damages paid by employers in age discrimination cases are typically small (making the penalties for discrimination insignificant).[60]

Other Employment Barriers. Earlier we discussed the matching of older workers with available jobs. Our conclusion was that matching was far from hopeless, given the broad profile of jobs projected for the future. But often older workers do lack the necessary skills to qualify for some of the available new jobs. Or they are not living in areas where suitable job opportunities exist. Competing for jobs in the growing electronics and computer industries, for example, is difficult for many older workers, given their educational backgrounds. Often skills developed in the older long-established industries cannot be readily used, for example, in the new high-technology industries. And, although lots of evidence exists to indicate older workers can learn new skills, no large-scale programs exist in the United States to provide older workers with the newer skills often required (we discuss training programs below).

Moreover, the problems arising from this incompatibility of skills have been aggravated by shifts in industries from their former locations in the Northeast, Middle Atlantic, and North Central states to the Southeast, Southwest, and West. Older workers with marketable skills are often reluctant to leave communities where they have established "roots"; the result is that as the economy shifts, they are left behind with little hope for suitable new employment in economically stagnating areas of the country.

Another barrier arises from benefits issues. Employee benefits (pensions and health insurance) are still an important part of many workers' total compensation at all ages. But many employers are reluctant to hire older workers because it is often more costly to provide such workers with benefits. For example, the higher costs of "defined benefit" pensions for older workers result primarily from two factors: (1) a shorter work history over which employer pension contributions will be made and thus lower investment income arising from the pension contributions, and (2) a declining probability, with age, of employee withdrawal (job turnover) between hiring and retirement.

Perhaps the biggest factor influencing employer hiring decisions is health care insurance. Especially among small businesses, rising health care costs are of major concern. General costs of health care insurance are rising at double-digit rates, much higher than the general rate of inflation. Data analyzed by Towers Perrin shows that in 2005, annual average medical claim costs for employees and dependents varied greatly by age—from a low of $2,148 (ages 25 to 29) to a high of $7,622 (ages 60 to 64).[61]

The cost of employer health insurance is typically determined largely by the age and health experience ratings of a company's work force. In this regard, the *New York Times* reports: "Businesses with a slightly older work force or a handful of employees with significant medical bills can see their rates [from year to year] soar 20 or 30 percent."[62]

Given sharply rising health care costs, it is not surprising that employers are reacting. Currently, companies are (1) eliminating health care benefits,

(2) hiring more temporary or part-time workers (with no benefits provided), and/or (3) requiring that workers pay more of both insurance costs and actual health care bills. Also, with regard to older worker, we do not know the extent to which some employers are not raising their salaries as much as those of younger workers or are hiring older workers at lower wage levels.[63] Some employers are just not hiring workers (young or old) who are likely to raise the company's health insurance premiums. For example, in a 2005 memo to Wal-Mart's Board (leaked to the *New York Times*), company executives recommended a variety of ways "to dissuade unhealthy people from coming to work at Wal-Mart."[64]

Less Productive? One assertion we often hear is that older workers are less productive. But the available evidence on this complex question indicates that one should be cautious about making generalizations. There are a large number of research studies bearing on this issue. Most of this research casts strong doubt on the validity of the common generalization that dominates much of employer and public thinking on the issue—older workers are not as productive as younger workers. The research findings summarized in the box below counter the myths that older workers are less productive.

---

1. You don't have to be old to be stupid or lazy:
   - Studies show chronological age is a poor indicator of ability.
   - Mental and physical capacity varies widely at all ages.
   - Good attitudes and job performance know no age limit.
   - Older workers are often superior to average younger workers.
2. What research testing says about older workers:
   - They score as well as or better on creativity and flexibility.
   - They are able to learn new skills.
   - Lower rates of absenteeism, accidents, and job turnover.
3. Experience counts:
   - Potential performance declines are often offset by experience.
   - A mature workforce embodies high productivity.
4. Beware averages:
   - While some studies found that *average* productivity declined with age in some industries, the decline was generally small for workers in their 50s and 60s and varied significantly from person to person.

In general, it is clear that there are certainly differences in productivity among workers. *But age is not the key factor* that determines whether a worker's productivity is high or low. There are "good" and "bad" workers at every age. Moreover, to the extent that studies have found that productivity in certain jobs has fallen with age, the declines, typically, have been very small.

Also, it is important to keep in mind that work settings are constantly changing. As pointed out in a recent report by the management consultant firm Towers Perrin, for example, "the era in which productivity demands strong backs has largely passed, replaced by a world in which (for most organizations) employee commitment and the knowledge that comes with experience are far more important drivers of workplace contributions."[65]

Research by Towers Perrin on worker contributions has found that "motivation and engagement" (factors demonstrated to be related to firm financial success) "not only do not decline with age, but, in fact, increase." According to the data collected by Towers Perrin, "workers age 55 and older are the most motivated, while the youngest workers are the least motivated."[66]

Many employers recognize that the productivity of some of their older employees is as high, or higher, than that of younger workers. These same employers often argue, however, that it is difficult (and costly) to identify such workers and that older workers are typically higher paid workers. They argue that (in dealing with these complex matters) retirement rules and pensions have provided a practical administrative procedure that is an objective, impersonal, and impartial way of transitioning workers into retirement. Before passage of the Age Discrimination in Employment Act, for example, employers used mandatory retirement rules to avoid charges of discrimination, favoritism, or bias in the termination process. This option, however, is no longer available to them.

Without mandatory retirement rules, employers are faced with either allowing workers to decide when to retire or undertaking potentially expensive activities for sorting out (given pay levels) the insufficiently productive older workers. More importantly, the employer must justify these termination decisions so that general worker morale will not be adversely affected.

With the passage of legislation prohibiting employers from using age as a basis of job termination, there has been more interest among management in techniques of measuring job performance and using such information as part of any termination process. However, such efforts remain quite minimal, and the "pension carrot" still remains the principal management tool. Setting pension eligibility ages lower has been, and still is, a major policy tool. In fact, it is clear that in most cases pensions have been designed in a way to deliberately encourage retirement.

Again, of course, the question arises as to whether the nation can afford to continue these policies discouraging work at later ages? Or do we need to begin to find ways of retraining and retaining older workers longer in the labor force?

TEACHING OLD "DOGS" NEW TRICKS

Certainly, concern about population aging in recent years has increased interest in dealing with the employment problems of older workers and encouraging these workers to work longer. For example, the *Economist* in 2004 argued that "the whole idea of retirement at a pre-fixed age needs to be put out to grass.... [But] if older people are to work longer, they need to retrain and update their skills and expertise.... Lifelong education should be turned from a political slogan into a reality."[67]

It is true that lifelong learning is one of those ideas that many people talk about but few people take seriously. The lack of serious commitment to lifelong learning and the great enthusiasm in past decades about early retirement are intimately related. Up till now, government and business have thought it was cheaper to terminate workers at early ages than to retrain them for the new jobs being constantly created.

Thomas Friedman in his book *The World Is Flat* argues (as have others) that to stay on top in economic terms, the United States must spend more on research and development and train more students in science and engineering. In addition, he argues that we need to change our views on employment, shifting from a focus on lifetime employment to what he calls "lifetime employability."[68] He goes on to recommend that, "the social contract that progressives should try to enforce between government and workers, and companies and workers, is one in which government and companies say, 'We cannot guarantee you any lifetime employment. But we can guarantee that government and companies will focus on giving you the tools to make you more life-time employable'."[69]

Unfortunately, we are quite far from any policy of this sort. In fact, the United States was placed dead last in a 2003 international research study that measured the amount of money various countries spent on assisting persons in the labor force.[70]

As far as workers are concerned, surveys have found that a great many of them value training. When workers are asked to rank the most important factors that influence their decision to stay or move from a job, the opportunity to learn new skills is generally at the top of their list; the amount of money they will receive on the job is usually lower. In this regard, management expert Rosabeth Moss Kanter argues that companies need flexibility in hiring and firing policies, but she argues that at the same time there needs to be an explicit commitment to actions in the workplace that focus *not* on promoting "narrow skills to fill today's slots" but on providing abundant learning opportunities to promote *increased* competence with age.[71]

Although there seems to be general agreement that we need to do a better job of educating our *youth* for entry-level jobs, there is less agreement on the need to commit resources nationally to updating those skills over time, especially in the later work years. Yet, research clearly shows that individuals have the ability to learn at any age (Table 7.1).

Why So Little Retraining? Why have we given only lip service to the idea of learning throughout a worker's life-time? First, over the years there has been a widespread belief that the wonders of science have created a situation where there is no longer enough work for everyone. Technological innovation and modern production methods—such as mass production, new energy sources, computers and other complex machines, and robotics— are seen as creating a surplus of workers (and leaving only "hamburger jobs"). Many people have argued over the years that there are just too many potential workers and that we need to spread the available work around, creating shorter workweeks and promoting earlier retirement. In fact, in 1982 France reduced the Social Security normal retirement age to 60 based primarily on this type of reasoning.

Given the seemingly unlimited desire of people for old and new products and services, economists argue that this view is erroneous—that in the long run scarce resources (including labor) will never be sufficient to keep up with growing demands. But the idea of labor surplus as a result of technological revolutions remains strong among many noneconomists. In such a world of labor surplus, there would seem to be no need for workers to be retrained, especially as they get older—and also given that there often seems to be no shortage of workers when unemployment is high.

A second reason for scant training of older workers is that even if a need for labor develops, the dominant view among employers is that older workers are not as likely to be suitable for the new jobs. As we have discussed above, this is not so much because all the jobs of the future will be computer jobs requiring high-level training but rather because of cost factors and because most employers believe that work performance declines with age. To repeat what we said earlier, the reality is that up till now unions, government, and business have generally thought that it is cheaper to terminate workers at early ages than to retrain them for the new jobs being constantly created.

Third, as we have stressed repeatedly in this chapter, retirement policy to date has been determined over the past 60 years in large part by efforts to deal with chronic unemployment. Why retrain workers, it is sometimes argued, when the country cannot even employ the workers already looking for work?

All the above factors have dampened interest in older worker retraining. Many people think, however, that in the future there is likely (given the changing demographics) to be pressure on governments and employers that will cause them to reverse this disinterest. There is much talk of potential labor shortages in the future and proposals to raise the retirement age to help deal with pension costs. But we have pointed out that there are many factors operating that push in the opposite direction, making it very hard to predict what will actually happen.

Be Prepared to Learn New Skills;. But What Skills? A study by Erica Groshen and Simon Potter, two economists at the Federal Reserve Bank of New York, reports that there has been a rise over the past decade in what economists call "structural unemployment"—that is, major economic factors constantly changing the nature and skills associated with various jobs and making many jobs obsolete.[72] In 1990–1991, 60 percent of workers in the United States were in industries that were undergoing structural unemployment. In contrast, Groshen and Potter estimate that in 2001, the percentage had risen to almost 80 percent.[73]

At the beginning of this chapter we pointed out that few jobs are safe from a tenure point of view. The standard advice to workers is to expect change, be ready to learn new skills, and learn how to look for new jobs.

But older workers have an especially difficult time upgrading their skills. They are pretty much on their own; nobody is rushing to help them. Even with skills, age discrimination dramatically reduces the chances of an older worker being hired.

It is important to remind ourselves of the difficulties workers *of all ages* face with the ever-changing labor market. *Newsweek* magazine ran a story in 2004 titled "Help Not Wanted."[74] Among other things, the article tells the story of a 46-year-old woman, Lisa Pineau, who was a mainframe programmer in Plano, Texas. She was laid off unexpectedly in late 2002. In this case, however, the job did not disappear. Before she left the company, she was forced to train a replacement worker brought in from abroad!

A new reality is the fact that there has been a widespread phenomenon of companies firing American workers and bringing in workers from other countries under the H-1B immigration visa program. There is an annual quota for these H-1B visas; in 2003, the quota was 195,000 workers.

Another serious dilemma illustrated so well by Lisa Pineau's experience relates to the problem individuals face in planning for jobs they might fill in the future. Many individuals think they are doing it right, the way policymakers advise—getting educated and trained in high-tech or professional jobs. Often at great sacrifice, young people (and their parents), spend large amounts of time (and money) for education and training to obtain the skills necessary for the jobs of the future. They prepare, for example, for high-tech jobs like computer programming. And then, like Lisa Pineau, many suddenly wake up one day to find (in Lisa's words) that "anything on a computer is getting off-shored" or taken over by cheaper imported foreign workers.

Or look at the example of highly skilled engineers. The engineering field has always been one of turmoil and change. "The half-life of engineering knowledge, the time it takes for something to become obsolete, is from 7 to $2^{1}/_{2}$ years," says the President of the National Academy of Engineering, William Wulf.[75] Given a flood of engineers brought in from abroad, outsourcing, and the dotcom-tech bust—the *Christian Science Monitor* reported that many engineers are dropping out of the field and engineering school enrollments are declining. "I spent seven years in school, and it resulted in a six-year career," observed a masters degree engineer after being terminated by Nortel Networks.[76]

One of the most difficult problems facing individuals—and also educational institutions and job retraining programs—is determining what to train for. Very often jobs that people train for are "not there" when they begin to look, or they disappear a short time after they are hired.

That reality is indeed a challenge.

The Sad History of Training Programs. As we have pointed out earlier, despite the evidence to the contrary, most government officials and employers over the years have not considered it worthwhile or cost effective to train older persons (compared with younger persons). Comprehensive Employment and Training Act (CETA), a major federal job skills program until 1983, did little to help older workers. Only 1 percent of the approximately 7 million persons age 45 and older who were eligible for CETA training *actually participated* in the program.

CETA was replaced by the Job Training Partnership Act (JTPA) of 1982. JTPA established a nation-wide network of job training programs, some of which were targeted specifically to older workers. In addition, under Section 124 of JTPA, states were required to set aside a little money for the training of economically disadvantaged workers age 55 and older.

But again, the actual number of persons trained under this program was very small. For example, between July 1992 and June 1993, only 8,423 older workers *in the entire country* were involved in regular JTPA programs and 27,800 were participants in special "set-aside" programs.[77]

The Workforce Investment Act of 1998. Still another major program was legislated in 1998 by the federal government to deal with employment problems. At the heart of the new program are "one-stop career centers" promising comprehensive, easy-to-access information on training and employment opportunities.[78] Unfortunately, older workers are barely mentioned in the new legislation. Moreover, they are never singled out as an underserved population. Yet, the U.S. Bureau of Labor Statistics projects that by 2008, over 40 percent of the labor force will be 45 or older (16 million more in 2008 than there were in 1998).[79]

There is one program that is set up solely for older workers. This is the Senior Community Service Employment Program (SCSEP). Persons participating must be age 55 or older, unemployed, and legally able to work in the United States. In addition, family income cannot be more than 125 percent of the official poverty level, although priority is to be given to "the most needy."

SCSEP currently enrolls only 100,000 seniors each year.[80] Participants in the program are involved in part-time, subsidized employment in the community, job training, and other job placement activities. The bottom line, however, is that few workers are served by the program, and those older persons with higher (but typically modest) incomes are not served at all.

Private Sector Help for Older Workers. A number of private agencies specialize in job services for older persons seeking employment. However, older workers using these services are typically not hired in jobs that utilize their existing skills and abilities to any large degree. Instead, they are more likely to be placed in low-skill and part-time positions, usually with small employers in various low-paying service occupations.

A few private companies have made *special* efforts to hire older workers. A 1991 study by the Commonwealth Fund looked in depth at the experiences of three major companies: Days Inn of America (hotels/motels), The Travelers Corporation (insurance and other financial services), and B&Q plc (a chain of do-it-yourself stores in Great Britain).[81] The study provided empirical evidence that older workers can work effectively, learn new technologies, and be cost-effective in a variety of service-providing settings.

However, the Commonwealth study focused on unusual companies. Researchers Barbara Hirshorn (University of Nevada) and Denise Hoyer developed a much larger national sample of private sector employers with twenty or more employees. They found little "purposeful" hiring of older workers in the United States.[82] They did find, however, that the hiring of retirees was widespread and common: over 46 percent of the firms had hired retirees. But few firms "targeted"—that is, undertook any particular efforts to hire—older workers for their special qualities, in general, such as experience and low absenteeism. Not surprisingly, most firms that did in fact hire older workers did so because they possessed certain specific skills or backgrounds. An interesting finding by Hirshorn and Hoyer was that many companies said that they wanted to hire retirees because of their experience, skill, reliability, and so forth but also said they did not know how to find them in the job market.

AARP has been a leader in promoting activities to address older workers' issues. For example, the organization initiates and supports legal action in the area of discrimination. It conducts (or finances) research on employment issues. AARP has also developed an extensive Web site with a lot of information for both workers and employers. And it has taken the leadership in the formation of an organization called the Alliance for an Experienced Work Force. The alliance, whose members are mostly trade associations (such as the U.S. Chamber of Commerce), "helps employers understand, plan for and create workplaces that successfully engage and utilize the skills of the workers over the age of 50 both now and in the future."[83]

WORK AND RETIREMENT IN THE FUTURE

We are now ready to draw from the above discussion some of the probable characteristics of work and retirement when the baby boomers retire. As the World Health Organization (WHO) stated in a discussion paper for the 2002 UN World Assembly on Aging: "It is time for a new paradigm, one that views older people as active participants in an age-integrated society and as active contributors.... [The paradigm should challenge] the traditional view that learning is the business of children and youth, work is the business of midlife, and retirement is the business of old age."[84]

Attitudes toward retirement in the future are likely to (and should) move sharply away from the simplistic view of all work before retirement and no work after. As William Novelli, the Executive Director of AARP, recently wrote: "The economic foundation for retirement was the traditional three-legged stool [Social Security, a company pension, and voluntary savings].... That model is out-of-date and rickety. Today, boomers and those slightly older, view retirement not as a termination, but as a transition. In response, we need to rethink work and retirement together."[85]

There are a number of changes we can expect to see:

More Part-Time Work. At the same time as rates of retirement have increased, there has also been a large increase in the number of older workers who are employed (or want to work) part-time[86] Although surveys of boomers approaching retirement find them looking forward to more leisure, hobbies, time with their families, and so forth—boomers also overwhelmingly insist that they expect to work in retirement.[87] One survey of preretirees found that only 5 percent expected, in what they regard as their retirement years, to work full-time doing "the same type of work I do now." However, almost 90 percent said that apart from income, a major factor in their decision to work would be the desire to stay mentally and physically active, and three-quarters wanted to do some kind of job that was fun or enjoyable. Other major reasons for working given by more than half the interviewees were a desire to "remain productive," wanting to be around other people and helping people, and finally a desire to learn new things.[88]

Expanded "Citizen Participation." If part-time employment increases in future years, will the proportion of elderly working increase *significantly?* Probably not.

Many will undertake activities that are not part of what is considered the "formal, paid labor market." Many people in the retirement years see it as an attractive period for exploration, reflection, and civic participation. Relieved of most of the pressures to work "to survive," more older people are likely to participate in volunteer work, be more heavily involved in giving assistance to other family members, and become involved in the rising national concern and action related to various societal problems—such as the environment and the quality of American life.

Most baby boomers in the coming decades will not just sit in their rocking chairs and watch television. We predict that most will continue to be active but with a new combination of leisure, volunteer, and work activities—new forms of what might be called "civic engagement."[89]

In that regard, Marty Martinson and Meredith Minkler, two researchers at the University of California, Berkeley, argue that "although volunteerism and other forms of civic engagement should not be required of older adults, those who are interested in participating should be encouraged and enabled to do so. For low-income individuals who wish to volunteer but for whom there may be economic impediments, the provision of government stipends to make such participation possible should be expanded."[90]

More Flexible Pensions. Pensions were an invention of the nineteenth and twentieth century, designed to provide more secure and more adequate income for various nonworking people. They were in large part a reaction to opportunities arising with economic growth. They were also the result of a concurrent growing need: the necessity to moderate the growing insecurity arising out of the industrial revolution and the inability of families to cope with it alone. One almost accidental consequence of creating pensions was a dramatic decline in labor force participation at later ages and the introduction of a new phase of life: retirement.

The first pension schemes were very rigid. Public schemes set an eligibility age for retirement and often financially penalized workers who deviated from it. Ages of eligibility were relatively high. In addition, employer-sponsored pensions typically rewarded only those workers who stayed with the company, and their provisions were equally rigid.

Over time this rigidity began to change. Pension provisions now generally allow retirement over a broad span of years without actuarially unfair penalties. The growth of portable defined contribution plans is often partly attributed to worker and employer desire for more flexibility. Most industrialized countries have now created a variety of mechanisms that provide flexibility and opened up many "pathways to retirement."[91]

WORK IN OLD AGE: A MEANINGFUL CHOICE

To summarize. Looking ahead to the future, the hope is that there will be greater flexibility in the work and retirement patterns available to older workers. But we should not expect these changes to produce a dramatic upswing in labor force participation among the elderly. Market-oriented economies will still have to struggle with chronic unemployment problems and job turnover. As a result, there will continue to be strong pressures for retirement policy to "buffer" the impact of that unemployment. In addition, for most workers the choice between retirement and work, if income is minimally adequate, is not a hard choice; retirement is clearly the preferred option (with part-time work a middle ground for some).

One of the important gains from industrialization has been to fundamentally change the economics of old age. Instead of working (often at unpleasant jobs) until health forced them to quit, *many older people now have a meaningful choice between paid work and retirement.*

If economic growth continues at a reasonable pace, more (not less!) leisure than we enjoy today will be possible in the future. But will it happen? How will we divide the fruits of that growth between consumption and leisure? And between the young and old?

Like many other social issues, income distribution between "rich and poor" is at the heart of the matter. Inequality has risen to a point that almost half of total income in the United States goes to the wealthiest 10 percent of the population.[92] The very large tax cuts of recent years favoring upper income individuals constrain many government policy decisions. They prevent reforms that would use the income from future growth in support of collective social programs or more leisure for the majority.

It is not surprising, therefore, that some today, in the name of fiscal responsibility, would like to roll back our prior gains in retirement leisure time and make many people work longer. They call it a pension revenue crisis and demand immediate action. Even if the crisis were real (and that is debatable), we have argued that it is unlikely that workers would be willing to solve it by significantly decreasing the retirement/leisure period. Moreover, employers may not change their inherent wariness of older workers, given the various alternatives available. Time will tell.

· · · · · · · · · ·

CHAPTER 8

Health and Longevity: What Lies Ahead?

[W]e must avoid allowing long-term care for the elderly and medical care in general to crowd out every other civic good—such as educating the young, promoting human excellence in the arts and beyond, and providing for our common defense.
—The President's Council on Bioethics[1]

But I'm a baby boomer. I intend to live to be 100.
—Susan Ferraro[2]

Alzheimer's is perhaps the most frightening problem one encounters in old age. Many were shaken when it was announced after he left office that President Ronald Reagan was ill with the disease. On June 16, 2004, less than two weeks after the former president's death, a bipartisan group of lawmakers introduced the Ronald Reagan Alzheimer's Breakthrough Act, with the aim of doubling government research funding from about $700 million annually to $1.4 billion. Senator Barbara A. Mikulski (D-Md.), who lost her father to Alzheimer's in 1987, called the initiative "a living memorial" to the former president.

The disease strikes silently and knows no barriers of income or class:

How long had our mother had Alzheimer's? My sister and I have asked ourselves that a thousand times since the diagnosis of dementia in 1993. We know it must have been at least fifteen, maybe even twenty years. Her memory had been going for a long time, *but she's just getting older*, we had thought. Her math skills went first, and she had been letting my sister take care of her checkbook and bills for several years. She had been repeating things she said for a long time, and getting things someone else had told her all mixed up when she tried to repeat them.[3]

So writes Brenda Sibley in a poignant remembrance of her mother. To experience and be aware of the gradual deterioration of ones brain, losing first mental and then physical function, is horrible. And no one knows if and when it will strike in the later years and how to prevent it.

As Thomas DeBaggio recalls in his book, *Losing My Mind*:

I looked forward to a life to rival my Midwestern grandmother's 104 years.... Then came a beautiful spring day later that year. It was the day after the tests were finished and the results reviewed. It was the day I was diagnosed with Alzheimer's.... At fifty-eight, I realize the foolishness of my dreams [of a perfect and healthy old age] as I watch my brain self-destruct.[4]

DeBaggio writes about his experiences with insensitive and cold-mannered doctors, the endless tests, and the unhelpful medicines. He talks about the problems he has interacting with family and friends. And he describes his declining ability to remember—and hence his declining ability to cope with life. He concludes his book with the following emotional words: "I am on the cusp of a new world, a place I will be unable to describe ... I must now wait for the silence to engulf me and take me to the place where there is no memory left and there remains no reflexive will to live. It is lonely here waiting for memory to stop and I am afraid and tired."[5]

According to the national Alzheimer's Association, Alzheimer's disease currently afflicts 5 million people in the United States. That number is projected to grow to between 11 and 16 million people by the year 2050, unless a cure or effective preventive measures are discovered.[6]

Alzheimer's and other dementias affect each person stricken in a different way. But there are some common threads. In the beginning, the symptoms of Alzheimer's are not much different from the problems of day-to-day living. In fact, many people as they move into middle-age and the later years often erroneously fear that the forgetfulness we all experience as we grow older is, in fact, something much worse. For those with the disease, however, the symptoms of the disease gradually become more pronounced. They typically include difficulties with language, time disorientation, difficulty in making decisions, depression and aggression, lack of initiative and motivation, and—of course—significant short-term memory loss. Finally, in the later stages of the disease, there is usually urinary and fecal incontinence, loss of speech, and eventually an inability to walk or even sit up.[7]

LONG-TERM CARE: HOW TO PAY FOR IT?

The impact of Alzheimer's is not just mental and physical; also extremely challenging are its economic impacts on the family as well as the physical and emotional demands it places on loved ones who are (at least in the early stages of the disease) the primary caregivers. Wives and daughters, especially, often give up employment (and its income) and other activities to take on these new responsibilities.

Of course, the most dreaded economic costs are the expenses related to care in a nursing home—where many Alzheimer's patients often end their lives. Unfortunately, community and general government support to deal with the costs of care that families face remains relatively minimal in most parts of the country. And, as we discuss later in this chapter, significant financial help from government to deal with the cost of institutional care comes only when one has no assets and insufficient income to pay the costs of care.

Alzheimer's is but one of many medical problems associated with old age that disable us and often make it difficult, if not impossible, to carry out the needs of daily living. Among the chronic conditions prevalent at older ages are heart disease, diabetes, stroke, cancer, arthritis, and Parkinson's disease. Given our mention of these diseases, however, we want to warn the reader not to fall for the stereotypical notion that when you get old, you are sick and feeble. Most older people remain relatively healthy during most of their later years. Although there are often chronic ailments to deal with, they usually do not stop older people from working, playing, volunteering, and doing many other activities. But, of course, with advancing age the probability of serious illness increases.

In fact, if you are lucky enough to live a long life, then you are likely to end up needing some form of long-term care. A person who reaches the age of 65 has a four out of ten chance of spending some part of his or her remaining life in a nursing home.[8] Currently the overwhelming majority (75%) of people age 85 and older has long-term care needs,[9] and about one in five is in a nursing home on any given day.[10]

Whether you get your long-term care in a nursing home or through care services purchased at home, the cost is huge. In 2005, according to the MetLife Mature Market Institute, the national average annual cost of a private room in a nursing home was over $74,000. Rates ranged from an average low of $42,000 in Shreveport, Louisiana, to a high of $194,000 in Alaska. The highest *average* in the lower United States was $116,000 in New York City, where the most expensive home charged $154,000.[11]

Staying at home does not significantly reduce costs unless the bulk of hands-on care is provided on an unpaid basis by family or friends. In fact, numerous studies have shown that round-the-clock long-term care in a home setting—in effect, a one-person nursing home—costs just as much as a nursing home institution.[12]

Long-term care costs are rising at a rate much faster than inflation. If the trend continues, long-term care costs will be even more astronomical and will quickly wipe out any savings of all but the wealthiest older persons needing such care.

Many people think the huge expenses of long-term care are covered by Medicare. They are not, even though the bulk of *other* older persons' health care costs are insured by the program. Medicare payments for nursing home care are limited to short-term skilled nursing care that follows a hospital stay of at least 3 days.

In the early decades of U.S. private sector health insurance, long-term care was not covered. Long-term care was eclipsed by the glamour and prestige of hospital-based medical care. Hospital services are inherently dramatic because they deal with acute episodes of illnesses and trauma and their relatively "high-tech" and "quick-fix" dimensions of diagnosis and intervention. Long-term care, however, tends to be undramatic, low-tech, and drawn out over time, primarily involving large numbers of unskilled workers. Moreover, the bulk of long-term care costs are associated with board and care aspects rather than medical interventions.

Much concern is expressed today about the fact that 46 million Americans, 16 percent of the population, are not covered by health insurance.[13] Yet, coverage for long-term care (for disabled and dependent persons of any age) is not part of the discussion.

"Spending Down." So how is an older person to cope financially with the need for long-term care? Even individuals with a decent amount of savings, theirs or those of their family, find that the expenses and consequences are daunting. Savings, and even home-ownership, can easily be wiped out.

Consider the rather typical case of Laura Butler, a middle-class widow in the Chicago area. She had contracted Alzheimer's disease and was unable to do several basic activities of daily living without help from someone else. When she began to employ round-the-clock home care in 1994, she had an annual income of about $40,000. Social Security and a private pension provided her with $30,000. Laura had roughly $250,000 invested in stocks that yielded another $10,000 in dividend income annually, and she also owned a condominium. However, her not insignificant income ($3,300 a month) was insufficient to meet her total expenses when her 24-hour care began.

In this situation Laura quickly began to "spend down" her assets. That is, each month her son, who had her power of attorney, had to sell off some of her stocks in order to raise cash to meet her bills. But the stocks he sold off had been sources of dividend income that would no longer be available. So every month the gap between Laura's total income and her bills widened more than the last, and larger and larger amounts of stock had to be sold off.

Eventually, the progressively larger monthly sell-off of stocks meant that her savings were completely gone. So now, in order to keep paying the long-term care bills, Laura's son had to arrange for a "reverse mortgage" line of credit from a bank, with the $220,000 value of her condominium as collateral. Finally, the condo had to be sold to pay off both her ongoing long-term care expenses and the debt incurred from the line of credit.

Long-Term Care Insurance. If Laura had purchased a long-term care insurance policy, she might have held on a little longer to some or all of her savings, as well as her home. Current policies pay daily cash benefits for long-term care at home, in nursing homes, or in other residential settings such as assisted living complexes. In the typical policy, the policyholder becomes eligible for these benefits if he or she has Alzheimer's disease requiring round-the-clock supervision, or needs hands-on help with two or three basic "activities of daily living" (such as bathing, dressing, toileting, eating, and transferring in and out of a bed, chair, or wheelchair). The size of the benefits ($100, $150, $200 a day, or more), and the number of months or years that they will be paid, depends on how much one is willing to pay in annual premiums to the insurance company. For an additional cost, an optional (and wise) purchase of inflation protection is available, which annually increases the size of the benefits at a compounded rate of typically 5 percent. A person who purchased a $150 benefit 5 years ago with such inflation protection would have a benefit today worth $191 a day. Unfortunately, many individuals cannot afford, or are unwilling to pay, the premiums for higher levels of benefits that would cover the bulk of long-term care costs. As a consequence, for example, private insurance paid for only 4 percent of all U.S. long-term expenses in 2004.[14] The rest was paid for out-of-pocket by individuals who had no insurance, and by public sources such as Medicaid, a program for the poor.

Since first offered in 1970, a total of 9 million policies have been sold, but only around 4 million individuals are currently insured.[15] There was substantial growth in the number of polices sold between 1987 and 2002, but the industry has experienced a distinct downturn since then.[16] The low rate of long-term care insurance purchases was confirmed in a recent study by the U.S. Government Accountability Office (GAO). A long-term care insurance benefit was made available to federal employees starting in 2002. GAO reported that only 5 percent of federal employees have elected to participate, even though the premium rates were less expensive in this group setting than for policies sold to unaffiliated individuals.[17]

Why haven't more people bought long-term care insurance? After all, there are presently some 36 million Americans age 65 and older. And the millions of people in their late 50s and early 60s might be expected to be a prime market as well.

One reason may be widespread psychological denial of the eventual need for long-term care and the expenses involved. Another is that some people who apply for polices are excluded from coverage because the insurance company learns from medical records that they have a "pre-existing condition" that is likely to lead to the need for long-term care fairly soon, and for a relatively long time.

Still another barrier for many potential customers is the high cost of purchasing a policy. A 65-year old who purchases 36-months of benefits at $150 a day, with 5 percent inflation protection, will likely have to pay nearly $3,000 a year in premiums. If both members of a couple insure themselves, the price is almost double (most companies offer a 10% discount for spouses). The older the customer, the higher the price; with advancing age the odds of needing long-term care are higher. Relatively young customers get a relatively low price but, of course, they are likely to pay the premium for many, many years.

Insurers encourage purchase of the policies at a young age by promoting the notion that they will never raise your premium. Yet, the premiums for these policies (for both younger and older customers) can and have been raised dramatically.

How could this happen, you ask? A very careful reading of policies makes it clear that the promise to never raise *your* premium is a promise not to charge you more *individually* as your age advances or your medical claims history changes. In fact, "buried in the fine print... [is the] reserved right to ask state insurance commissions for across-the-board increases based on total claims."[18] And the commissions have been granting major rate increases, as high as 50 percent in some cases.

Will insurance play a larger future role in paying for long-term care? One expert in this area is Robyn Stone, director of the Institute for the Future of Aging Services at the American Association of Homes and Services for the Aging. She observes that: "The role of private long-term care insurance remains the subject of much debate. One camp argues that it will never be more than a "niche" market for relatively prosperous young-old. Others anticipate substantial growth in the market as baby boomers and their children age."[19]

Medicaid to the Rescue. So, what happened to Laura Butler after her savings were gone and her home was sold? She didn't die. Ultimately, not long before her home was sold, it was necessary for Laura to enter a nursing home because of the effects of a stroke that made home care impossible. She went on to live another 4 years. But how did she pay the nursing home costs after the proceeds from selling her home were used up?

This is where Medicaid stepped in to help her out. Medicaid is a jointly funded federal/state program of health insurance for selected categories of very poor Americans that are specified in federal legislation (Title XIX of the Social Security Act). Older persons are one of the categories of citizens eligible for benefits if they meet the program's stringent low-income and low-asset eligibility requirements (that is, satisfy "means tests") administered by the states.

Even after Laura was devoid of assets, she still had an income of about $30,000, which meant she was too prosperous under one set of rules to pass the low-income test for Medicaid eligibility. Yet, because she was in a nursing home, other rules applied. The income test applied in her case was a determination as to whether her income was sufficient to pay the roughly $70,000 annual cost of her nursing home care. Obviously, it wasn't, and she no longer had assets to draw on. So the Illinois Department of Public Aid (the state's welfare agency) approved her application for Medicaid.

After a lifetime of middle-class self-sufficiency, Laura Butler was now, officially, a welfare case. Each month she was allowed to keep about $40 from her Social Security check as spending money (for personal items such as toothpaste and sundries). The balance of her income, together with Medicaid payments from the state, financed her care. And, of course, she had no assets to pass on to her children or grandchildren as she had once expected to do.

Laura's spending down of her assets is such a common experience among older Americans that Medicaid currently pays 35 percent of overall long-term care expenses nationally for older adults and 40 percent of nursing home costs.[20] But not every older person whose nursing home care is at least partially financed by Medicaid has spent down like Laura. Some have been poor for most of their lives and have little or no savings when they enter a nursing home or need round-the-clock home care. Others are relatively wealthy individuals who are able to become technically "poor" so they can become eligible for Medicaid when they need long-term care and still provide a legacy for their heirs.

Asset Sheltering. An unknown number of individuals become eligible for Medicaid by sheltering their assets with the assistance of attorneys who specialize in so-called Medicaid Estate Planning. Because sheltered assets (and the income they generate) are not counted in Medicaid eligibility determinations, such persons are able to take advantage of a program for the poor, without being poor. As the title of one of many books on the subject baldly states, *The Medicaid Planning Handbook: A Guide to Protecting Your Family's Assets from Catastrophic Nursing Home Costs.*[21]

Because Medicaid expenditures on long-term care have been increasing rapidly, asset sheltering has become a source of considerable concern to the federal and state governments. Congress has enacted a law which makes it a federal crime to shelter assets in order to become eligible for Medicaid, and keeps tightening loopholes to make the activity more difficult. But practically speaking, the law up till now has been virtually unenforceable.

The frequency of asset sheltering and the sums involved—like the extent of unreported income at tax time—are difficult to ascertain. Although studies and various observers agree that this activity is occurring at some level,[22] there is no compelling evidence about its overall scope and magnitude.[23] There is enough overall asset-sheltering activity, however, to support Medicaid Estate Planning as a legal specialty.

Of course, some amount of evasion is not surprising given the major impact long-term care needs have on a family's economic situation and plans for inheritance giving. Once again we see a special risk confronting many individuals, and the fact that there is no universal program, except welfare, to meet the threat. Clearly these risks, together with the steadily rising costs currently confronting governments, raise the question of possible reform in paying for long-term care.

Reforming the System? Although the older population will grow significantly during the next two decades, it is not until the 2030s that a substantial proportion of baby boomers will be 80 and older. But then, the demand for long-term care will grow dramatically. By 2040 the number of persons aged 85 years and older—in the age range where the elderly are most likely to need long-term care—is projected to more than triple from about 4 million, today, to about 14 million. By then, the number of *disabled* elderly is projected to increase up to twice as much as today, reaching a high of 12 million. Likewise, spending on long-term care is expected to increase nearly four times by the 2040s, to about $380 billion (in constant dollars).[24]

One might think that now is a good time to reform the current way we finance long-term care, before the huge increase in demand occurs in the 2030s and 2040s. A number of other countries have done just that. Many of them have used a social insurance (risk sharing) approach to the problem: Austria, Belgium, Germany, Israel, Japan, Luxembourg, and the Netherlands. Germany, for instance, has spread the risk of long-term care costs by including payments for them within its Social Security system.[25]

In the United States, however, the last major political efforts to develop a better approach to financing long-term care occurred between 1989 and 1994. During that period a number of legislative bills—including President Bill Clinton's failed proposal for health care reform[26]—were introduced to provide some governmental support for long-term care to individuals not poor enough to qualify for Medicaid.

One major factor standing in the way of reform, paradoxically, is the fact that much of long-term care has been provided by the family, especially women, on an unpaid basis. The 1994 National Long-term Care Survey found that more than 7 million Americans (mostly family members) provided 120 million hours that year of unpaid care to elders outside formal care institutions. Almost 75 percent of the "primary care givers" were women, 36 percent were adult children, and 40 percent were spouses.[27]

Policymakers, already concerned about the size of spending on old-age benefits, worry that any general government financing of long-term care (beyond Medicaid) will open the floodgates, with informal caregivers cutting back on their efforts and sending government costs for care through the roof. This fear has been a major factor in policy discussions for two decades or more.[28]

This concern appears ill-placed, however. Research over the years has found that making formal services available to families, rather than discouraging family caregivers, actually helps them sustain their caregiving efforts by providing respite and helping them cope with the increasing amounts of care necessary as the "patient" becomes frailer and sicker over time. "No study has found that provision of skilled and home-based support services led family caregivers to neglect or abandon their elder."[29]

Yet, family caregiving may very well decline in the years ahead because of other, broader developments in the social structure of family life. There have been steady increases in the proportion of marriages that end in divorce and reductions in remarriage by divorced persons. With an eye to these trends, demographer Douglas Wolf notes:

> Research has shown that divorced elderly parents are less likely than widowed parents to occupy shared housing with a child and are less likely to receive help with either personal care or household chores from their children. In short, there is a good deal of evidence to support the claim that the children of tomorrow's elderly parents may be comparatively less interested in meeting their parents' chronic care needs than their current counterparts are.[30]

Wolf's overall analysis, which looked at many demographic factors, leads him to an important conclusion: there will be a significant shrinkage in the supply of informal eldercare in relation to the growing demand in the decades ahead. He concludes, therefore, that there needs to be a formal effort to address what is likely to be a growing national problem—the declining availability of relatives to provide assistance and increasing amounts of care when we grow frail.

Since the failure of the Clinton health care plan in 1994, however, there have been no significant efforts on the national level to address this issue. In 2005 the President's Council on Bioethics did attempt to draw attention to the challenges of caregiving by publishing a report entitled *Taking Care: Ethical Caregiving in Our Aging Society*. After acknowledging that "public policy must address these issues directly," it called for the establishment of a Presidential Commission on Aging, Dementia, and Long-Term Care. But its vision for this Commission was very timid; the Council had predetermined that the option of significant expansion of government support for long-term care should be off the table. So it recommended that this new Commission's charge would be to recommend reforms, "whose primary aim would be to improve the capacity of families to care for their loved ones, rewarding and supporting their efforts by promoting institutions and practices...that can assist caregivers in their tasks."[31]

In short, the President's Council *totally ignored options for major public policy reforms* to deal with long-term care such as those that have been undertaken in other first-tier industrialized nations. Clearly, developing better policies to deal with the enormous risks of long-term care facing baby boomers—as well as today's elderly and their families—is not on the contemporary policy agenda of the Aging Nation.

WARDING OFF DECLINE AND DEATH

Leroy "Satchel" Paige may have been the greatest baseball pitcher of all time. Paige, an African-American, played most of his career in the Negro Leagues (the mid-1920s to the mid-1940s), prior to Jackie Robinson integrating the major leagues by playing for the Brooklyn Dodgers beginning in 1947. The next year, Satchel Paige was signed at age 41 by the Cleveland Indians and helped pitch them to the 1948 world championship. Incredible as it may seem, Paige continued pitching for major and minor league teams until he was 60 years old. Toward the end of his career he was asked for the secrets of his ability to keep pitching effectively at an advanced age. His classic advice was:

> Avoid fried meats which angry up the blood. If your stomach antagonizes you, pacify it with cool thoughts. Keep the juices flowing by jangling around gently as you move. Go very lightly on the vices, such as carrying on in society, as the social ramble ain't restful. Avoid running at all times. Don't look back, something might be gaining on you.[32]

Satchel Paige's lifestyle recommendations for health and longevity are part of a continuing stream of such advice through the ages. One of his notable (though less colorful) forebears was Luigi Cornaro, a Venetian whose book *The Art of Living Long* was first published in 1558 in Padua, Italy. Over the centuries, it has enjoyed tremendous popularity—a testimony to the strong interest in this topic by the human race. According to biologist Leonard Hayflick of the University of California, San Francisco, fifty editions of Cornaro's book were published during the eighteenth and nineteenth centuries in England, alone. The most recent edition was published in English in 2005.[33] As Hayflick explains, "The book's popularity derives from Cornaro's description of how he reached 98 years after abandoning, at age 50, a life of debauchery and gluttony for an abstemious and ascetic lifestyle. His new life of sobriety and temperance included a diet of a small amount of bread, meat, broth with eggs, and new wine."[34]

Among the many lifestyle tips that Cornaro offers in his book is that "the food from which a man abstains, after he has eaten heartily, is of more benefit to him than that which he has eaten."[35]

Seeking the Fountain of Youth. The quest for the "fountain of youth" has been part of human culture since early civilizations. Perhaps the oldest written record of attempts to reverse aging is an Egyptian papyrus, from about 1600 BC, which provides instructions for preparing an ointment that transforms an old man into a youth of 20 and claims that it has been "found effective myriad times."[36]

Through the centuries, a variety of antiaging approaches have recurred. Among them have been:

- Alchemy, the use of precious metals (e.g., as eating utensils) that have been transmuted from baser minerals;
- "Shunamatism" or "gerocomy" (cavorting with young girls);
- Grafts (or injected extracts) from the testicles, ovaries, or glands of various animal species;
- Cell injections from the tissues of newborn or fetal animals;
- Consumption of elixirs, ointments, drugs, hormones, dietary supplements, and specific foods;
- Cryonics (preservation of the body in liquid nitrogen for later medical restoration of life and health); and
- Rejuvenation from devices and exposure to various substances such as mineral and thermal springs.

Antiaging aspirations and efforts flourish today, perhaps more than ever, in two major forms: first, a commercial and clinical movement that offers antiaging products, regimens, and treatments; and second, research and development efforts of biogerontologists (scientists who study the biology of aging).

The goals of the commercial and clinical antiaging movement are essentially to extend the time its customers and patients can live without the common morbidities of aging such as: wrinkling of the skin, hardening of the arteries, memory loss, muscle loss, visual impairment, and slowed gait and speech. Although biogerontologists generally share these objectives, they also have even more ambitious aims. They seek to achieve a significant extension of average human life expectancy and/or maximum lifespan without extending the period of infirmity and dependence.

The Commercial and Clinical Antiaging Movement. The use of antiaging products in the United States, particularly dietary supplements, soared in the years following the enactment of the federal Dietary Supplement Health and Education Act of 1994, which relaxed regulation of such products.[37] During the same period, several dozen antiaging books were published.[38] A number of journals with names like the *Journal of Anti-Aging Medicine* began publication. And dozens of Web sites like "Youngevity: The Anti-Aging Company" began marketing products—such as "The Vilcabamba Mineral Essence" to enable people to live their lives "in a state of youthfulness."[39]

There are no hard statistics on the size of the overall antiaging market in the United States, but estimates suggest that it is robust. A research report prepared by a "knowledge services company," FIND/SVP, estimates that the antiaging market was about $43 billion in 2002 and could increase to $64 billion by 2007.[40] It defines the market in terms of five categories: cosmetic treatments and surgery; exercise and therapy, food and beverages; vitamins, minerals, and supplements; and cosmetics. Whatever the magnitude of this market, it seems likely to grow as the baby boom cohort ages.

A clinically oriented element of the antiaging movement is the American Academy of Anti-Aging Medicine (A4M), which proclaims that "anti-aging medicine is ushering in the Ageless Society."[41] The stated mission of A4M is "the advancement of technology to detect, prevent, and treat aging related disease and to promote research into methods to retard and optimize the human aging process."[42] The president and the chairman of A4M are Chicago-based osteopaths who have published nearly a dozen books. One of the books, for example, is *Ten Weeks to a Younger You,* the cover of which promises "age reversing benefits of the youth hormones" such as enhancing IQ, eliminating wrinkles, increasing memory, and enhancing sexual performance.[43]

Founded in 1993, A4M claims it has 11,500 members in sixty-five countries and receives 1.8 million hits per month on its Web site.[44] The organization sponsors national and international conferences, including an annual meeting each December in Las Vegas. Publicly available income tax returns show that it had accumulated net assets of $4.7 million by 2004.[45]

Although A4M is not recognized by the American Medical Association or the American Board of Medical Specialties, it has established certification programs of its own. Under its auspices, certification is given to physicians, chiropractors, dentists, naturopaths, podiatrists, pharmacists, registered nurses, nurse practitioners, nutritionists, dieticians, sports trainers and fitness consultants, and PhDs. A4M certification enhances the ability of these practitioners to promote themselves as antiaging and "longevity" specialists.

Antiaging products and treatments are certainly not new; there has clearly been consumer interest in interventions to prevent, arrest, or reverse aging throughout human history. However, Carole Haber, a historian specializing in issues of aging, asks, "Why this sudden resurgence in the notion that aging is an abhorrent disease that must be eliminated?"[46] She suggests that a key factor is that antiaging interventions may have a special appeal to aging baby boomers because they grew up in an especially youth-oriented period in mass culture.

Can Consumers Be Better Protected? Some contemporary interventions undertaken by the antiaging movement—such as cosmetics, exercise programs, and nutritional regimens—can be beneficial, benign, or not greatly harmful in terms of economic loss to the consumer. Moreover, even if the effectiveness of some interventions has not been established through conventional medical evidence, they may have beneficial health results for consumers through placebo effects—that is, the mere process of taking them in the belief that they will be beneficial.

Nonetheless, antiaging interventions raise a number of concerns for patients, practitioners, and the larger society. Health law professor Maxwell Mehlman and colleagues at Case Western Reserve University have addressed many of these concerns in an article entitled "Anti-Aging Medicine: Can Consumers Be Better Protected?"[47] They argue that foremost is the question of safety for those older persons and aging baby boomers who use the products and undergo treatments. The wares being sold and techniques being endorsed include powerful drugs that have the potential to cause serious physical and/or mental harm. For example, studies indicate that some short-term antiaging hormone treatments can have adverse effects such as diabetes and glucose intolerance.[48] There is also the potential that long-run administration of growth hormone to older persons may elevate the risk of cancer.[49]

In addition to issues of harm, the mere ineffectiveness of some antiaging interventions can have deleterious consequences for the welfare of patients and consumers. Engaging in an ineffective antiaging therapy may preclude patients from participating in other regimens that could be beneficial. Consumers may also waste money that could be used for helpful medical interventions. For instance, older persons may choose to undergo growth hormone treatments because they are mistakenly led to believe that this will increase their muscle strength. This may divert them from undertaking regimens such as resistance exercise training, which has been shown to increase muscle strength significantly.[50]

For some treatments the sums involved can be substantial. Growth hormone treatments cost between $7,500 and $10,000 annually according to one report,[51] and "longevity clinics" are charging as much as $2,000 per day.[52] Granted, the majority of older people and baby boomers are not able to spend such sums. But even those who only buy comparatively inexpensive mineral waters and ineffective dietary supplements suffer some degree of economic harm.

There is growing awareness of the problems. The federal government has disseminated public health messages in an effort to protect consumers of antiaging products and treatments. The U.S. General Accounting Office (now called the U.S. Government Accountability Office) issued a report in 2001 on the physical and economic harms wrought by antiaging products.[53] The National Institute on Aging (NIA) has produced an "Age Page" called "Life Extension: Fact or Fiction" in which it discredits the "very much exaggerated" antiaging claims for pills containing antioxidants, DNA, and RNA—as well as for dehydroepiandrostene (DHEA) and growth hormones.[54] And the Web site of NIA has promoted a free fact sheet on "anti-aging miracle drugs"[55] as part of an educational effort urging consumers to use caution when it comes to antiaging hormone supplements. Also, the U.S. Senate Special Committee on Aging held a hearing in 2001 focused on fraudulent marketing tactics for antiaging medicines.[56]

To date, however, there are no indications that market forces are weeding out risky, ineffective, economically harmful, and fraudulent antiaging interventions. In principle, one possible approach to achieving greater consumer protection is governmental regulation. But there are a number of distinct barriers to effective governmental regulation of antiaging medicine. These are discussed in detail by Mehlman and his colleagues.[57] They argue that in view of the limited capacity of government to act in this arena, physicians and other health care professionals will need to bear a major responsibility for protecting antiaging consumers.

To this end they recommend a number of steps for self-regulation by individual physicians and by medical organizations and journals. In addition, they pointedly challenge organized groups of gerontologists and geriatricians to undertake much more vigorous leadership than they have so far in the arena of antiaging medicine, because professionals in these specific fields are, and should be, most concerned about the impact of antiaging interventions on older adults and aging baby boomers.

Lifespan Frontiers in Biogerontology. In an era in which the human genome has been sequenced and great advances have taken place in numerous areas of molecular biology, it is likely that many more medical miracles are "coming down the pike." The challenge for any one of us is to still be "on the pike" when those miracles materialize.

One area of these advances watched closely and anxiously by demographers, actuaries, economists, and others concerned about the economics of aging is upward trends in life expectancy. Recent developments with regard to the "lifespan frontiers" may cause many of them to worry even more.

Simultaneous with the entrepreneurial and clinical antiaging medicine movement are the efforts of biogerontologists to develop interventions that will dramatically extend the average life expectancy and maximum life span of our human species. Many of them are encouraged and financially supported by highly reputable scientific institutions such as the U.S. National Institutes of Health (NIH).

In 1999, for example, two NIH institutes jointly convened a working group of over fifty scientists. The group was challenged to explore the significant possibilities for applying to humans the life extension results that have been achieved in caloric restriction (CR) experiments with laboratory animals. Hundreds of studies have shown that a regimen of 20 to 50 percent reduction in caloric intake leads to substantial increases in average life expectancy in a variety of species, especially in rodents (one of the primary types of animals used in laboratory research on the biology of aging). In addition, CR "decelerates aging"—that is, it slows many of the physiological problems associated with aging.[58]

The NIH working group on CR produced a substantial agenda of promising opportunities for research on the implications for humans.[59] Among the most interesting explorations underway are three CR pilot research projects, with one subject group restricted to a very low diet of 890 calories a day.

In 2006, one of these projects published some results in the *Journal of the American Medical Association*. The study found that dietary CR had a positive effect on two "biomarkers" associated with slowed rates of aging. But, not surprisingly, it concluded that, "studies of longer duration are required to determine if calorie restriction attenuates the aging process in humans."[60]

And therein lies the rub! Would many of us be willing to undergo decades of very restricted diets—perhaps for 40 or 50 years of adult life—in order to find out whether we will make it to be super centenarians and beyond? Faced with that question, some biogerontologists are now working on the development of pills—so-called "CR mimetics"—that would elicit the effects of dietary CR without the need for the continuous restriction of food intake.[61] Slowing the fundamental processes of aging in humans through a CR mimetic would not only delay age-associated diseases and disabilities, but would also greatly increase both average life expectancy and maximum life span beyond the prior experience of our species.

The current U.S. average life expectancy from birth is 77.9 years (80.4 years for women and 75.2 for men).[62] The oldest human identified to date was Frenchwoman Jeanne Calment, who died in 1997 at the age of 122.[63]

Biogerontologist Richard Miller of the University of Michigan estimates that an effective CR mimetic intervention to achieve decelerated aging "might increase the mean and maximal human life span by about 40 percent, which is a mean age at death of about 112 years for Caucasian American or Japanese women, with an occasional winner topping out at about 140 years."[64]

In addition to CR, another antiaging intervention that has been successful in a variety of animal experiments is "genetic manipulation." As University of Colorado biologist Thomas Johnson has pointed out, "mutating a single gene can lead to a more than twofold extension of average life expectancy and maximum life span in animal models."[65] Thus, a number of companies are trying to develop pharmaceuticals that can have the effect in humans of mimicking the action of genetic mutations that have led to dramatic life extension in animals.[66] Stem cell transplantation is still another avenue that has the promise of substantially increasing average life expectancy by treating effectively the many diseases from which we die at older ages, though long before we have achieved maximum life span.

The most radical antiaging prospect—a "strategy for engineering negligible senescence" (SENS)—is championed by Aubrey de Grey, a laboratory technician at the University of Cambridge. De Grey, and a handful of biologists who share his vision, propose that an engineering approach can ultimately *arrest aging* by continually *restoring* vitality and function. This is to be done by reversing the processes of aging as they occur in adults, thereby removing the damage inevitably caused by basic metabolic processes.[67] De Grey and his colleagues expect that substantive progress toward this objective will be feasible within about a decade. De Grey asserts that it is "inevitable, barring the end of civilization, that we will eventually achieve a 150-year mean longevity."[68]

Confronting Implications of "The Impossible." As improbable as any of these antiaging aspirations may seem at present, developments in science—such as the cloning of mammals—can catch society unawares by accomplishing what seemed to be "the impossible."[69] Even while our nation is focused on the implications of an aging baby boom, it is none too soon to undertake anticipatory deliberations concerning issues generated by the potential consequences of the antiaging interventions being pursued by biogerontologists.

Eric Juengst and his colleagues in the Department of Bioethics at Case Western Reserve University have identified a number of such issues.[70] If dramatic increases in healthy life expectancy and life span become feasible, how should the interventions that achieve them be allocated in society? Serious ethical issues would be created if the interventions were not universally available, but allocated instead in accordance with wealth, social or political status, ascribed "merit," or some other distinguishing criteria. Alternatively, if access to effective antiaging interventions were unlimited, *radical societal changes would take place* in the nature of the labor and housing markets, family life, politics and public policies, the law, and almost every social institution. Wow!

These and other potential consequences of effective antiaging interventions have much more profound and far-reaching implications than other current biomedical policy issues, such as the highly publicized concerns about the ethics of human cloning. If biogerontologists succeed in their aspirations to decelerate or arrest aging, the consequent transformations in the nature of individual and collective life will be far reaching, many of them extreme. Yet, they have rarely been addressed to date, and certainly not in forums that reach a wide public.[71]

You might be surprised to learn that the National Institute on Aging has been using taxpayer dollars to support antiaging research by biogerontologists. In fact, one of the priorities declared by NIA in its 2001–2005 official strategic plan was to "unlock the secrets" of aging, health, and longevity, including the identification of factors that "slow the clock" of aging.[72]

In our view it would be appropriate for NIA to also take the lead in promoting public dialogue on these issues—a dialogue that reaches beyond the scientific and academic community to include the general public. Through such discussions our nation may be able to wisely shape the future of developments in antiaging science and their social consequences. NIH has had a longstanding program that explores the ethical, legal, and social implications of genetic research and interventions for our citizenry and institutions. It is time to develop a similar program focused on the social and ethical implications of significant, healthy life extension.

RATIONING HEALTH CARE FOR THE ELDERLY?

On April 25, 1983, Alan Greenspan was an invited speaker at the annual meeting of the Health Insurance Association of America. In his speech he stated that 30 percent of Medicare funds are annually expended on 5 to 6 percent of Medicare enrollees *who die within the year*. He pointedly asked his audience "whether it [the money we spend] is worth it."[73]

Because Greenspan raised this issue in public, it was a significant event. He had just finished a several-year stint as chairman of a National Commission on Social Security Reform created by President Reagan. Previously, he had served as chairman of President Ford's Council of Economic Advisers (and later, of course, he was to serve for many years as chairman of the Federal Reserve Board). Newspapers all over the country noted his comments. Although Greenspan's figures were slightly inaccurate,[74] he certainly made his point.

About a year later, the Governor of Colorado, Richard Lamm, was widely quoted as stating that "older persons have a duty to die and get out of the way."[75] Although Lamm subsequently stated that he had been misquoted on this specific statement, he has been delivering the same message repeatedly since leaving office, in only somewhat more delicate fashions.[76]

These widely disseminated quotes from Greenspan and Lamm were the opening shots in a campaign—by some public figures, economists, and bioethicists—to limit health care for older Americans—a campaign that has persisted to this day. And there can be no doubt that such comments, and the campaign in general, are part of the changing tide of hostility regarding government benefits going to older Americans. As we described in Chapter 1, in the space of a few years, "the elderly" were transformed from sympathetic objects of compassionate stereotypes—such as poor and deserving grannies and grandpas—into greedy geezers and scapegoats for a variety of social and economic problems—including soaring health care expenditures.

The growing costs of Medicare were very much a part of the "graying of the budget" concerns that emerged during the Carter and Reagan presidencies. From 1970 to 1980 the costs of the program increased at an annual rate of 17 percent, and expenditures rose from $8 billion to $38 billion a year.[77] The rate of growth has slowed since that period, although it is still much higher than the rate of inflation. The steep upward trajectory of Medicare costs has produced some attention over the years on how to control the program's expenses, although the big attention, of course, has been on Social Security pension costs.

The Specter of Rationing. In the years following the provocative statements by Alan Greenspan and Richard Lamm, the idea of rationing health care of older people did became a frequent topic of discussion among policy analysts. Conferences and books explicitly addressed the subject of limiting health care of the elderly, with titles such as *Should Medical Care Be Rationed By Age?*[78] At the same time, ethicists and philosophers began generating principles of equity to govern "justice between age groups" in the provision of health care, rather than, for instance, justice between rich and poor, or justice among ethnic and racial groups.[79]

The most prominent proponent of old-age-based rationing has been biomedical ethicist Daniel Callahan, whose 1987 book entitled *Setting Limits: Medical Goals in an Aging Society* received substantial popular attention. True to the title of his book, Callahan urged the use of "age as a specific criterion for the allocation and limitation of health care." This would be accomplished by denying life-extending health care—as a matter of public policy—to persons who are aged in their "late 70s or early 80s" and/or have "lived out a natural life span."[80] Specifically, he proposed that the Medicare program not pay for such care, and hoped that other insurers would follow suit.

Of course, even such rationing of health care would not result in restrictions on everyone. As in other areas of life, "money talks." Life-saving care for wealthy individuals, who are able to pay for expensive health care out of their own pockets, would always be available, regardless of Medicare policy.

Although Callahan described "the natural life span" as a matter of biography (the personal details of one's life course experiences) rather than biology, he used chronological age as an arbitrary marker to designate when, from a biographical standpoint, the individual should have reached the end of a natural life. More recently, in an article in the prestigious *New England Journal of Medicine*, he expressed the view that the only deaths that are "premature" are those that occur before age 65.[81]

Callahan's rationing proposal attracted a lot of attention. It provoked widespread and ongoing discussion in the media and directly inspired a number of books and scores of articles published in national magazines and academic journals.[82] Many of these books and articles strongly criticized the idea of old-age-based rationing. Nonetheless, the notion of limiting the health care of older people through rationing is now firmly embedded in public discourse about U.S. health care policies.

From a societal point of view, the rationing debate has produced one important result. It has explicitly introduced the idea that the power of government might be used to limit the health care of older persons. It has been long acknowledged by medical care experts that informal rationing does occur. Physicians do this, especially with regard to the health care of older persons, through day-to-day, case-by-case decisions in various types of circumstances. But these practices are not official policy.

Why Ration? Proponents of old-age-based rationing have set forth both economic and philosophical rationales for their views. Their economic argument is essentially that the costs of health care for older people will become an unsustainable burden for the United States during the next few decades because of population aging. They see this as posing grave problems for the economy and making it very difficult for government to spend funds on other worthy social causes.

The philosophical arguments for old-age-based rationing are more varied than the economic arguments. Harvard philosopher Norman Daniels, for instance, poses an abstract, artificial problem of justice by depicting a society in which each individual has available a fixed sum of money for his or her life-long health care.[83] Without our knowing our particular individual positions in such a society, he asks: How would we allocate, in advance, the availability of funds for care at various stages of life? His answer is that we would choose to make sure that we had enough for health care in our early and middle years, and allocate very little for our old age. Others would disagree.

In contrast to Daniels, Callahan propounds a communalist philosophy. He argues that it is inappropriate for older people to pursue their individualistic needs and aspirations. As he sees it, the meaning and significance of life for the elderly themselves is best founded on a sense of limits to health care, and recognition that life cannot go on for long and that death is on the way. This meaning of aging envisioned by Callahan requires older persons to adhere to a value of serving the young through politics and more directly in one-on-one relationships. In Callahan's view, limiting lifesaving care for older persons would affirmatively promote the welfare of both the elderly and younger generations. Similarly, humanist philosopher Leon Kass, until recently chairman of the President's Council on Bioethics, believes that "the finitude of human life is a blessing for every human individual, whether he knows it or not."[84]

Busting the "High Cost" Myths. The idea of rationing the health care of older people has become an established currency in the marketplace of ideas, but it is clearly controversial. As interest in this idea grew, the Alliance for Aging Research, a Washington-based nonprofit advocacy group, set out to counter the economic arguments for rationing—particularly those that focus on the high costs at the end of life. To do so, it established an advisory panel of nine national experts on the subject to guide its work. Particularly notable was that the panel included James Lubitz, Chief of the Analytical Studies Branch of the agency administering the Medicare program. Over the years, Lubitz has conducted extensive research on Medicare costs at the end of life.

The Alliance's group of experts issued a report[85] that debunked common myths regarding health care costs and older persons. Based on a number of technical studies of health care expenditures on older people, the experts made the following important observations:

> "*Myth:* It is common for older people to receive heroic, high-tech treatments at the end of life. *Fact:* Only a fraction of people over age 65 receive aggressive care at the end of life. The older people are, the less likely they are to receive aggressive care when dying. . . . In fact, *only about three percent of Medicare beneficiaries who die incur very high costs* [emphasis added], of the kind that suggest aggressive care."

> "*Myth:* The majority of older Americans die in hospitals. *Fact:* The majority of older Americans do not die in hospitals, and the older people are, the more likely they are to die in nursing homes."

> "*Myth:* Aggressive hospital care for the elderly is futile; the money spent is wasted. *Fact:* Many older people who receive aggressive care survive . . . [and] do well for an extended period. . . . At present, physicians do not have a reliable way to predict the outcome of treatment in elderly patients or, with the exception of terminal cancer, to predict how long a patient has to live with much accuracy."

> "*Myth:* Putting limits on health care for the very old at the end of life would save Medicare significant amounts of money. *Fact:* Limiting acute care at the end of life would save only a small fraction of the nation's total health care bill. . . . According to one rough estimate, if society did limit aggressive care for all persons 65 and older who died, while implementing advance directives [such as living wills] and using hospice care, the savings would amount to only 6.1 percent of annual Medicare expenditures and less than one percent of total national health expenditures." (Note that this latter estimate is for denying aggressive care for all persons age 65 *and older*, not 80 *and older* as proposed by Callahan; limiting care at age 80 and older would save far, far less than rationing at age 65.)

> "*Myth:* The growing number of older people has been the primary factor driving the rise in America's health care expenditures over the

past few decades. *Fact:* Population aging does not so far appear to be the principal determinant of rising health care costs." (We will have more to say about the sources of health care costs later on in this chapter.)

"*Myth:* As the population ages, health care costs for the elderly will necessarily overwhelm and bankrupt the nation. *Fact:* Population aging need not impose a crushing economic burden.... In other countries that have already experienced a sharp rise in the older population, health care spending has not risen proportionately. For example, Japan's population aged 65 and older increased by 31.9 percent from 1980 to 1990, but its proportion of gross domestic product (GDP) spent on health care rose only 1.6 percent."

As this brief summary of the Alliance's report indicates, *no simple rationing scheme like using an age-based cutoff to deny Medicare coverage for expensive procedures will make a major difference in the growth of Medicare expenditures.* Theoretically, limiting aggressive care for people aged 65 and older might save 6 percent of Medicare costs annually. But realistically, the establishment of such a policy would hardly be feasible politically.

In addition, a number of studies have demonstrated that people at older old-ages, in their late 70 and 80s, receive aggressive care much less frequently than those aged between 65 and 70. In fact, "Medicare payments in the last year of life fall as age at death increases."[86] Moreover, a policy that tried to preclude care to high-cost patients of any age who are going to die within a short period of time would not be feasible for physicians to implement. As indicated above, except in the case of certain cancers, physicians are not able to predict accurately who is going to die within a few months or even a year, with or without high-cost treatment.[87]

There are other, more complex ways that Medicare coverage can be limited, however. We will discuss these shortly as we consider the future of Medicare within the context of the larger American health care system.

Social and Moral Consequences. Economics aside, there are social and moral costs involved in policies that would ration health care on the basis of old age. One possible consequence of denying health care to elderly persons is what it might do to the quality of life for all of us as we approach the "too old for health care" category. Societal acceptance of the notion that elderly people are unworthy of having their lives saved could markedly shape our general outlook toward the meaning and value of our lives in old age. At the least it might engender the unnecessarily gloomy prospect that old age should be anticipated and experienced as a stage in which the quality of life is low. The specter of morbidity and decline could be pervasive and overwhelming.

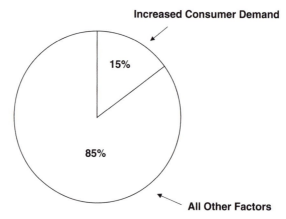

Increased Consumer Demand

Figure 8.1. Consumer demand as a source of rising health care costs, as compared with all other factors. *Source:* Price Waterhouse Coopers, *Factors Fueling Rising Health Care Costs.* Washington, DC: American Association of Health Plans, April 2002.

techniques. Dr. John Abramson, on the clinical faculty of Harvard Medical School, points out the serious implications of the changes for our health and the nation's health bill.[96]

Starting with major cutbacks during the Reagan years, publicly funded university clinical drug trials have declined rapidly. The result is that now most of such research is funded by drug companies (financially interested in "good outcomes") and is no longer done in universities with a long tradition of impartiality and academic freedom. For example, "the editors of the most respected medical journals have warned that they cannot protect their readers [mostly physicians seeking prescribing guidance] from the pro-industry bias seeping into many of the scientific articles they publish."[97] That's certainly a sad state of affairs. As Abramson sees it, the heart of the problem is "the changed purpose of medical knowledge—from seeking to optimize health to searching for the greatest profits."

It is important to see that the increasing costs of drugs and the innovations in high tech diagnostic and interventional tools *have nothing to do with population aging* but have a lot to do with mushrooming general expenditures on heath care in the United States. Total health care expenditures were "only" $255 *billion* in 1980 but reached nearly $1.9 *trillion* in 2004.[98] As graphically depicted in Figure 8.1, 15 percent of rising health care costs have been fueled by increased consumer demand from patients of all ages. Increased consumer demand, of course, includes more than increases in the number of patients served. It also encompasses growth in the intensity of service use per patient, attributable in part to factors like the practice of "defensive medicine" by physicians who take care to avoid malpractice lawsuits. Think also about the role played by aggressive direct-to-consumer marketing by elements of the health industry, such as the explosive proliferation of television commercials for pharmaceuticals.

Medicare's Cost Control Campaign. Since the early 1980s, Congress and the agency that administers Medicare—now called the Centers for Medicare and Medicaid Services (CMS)—have continually looked for and implemented measures designed to control the program's costs. In the early 1980s, a new "prospective payment system" was established for paying the hospital costs of Medicare patients. In the past, hospitals had billed Medicare *retrospectively* for patients' hospitalization expenses that often included lengthy hospital stays.

Under the new system, the Medicare agency delineated nearly 500 "diagnosis related groups" (DRGs) into which a patient's reason for hospitalization might fall, and established a fixed fee that it would pay the hospital for the patient's DRG. It didn't matter if the patient's hospital stay was short or long, or how many tests or procedures were performed on her, the hospital received no more or no less than the prospectively specified payment for the DRG assigned to her.

One result of this payment system has been that the annual rate of growth of Medicare hospital expenditures has slowed over the years.[99] In addition, because of the fixed payment for each diagnosis, hospitals now had a financial incentive to discharge their patients as quickly as feasible. So the length of hospital stays for Medicare patients has declined. (Hospital stays for other patients also declined; once Medicare had demonstrated that shorter stays were feasible, insurance companies successfully pressured hospitals to reduce lengths of hospital stays for private sector insurees, too.)

The prospective payment approach has been extended to other sectors of Medicare over the years, most recently to services for home care patients and patients who receive skilled nursing care in institutions as a follow up to their hospitalizations. The specific conditions of each patient case are assembled and, on the basis of comparable cases, the federal agency administering Medicare then establishes the services that the program will pay for.

Physicians have also been a target of efforts to contain program costs. In 1992, Medicare implemented a Resource Based Relative Value Scale (RBRVS) for establishing what it would pay in the way of physicians' fees. Prior to this physicians' fee scale, doctors had charged fees to Medicare that they had established in their medical practices. Under RBRVS, fees are established by Medicare for the many different physician specialties and services. Physician fees and the other Medicare fee-for-service payments are continuously monitored by a Medicare Payment Advisory Commission, which makes recommendations to Congress several times a year.

Over the past several decades Congress and the executive branch have embraced the strategy of trying to control costs by encouraging Medicare program participants to abandon the traditional fee-for-service sector of medical care to enroll in Medicare managed care organizations (MCOs)—such as health maintenance organizations (HMOs). In contrast to the traditional fee-for-service (FFS) reimbursement system under Medicare, MCOs limit the federal government's financial risk in that Medicare makes a fixed per capita payment to these organizations for each Medicare participant they enroll; in turn, the MCOs are responsible for providing all needed services that are covered by Medicare.

This strategy was right in step with trends in private-sector health insurance. During the 1990s, many employers that sponsored health insurance for their workers flocked to managed care arrangements in the hope that the per capita fees they paid for their employees would stay lower than the sharply escalating premiums they had been paying for traditional fee-for-service insurance. In fee-for-service, the health care providers have an economic incentive to overtreat their patients; in managed care, with the money for care paid upfront, providers have an incentive to undertreat.

The Medicare managed care strategy, however, has largely failed. For a time, it seemed like MCOs would be popular among Medicare participants. Enrollment of Medicare beneficiaries in MCOs grew to a peak of 16 percent in 1999, but then it dropped to 11 percent by 2003.[100]

In some measure this decline was due to the MCOs withdrawing from the Medicare program; they found they could not make a go of it financially, due to the low per capita payments made to them by Medicare. The decline was also due to the millions of Medicare beneficiaries who chose to return to the traditional fee-for-service sector because of their dissatisfaction with managed care.

Congress and the President tried to revive the managed care strategy for containing Medicare costs with the Medicare Prescription Drug, Improvement, and Modernization Act (MMA) of 2003. The legislation provided substantial subsidies for Medicare MCOs and tried to improve marketing for them and other nontraditional entities (such as Medicare "preferred provider organizations") by dubbing them "Medicare Advantage" (previously they had been called "Medicare+Choice"). Perhaps the subsidies will attract more MCO providers, and the word *advantage* will lure more Medicare participants. But any cost savings achieved through this strategy will undoubtedly be offset by enormous new expenditures for the new, outpatient prescription drug coverage also established in the MMA legislation.

Various estimates have placed the cost of this drug coverage at $50 to $60 billion a year over the next 10 years. One big reason for this huge cost arises from the fact that the MMA had the footprints of the pharmaceutical industry all over it; for example, the legislation explicitly prohibits the Centers for Medicare and Medicaid Services from bargaining for lower drug prices for its 42 million program participants, even though the Veterans Administration health care system has successfully done this for years.

At this point, there are no grand ideas—no sweeping magical solutions—for significantly containing Medicare costs. However, a noted health economist, Uwe Reinhardt of Princeton University, has put forth an approach to the ongoing challenge, which, though not dramatic, may prove to be feasible. Reinhardt suggests:

> The pressing challenge is to determine what real resources actually would be required to provide all elderly Americans with high-quality, cost effective health care and then to act on those insights. If the gradual aging of the U.S. population over the next three decades is accompanied by a gradual switch in medical practice styles from those preferred in the high-cost regions to the more conservative practice styles preferred in the lower cost regions, then the United States might be able to manage the impact of its retiring baby-boom generation on its health sector . . . .[101]

It's the Total System, Stupid! As Reinhardt's proposal for reform suggests, Medicare is only part of the overall American health care system—a system that has many flaws. It is not just that we spent 16 percent of our GDP on health care in 2004,[102] and are projected to spend 19 percent by 2014.[103] It is not simply because our per person annual cost for health care (that reached $6,280 in 2004)[104] is almost twice the median for the members of the Organisation for Economic Cooperation and Development (OECD), an organization that includes all the industrialized nations of the world.[105] Nor is it just because American employers are finding that the costs of providing health insurance for their employees is placing a great strain on their capacity to compete with international competitors in their respective industries.

The high cost of our approach to health care is just one issue. Another problem is that the results—what we get for our money—are not as good as we'd like. We lag behind many other industrialized countries with respect to important measures of health such as infant mortality and average life expectancy.[106] For example, twenty nations have a higher life expectancy at birth than the United States.[107]

In addition, most of the members of the OECD use the power of government to assure health insurance coverage for at least 99 percent of their citizens. But the United States rate of government assured health care is 33 percent, by far the lowest of the 30 OECD nations.[108] (Mexico and Turkey are the only other nations in this group that have no form of universal insurance.) As we have pointed out earlier, one of the consequences of our health policies is that 46 million Americans, 16 percent of our population, are uninsured.[109]

Americans, in the aggregate, are not at all content with their health care system. In a survey of satisfaction with health care systems in five nations—Australia, Canada, New Zealand, the United Kingdom, and the United States—nearly half of the American public (46%) felt that "there are some good things in our health system, but fundamental changes are needed to make it work."[110] It is astounding but true that an additional 33 percent of Americans expressed a considerably more negative view, saying that "our health care system has so much wrong with it that we need to completely rebuild it." In contrast, even though per capita spending on health care in the United Kingdom is only about one-third of what it is in the United States, only 14 percent of consumers in that nation felt that a complete rebuilding is needed.

A State-by-State Approach? In 2006, the state of Massachusetts decided to do something about one of the flaws in our health care system. Massachusetts adopted a bipartisan plan to achieve near-universal health insurance coverage within the state.[111] It is a complicated scheme involving a mandate for individuals to purchase health insurance, together with requirements for employers with more than ten workers to provide their employees with health insurance (or pay a fine to the state for each uninsured employee). Individuals who do not purchase health insurance will be financially penalized on their state income tax for not doing so. Government subsidies to private insurance plans will help the working poor buy insurance that they could not otherwise afford. The plan is projected to cover over 505,000 uninsured people in 3 years, leaving less than 1 percent of the population of Massachusetts uninsured. In addition, Massachusetts hopes that the plan will eventually help contain costs, too. Many uninsured individuals tend to avoid seeking relatively low cost care for early symptoms of illnesses that, when ignored, often lead to subsequent high-cost hospitalizations and medical interventions. The expectation is that such formerly uninsured individuals will now seek out care at an earlier appropriate stage of illness and thereby avoid serious and very expensive adverse health situations later on.

This innovative Massachusetts approach to health care reform will undoubtedly be scrutinized carefully by states throughout the nation as it is implemented.[112] At the very least, the legislation has already demonstrated that a wide variety of parties—business, labor, insurance companies, the health care industry, consumers, and Republicans and Democrats—could come together and fashion an attempt to solve one of the major problems with our health care system, access to health care for a large number of uninsured citizens. Before the law was passed, of course, some critics said it would not work. And, not surprisingly, the day after Massachusetts enacted this reform, the Director of Health and Welfare Studies for the Cato Institute, an antigovernment Washington think tank, was condemning individual mandates for health insurance as a "slippery slope to national health care," an anathema to his constituency.[113]

Health care reform is indeed a difficult nut to crack. And it is a very expensive item on our agenda for future social welfare costs. Why then is there no serious national plan on the public policy agenda?

The answer of course is contemporary politics. But also, much of the answer in the future regarding Medicare and our total health system will depend on the politics of "an aging nation"—both the politics of older persons and old-age-based organizations, and the politics of our nation as a whole. These are the main focus of our final two chapters.

CHAPTER 9

A Gerontocracy? The Politics of Aging

Will global aging enthrone organized elders as an invincible political titan?...Picture retiring boomers, with inflated economic expectations and inadequate nest eggs, voting down school budgets, cannibalizing the nation's infrastructure, and demanding ever-steeper hikes in payroll taxes.

—Peter Peterson[1]

"The elderly" is really a category created by policy analysts, pension officials, and mechanical models of interest group politics.

—Hugh Heclo[2]

About three decades ago (in 1974), the prestigious American Association for the Advancement of Science (AAAS) sponsored a symposium entitled "The 1990s and Beyond: A Gerontocracy?" It raised and seriously addressed the question of whether the United States would become a country dominated and ruled by elders.

Although many members of Congress and other political leaders are of advanced age, they were not the focus of the AAAS discussion. Rather, the symposium focused on the political consequences of population aging and presented different views regarding the likely effects of demographic change on the outcome of national elections. The general answer from the panelists was that an America with a much larger population of elders would see only a modest change in twenty-first-century American politics.

We agree. But the Merchants of Doom would not.

For example, contrast with the AAAS discussion the views expressed two decades later by MIT economist Lester Thurow. He addressed the political implications of population aging with the full-throated cry of a Merchant of Doom. He depicted aging baby boomers as a dominant bloc of voters whose self-interested pursuit of government benefits will pose a fundamental threat to our democracy:

> [N]o one knows how the growth of entitlements can be held in check in democratic societies. . . . Will democratic governments be able to cut benefits when the elderly are approaching a voting majority? Universal suffrage . . . is going to meet the ultimate test in the elderly. If democratic governments cannot cut benefits that go to a majority of their voters, then they have no long-term future. . . . In the years ahead, class warfare is apt to be redefined as the young against the old, rather than the poor against the rich.[3]

An equally frightening doomsday scenario was painted by another Merchant of Doom, *Washington Post* columnist Robert Samuelson. In 2005 he attacked the 36-million-member AARP, formerly called the American Association of Retired Persons. He dramatically proclaimed:

> Among AARP's 36 million members, there must be many decent people. . . . But I won't be joining, because AARP has become America's most dangerous lobby. If left unchecked, its agenda will plunder our children and grandchildren. Massive outlays for the elderly threaten huge tax increases and other government spending. Both may weaken the economy and the social fabric.[4]

As we will show, these apocalyptic political visions are based on a naive view of contemporary older voters and old-age interest groups. They see elderly voters as a powerful monolith of greedy geezers whose political priority is to squeeze more and more old-age benefits from government. We make clear in this chapter that this simplistic view is sharply contradicted by the facts. The modern history of old-age politics is far more complex, and the future will not be as scary as some predict.

Yet, the dire warnings of Thurow, Samuelson, and other Merchants of Doom indirectly raise important questions about the politics of our aging nation in the years and decades immediately ahead. As more and more baby boomers become eligible for Social Security and Medicare, greatly expanding federal expenditures on old-age benefits, proposals to limit those benefits will no doubt be more numerous and draconian than they have been up till now. In that context, it is important to ask the following questions. Will boomers band together with other older Americans to engage in generational conflict over government spending? Will boomers be able to use their numbers and organizational resources to protect the old-age benefits that exist today? Will boomers "greedily" expand in a substantial way the range and generosity of government benefits for older people?

Or will a very different outcome emerge? Will much of the old age welfare state that was constructed during the twentieth century be dismantled?

Although answers to such questions are necessarily speculative, we will develop the possibilities based on the facts to date. We begin our analysis by sorting out fact from fiction regarding the political behavior of older persons and old-age interest groups.

THE "SENIOR POWER" MODEL

Implicit in the gloomy scenarios that portray greedy geezers as a threat to American society is a specific way of looking at policy processes. It is often called the "senior power model" for interpreting the politics of aging. The model starts with the fact that older people constitute a numerically significant portion of the electorate. It then assumes that their political behavior is guided by their self-interests and that most of them perceive their interests to be similar to those of other older people.

The senior power model assumptions are based on the notion that older people are homogeneous in political attitudes and voting behavior and thereby, through sheer numbers, are and will increasingly be a powerful, perhaps dominating, electoral force. The senior power model also assumes that interest groups representing older people are very influential forces that can "swing" the votes of older persons and thereby "intimidate" politicians. Based on all these assumptions, it is not difficult to believe that older voters and old-age interest groups are able to exert substantial control over policies on aging and that they can elevate the relative priority of these policies in national politics.

Some of the many commentators who subscribe to this set of beliefs have put forth rather radical proposals for containing senior power. More than three decades ago, for instance, a professor at Brandeis University proposed that all Americans be disfranchised at retirement or at age 70, whichever came earlier.[5] In 1981, a former U.S. Assistant Secretary of Health and Human Services, voiced fears that the "gray lobby" would win a pitched battle against the children's lobby in a competition for shrinking social welfare resources. He proposed that parents with children under the voting age of 18 be enfranchised with an extra vote for each of their dependent children.[6]

Concerns regarding the voting power of older people are not confined to the United States. For example, Peter Peterson reports that a senior minister in Singapore's government proposed that "each taxpaying worker be given two votes" to balance the voting power of retirees.[7]

Some elements of the senior power model undergirding such proposals are reasonably accurate, but others are sharply contradicted by the facts. In order to consider what American politics may be like when baby boomers join the ranks of older voters, we start by first examining what we know to date about the politics of aging.

DO OLDER PEOPLE VOTE AS A BLOC?

During national election campaigns, pollsters and journalists throughout the country mobilize a perennial cliché: "*Senior voters are a key battleground in this election.*"

Why has this cliché developed? One reason is because older persons have a high voting participation rate. Since the 1976 presidential election, people aged 65 and older have constituted a larger share of all Americans who actually vote than they are of the voting age population. They have been (1) turning out to vote at a higher rate than the rest of the electorate and (2) increasing their participation rate while the rates for all other age groups are lower than they were in the early 1970s. Even so, the fact that older voters participate in elections at a higher rate than younger voters does not, by itself, account for the attention they receive. Older people are far from the largest age group in the electorate. In the 2004 presidential election, for example, Americans aged 45–64 cast 38 percent of the vote, and those aged 25–44 accounted for 34 percent, compared with only 19 percent by persons age 65 and older.[8]

Yet, another factor makes it easy to understand why older voters get so much attention. They are a readily identifiable benefits-program constituency that has been created by the very existence of Social Security, Medicare, and other old-age policies. Seniors are therefore a tempting electoral target—"the senior vote"—because in theory they may be swayed by campaign efforts focused on old-age benefits issues.

For some decades presidential campaigns have set up "senior desks,"[9] and the candidates have frequently addressed "senior issues" on the campaign trail. In the 1996 campaign, for instance, both President William Clinton and his opponent, Senator Robert Dole, claimed that they had "saved Medicare" during the previous 12 months. In the 2000 presidential campaign, both candidates—Vice President Albert Gore and George W. Bush—promised to secure insurance coverage for prescription drugs within the Medicare program. And in 2004, while President Bush promoted his proposal for partially privatizing Social Security, he took pains to assure current seniors (and also "near-seniors") that they would be protected from benefit reductions. Of course, not surprisingly, his opponent, Senator John Kerry, implied in campaign speeches that Bush's proposal would lead to large benefit cuts for these same groups.

What impact do these "senior strategies" have on older voters? Because election returns are not reported by age or any other demographic characteristic, the best available sources of information on age and voting decisions are nationwide election-day exit polls conducted for the media. Over many years these polls have been tracking votes by age groups, consistently using age 60 and older to define the oldest group (although off and on they have used age 65 as well). Although age 65 and over is commonly used to categorize "seniors," age 60 is a cutoff point that is highly relevant to old-age benefit policies. Persons age 60 (and their spouses of any age) are eligible for social and legal services, transportation, and meal programs provided through the Older Americans Act. They are also on the cusp of eligibility to choose "early retirement" benefits under Social Security from the age of 62 until the "normal retirement" age.[10] (The early retirement option is elected by about two-thirds of those who receive retirement benefits from the program.)

BUT SENIORS DON'T VOTE COHESIVELY

Despite election campaigns that specifically woo seniors, the exit polls reveal clearly that *targeting older persons through old-age benefit issues does not have much impact on their electoral choices.* As sociologist Debra Street has concluded, "There is no credible evidence that age-based voting blocs are a feature of national election landscapes."[11]

Voters age 60 and older tend to distribute their votes among candidates in about the same proportions as the electorate as a whole and members of other age groups. Older voters have consistently supported the winner of the popular vote by about the same percentage as the electorate as a whole.

Figure 9.1 compares the percent of votes cast by persons aged 60 and older with votes cast by the total electorate for Republican candidates for President in the last seven presidential elections (1980 through 2004). It shows that older voters and the entire electorate have distributed their votes pretty much the same, and in some years exactly the same. When the votes of various age groups are compared, the percentages have been virtually identical for the 30–44, 45–59, and 60 and older age groups, and never exceeding a difference of 3 percentage points during the 1980–2004 period. In fact, they have often been precisely identical.

Only the 18–29 year-old category has deviated somewhat from the others over this 24-year period. To the extent that attachments to political parties exist among voters in the youthful age range, those allegiances are relatively new and have not been reinforced over a long period of time. One consequence of this fact is that members of the youngest group of voters are far more inclined to vote for independent candidates than are their elders. In 1980, the 18–29 age group cast 11 percent of their votes for Independent

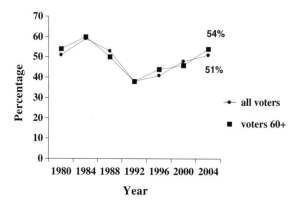

Figure 9.1. Percent of all voters and voters aged
60+ voting for Republican Presidential Candidates,
1980–2004. *Source:* M. Connelly. "How Americans
Voted: A Political Portrait." *New York Times*, p. 4wk,
November 7, 2004.

John Anderson, and in 1992 and 1996 they gave Independent Ross Perot 22
and 10 percent of their votes, respectively.[12]

The overall insignificance of differences in age-group vote distributions
can be appreciated by comparing them with the distributions of other demographic groupings. Over the same seven elections (1980–2004), for example, *men* consistently cast a higher proportion of their votes for Republicans
than did *women*, with the difference ranging from 7 to 10 percentage points
(except in 1992 when a great many men deserted the Republican Party to
vote for Perot).[13] This "gender gap" has held true, as well, among older men
and women.

A far more dramatic gap has persisted between African-American and
White voters. From 1980 through 2004, the African-American percentage
for Republicans has never exceeded 12 percent, while the White percentage
for Republicans has ranged from 64 to 40 percent (the latter in 1992 when
Perot attracted considerable support from usually Republican White men).[14]

THE "THIRD RAIL" MYTH

In spite of the overwhelming evidence to the contrary, the notion lives
on that there is a distinctive senior vote that responds to pocketbook issues
involving old-age benefit programs. For instance, print and television media
repeatedly assert that politicians who try to take benefits away from greedy
geezers will face dire consequences when they run for reelection. Perhaps
the most familiar of these journalistic warnings is that Social Security is "the
third rail" of American politics because politicians who "touch it" will be
"dead."[15] Yet, a dramatic test case in the 1980s belied this cliché.

During his first term President Ronald Reagan signed legislation that eliminated a year's cost-of-living increase in Social Security benefits. In addition, he proposed a general cut in Social Security benefits (an idea that was rejected by the Senate). When he ran for reelection in 1984, Democrats were confident they could gain votes from older persons because they had strong grounds for portraying Reagan as an enemy of Social Security and the elderly. But just the opposite happened. People aged 60 and older voted for Reagan *more heavily* in 1984 than they had in 1980, increasing their percentage for him from 54 percent to 60 percent.[16] In doing so, they were right in line with the electorate as a whole, which gave Reagan 59 percent of the vote. So, though Reagan "touched" Social Security, he was far from dead politically!

In fact, there is no evidence that the so-called greedy geezers have wreaked revenge on any other American politician in recent history. Moreover, a great deal of evidence indicates that the situation has been similar in European nations.[17]

WHY ISN'T THERE A SENIOR VOTE?

There are many reasons why the senior power model is wrong in assuming that older persons vote on the basis of self-interest, especially with regard to benefits made available by old-age programs. One reason is that candidates are on the ballot, but issues affecting Social Security, Medicare, and other national old-age policies are not.

Older voters can only vote for candidates, not for or against program features. Candidates are, first of all, individuals who may elicit feelings of trust or distrust and respect or disdain. Voters respond to a variety of other traits—candidates' personalities, appearances, their backgrounds, and their performances to date. Additionally, candidates usually identify themselves with a broad range of issue positions. Old-age policies are only one set of such issues. Also in the mix are issues related to national defense, foreign policy, the economy, taxes, civil liberties, the environment, energy, immigration, abortion, natural resources, education, scientific research, health and health care, agriculture, welfare, and a myriad of others. Older persons, like younger persons, may respond to any one or more of these types of issues.

Candidates also, of course, have political party affiliations. Older persons who identify with parties have strong partisan attachments because they have been reinforced over a long period of time. So the candidates' parties may be a more important consideration for an older voter than positions on old-age policies or other sets of specific issues.

In addition, evidence often contradicts the assumption of the senior power model that political attitudes and behavior of older people are predominantly shaped by common self-interests that derive from the attribute of old age.[18]

And also, logically, there is no sound reason to expect that a birth cohort— diverse in economic and social status, labor force participation, gender, race, ethnicity, religion, education, health status, family status, residential locale, and every other characteristic in American society—would suddenly become homogenized in self-interests and political behavior when it reaches the old-age category. Old age is only one of many personal characteristics of aged people, and only one with which they may identify themselves.

Moreover, among the elderly themselves, self-interest in relation to old-age policy issues, and the intensity of their interests, may vary substantially. Consider, for example, the relative importance of Social Security as a source of income for aged persons who are in the lowest and highest income quintiles. Social Security provides 83 percent of income for those in the lowest quintile but only 20 percent for those in the highest.[19] Clearly, some older persons have much more at stake than others do in policy proposals that would reduce, maintain, or enhance Social Security benefit payments.

And how about this surprise? In some cases the old can be more opposed than the young to federal programs for the old.[20] A study by Becca Levy and Mark Schlesinger of Yale University found, for example, that older persons (aged 65 and older) were more likely than younger persons (ages 21–64) to *oppose* increased funding for Social Security, Medicare, and Meals on Wheels for the elderly.[21] In this particular study the older participants held more negative stereotypes of the elderly than the younger participants did.

THE OLD "STRAW MAN"

Despite these facts, the image of older persons as bloc voters swayed by "senior issues" persists because it serves certain purposes. First, it is marketed by the leaders of old-age-based interest groups; they have a strong incentive to inflate the size of the constituency for which they speak, even if they need to homogenize it artificially in order to do so. Alternatively, the image is used as a "straw man" by those who would like to see greater resources allocated to their causes and who, in some cases, find it useful to depict a collective selfishness among the aged that they assert is the root of many societal problems. Finally, it is purveyed by journalists as a tabloid symbol that helps them reduce the intricate complexities of politics down to something easy to write about.

Most importantly, politicians also share the widespread perception that there is "a huge, monolithic, senior citizen army of voters."[22] This perception is reinforced by the fact that there are a great many older citizens who are generally quite active in making their views known to members of Congress, especially when proposals arise for cutting back on Social Security, Medicare, or other old-age benefits.[23] Hence, politicians are wary of (and eager to capitalize on) a potential cohesiveness of older voters. They strive to position themselves in a fashion that they think will appeal to the self-interests of older voters, and usually take care that their opponents do not gain an advantage in this arena. So even though older persons do not vote as a bloc, they do have an impact on election campaign strategies and often lead incumbents to be concerned about how their actions in the governing process, such as votes in Congress, can be portrayed to the elderly in subsequent reelection campaigns.[24] A classic example is the recurring increases in Social Security benefits that were legislated by Congress prior to the establishment of an annual cost-of-living adjustment in benefits that took effect in the 1970s.[25]

HOW POWERFUL ARE OLD-AGE-BASED INTEREST GROUPS?

In contrast with the flawed postulate that older persons vote as a self-interested bloc, the senior power model has some validity in its assumption that old-age-based interest groups or advocacy groups—casting themselves as "representatives" of a large constituency of older voters—have some power. This power has its roots, of course, in politicians' perceptions and journalists' portrayals of "older voters" as a potent electoral force. Although these interest groups have not demonstrated a capacity to swing the votes of older persons, they have played a role in the policy process, especially in recent years.

Old-age-based political organizations have been in existence since the beginning of the twentieth century. However, those founded in the early decades were primarily amorphous and transient social movements guided by charismatic leaders.[26] In Chapter 3, for example, we discussed the dramatic rise and impact on Social Security of the Townsend Movement.

Since the 1960s, however, the number of stable old-age advocacy groups has proliferated, and those that existed before the 1960s have become more politically active.[27] Today, dozens of old-age interest groups are more or less exclusively preoccupied with national policy issues related to aging, and many people believe that they are among the most powerful lobbies in Washington. This is especially true for AARP, an organization with a mass-membership of about 36 million persons.[28]

Numerous factors account for the proliferation and stability of political organizations focused on aging concerns. Government expansion in the aging policy arena generates interest group activity. This is not only because millions of older persons have a stake in old-age programs. It is also because providers of direct services to older persons, as well as the bureaucrats that administer the service programs, organize to mobilize political support for their programs. Grants and contracts from government agencies and support from private foundations also propel the growth and politicization of existing interest groups and the emergence of new ones.[29]

It is important to note, however, that since the 1930s, the enactment and amendment of major policies on aging such as Social Security and

Medicare can largely be attributed to top-down initiatives of Presidents and other administrative and legislative policy elites. These leaders' actions were based mainly on their own particular social policy agendas, rather than in response to pressures from old-age interest groups.[30] The impact of the old-age organizations was largely confined to promoting relatively minor policies in the latter half of the twentieth century, policies involving the distribution of funds to professionals and practitioners in the field of aging rather than directly to older persons themselves.[31] But more recently these old-age groups have been active in opposing cutbacks in Social Security and Medicare[32] and, as we discuss later in this chapter, AARP played a critical role in the passage of a major Medicare amendment in 2003.

Forms of Power. Although old-age political organizations have not initiated or shaped the major old-age policies over the years, their professed role as representatives of and advocates for "the elderly" has given them some entrée into the policy process. Public officials are willing to listen to the views of such organizations and often find it useful to invite such organizations to participate in policy activities. A brief meeting with the leaders of AARP and other old–age organizations enables an official to demonstrate that he or she has been "in touch" (symbolically) with tens of millions of older persons.

This symbolic legitimacy of old-age organizations affords them several types of power. First, they have easy informal access to public officials. Second, their legitimacy enables them to obtain public platforms in the national media, congressional hearings, and in other age-related policy forums. And third, old-age interest groups can mobilize their members when changes are being contemplated in old-age programs.

Perhaps the most important form of power available to the old-age interest groups is what we call "the electoral bluff." Although these organizations have not demonstrated a capacity to swing a decisive bloc of older voters, incumbent members of Congress are hardly inclined to risk upsetting the existing distribution of votes that puts them and keeps them in office. The perception of being powerful is, in itself, a source of political influence for these organizations. Hence, when congressional offices are flooded with letters, faxes, and phone calls expressing the (not necessarily representative) views of older persons, members of Congress do take heed.

Many old-age interest groups have attempted to enhance their power by banding together in a fifty-one-member Leadership Council of Aging Organizations (LCAO). The LCAO is a self-defined coalition of "national nonprofit organizations concerned with the well-being of America's older population and committed to representing their interests in the policy-making arena."[33] The coalition sends letters to members of Congress and the Administration on a broad range of policy issues, conducts issue briefings and forums, holds press conferences, and comments on presidential and congressional budgets affecting older persons (although not all members sign on to any given statement or letter).

Members of LCAO have tended to be liberal in their political orientation. That is, they have generally favored increasing or maintaining government spending on social programs—a stance that serves the self-interests of many of the LCAO groups because of their dependence on government programs to sustain and build their operations or those of their members. Conversely, they tend to oppose proposals that rely on the private market to deal with social issues. For example, the coalition has been squarely opposed to any privatization of the Social Security program.[34]

There have been occasions over the years, however, when these organizations have been divided on certain aging policy issues—such as Medicare coverage for catastrophic hospital expenses,[35] outlawing mandatory retirement,[36] and elimination of the Social Security "earnings test."[37] Such divisions have limited the effectiveness of the coalition.

In addition to the organizations that participate in the LCAO coalition, there are some conservative direct-mail organizations that do not publicize the size of their memberships. These include the United Seniors Association and the Seniors Coalition, both initially founded by conservative fund-raisers to oppose taxes on Social Security benefits.[38] The Seniors Coalition bills itself as "*the* responsible alternative to the AARP."[39] These conservative organizations are not as involved as LCAO members are in the day-to-day politics of old-age policies. Their main significance is that they represent to policymakers the notion that not all seniors are in favor of financing additional old-age benefits.

Many Types of Interest Groups. There is considerable diversity among the fifty-one organizations in the LCAO. In this sense they parallel the dozens of arenas in which large clusters of organizations pursue their interests through American politics—the environmental movement, the military industrial complex, the health care and health insurance industries, manufacturers, retailers, organized labor, and countless others

One grouping within the old-age arena is advocacy organizations that are highly focused on causes that affect selected categories of older persons. These include the Older Women's League and various organizations advocating for ethnic and racial subgroups of older people, such as the National Caucus and Center on Black Aged (NCBA). The latter organization was born in the months before the 1971 White House Conference on Aging was held in Washington. Its creation occurred when it became apparent that the Conference had nothing on its agenda dealing with issues affecting minority older persons. By threatening to stage a "Black House Conference on Aging," the NCBA was able to leverage the agenda of the White House Conference to include minority concerns. In general, however, these advocacy organizations for designated subgroups of older persons have only limited political power.

Other organizations represent persons afflicted by specific illnesses that usually affect older people. For instance, the Alzheimer's Association and the National Osteoporosis Foundation tend to lobby Congress armed with policy analyses highlighting their disease-oriented research and service concerns for their respective constituencies. Perhaps the most effective of these health-oriented interest groups has been the Alzheimer's Association. It has had an impact on long-term care policies at the state and federal levels and has managed, over the years, to have a significant portion of the biomedical research budget of the federal government's National Institute on Aging earmarked for research on Alzheimer's disease.[40]

Another grouping of organizations in the LCAO coalition is trade associations involved in providing programs and services to older persons as clients and customers. These include, for example, the American Association of Homes and Services for the Aging, the National Association of Area Agencies on Aging (N4A), and the National Association of Nutrition and Aging Services Programs (NANASP). Such trade associations draw on state and local political connections, as well as on their clients, to protest possible cutbacks in the programs that sustain their operations. In 1995, for instance, such protests led Congress to scrap its plan to bundle funds that were earmarked for congregate and home-delivered meals for the elderly. The proposal was to put the funds into broad nutrition block grants allocated to the various states. However, an effective protest was organized by N4A and NANASP, which included the mailing of empty paper plates by older persons to their members of Congress.[41] This salvaged the day for providers of meal programs for the elderly, as well as for older persons dependent on the programs.

There is also a cluster of professional organizations especially attuned in their public policy efforts to promoting aging-related research, education, and favorable conditions for professional practice in the field of aging. This group includes the American Geriatrics Society and the Gerontological Society of America. On occasion, some of these organizations have effectively lobbied Congress to fund programs to promote their professional activities, including a 5-year effort by the Gerontological Society of America (from 1970 to 1974) that established the National Institute on Aging (NIA) at the National Institutes of Health.[42] Thirty years later, the NIA has an annual budget of about $1 billion that funds gerontologists to conduct research and higher education in gerontology.

THE MASS MEMBERSHIP ORGANIZATIONS: VOICE OF THE PEOPLE?

The old-age interest groups that have the greatest potential for political power, of course, are those that have mass memberships of older persons. The members of such organizations are part of the latent constituency of older voters, which, in principle, might be influenced by their parent organizations in upcoming elections. Among these are the National Association of Retired Federal Employees (NARFE), the National Committee to Preserve Social Security and Medicare (NCPSSM), the Alliance for Retired Americans (ARA), and AARP.

NARFE is the smallest of the mass-membership organizations in the LCAO, with a membership of about 400,000. Its mission has remained the same since it was founded in 1921: "to protect and improve the retirement benefits of federal retirees, employees and their families."[43]

NCPSSM was founded in 1982, in the midst of a funding crisis in Social Security.[44] Its primary objective was "to serve as an advocate for the landmark federal programs of Social Security and Medicare."[45] Although it has only 1.2 million dues-paying members,[46] its Web site claims "millions of members and supporters."[47]

The Alliance for Retired Americans, with a membership of about 3 million retirees,[48] was created in 2001 as an organization in which all AFL-CIO union members automatically become members as they retire and to which all other retirees are welcome.[49] It is a successor to the liberal National Council of Senior Citizens, also an AFL-CIO creation, which was formed explicitly to promote government health insurance for older people.[50]

THE UNIQUE POSITION OF AARP

Although AARP is also a mass-membership organization, it deserves special attention because of its huge membership and sweep of activities. Moreover, its financial and staff resources are much larger than those of the other old-age interest groups. And above all, it has a reputation as a great power in Washington.[51]

AARP's 2004 annual report and financial accounting statements posted on its Web site placed its membership at about 36 million members and indicate the extent of its large business operation.[52] The organization offers a variety of commercial services: auto, health, prescription drug, and long-term-care insurance, mutual funds, credit cards, and support for travel (including hotel and automobile discounts). In addition, it sponsors a large amount of research (both in-house and through grants) and a number of volunteer programs, such as the "tax-aid" program staffed by 32,000 IRS certified volunteers in 8,000 sites across the United States.

AARP has a large staff based in its own office building in Washington, DC. It also maintains offices in all fifty states, Puerto Rico, and the U.S. Virgin Islands. It reported assets of $332 million at the end of 2004 and revenues of $878 million for the year. The largest portion of this revenue—40 percent ($350 million)—comes from "royalties and service provider relationship management fees" on the many products it markets to its members,

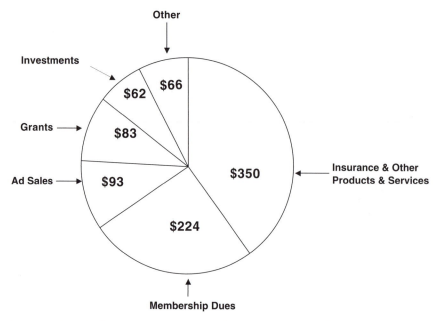

Figure 9.2. AARP income, 2004 (in millions). *Source:* AARP. *Annual Report 2004* and *Consolidated Financial Statements as of December 31, 2004.* Retrieved on January 8, 2006, from http://www.aarp.org/about_aarp/aarp/_overview/a2003-06-24-annualreport-03.html.

especially insurance policies. Other sources of revenue in 2004 were: membership dues, advertising in its publications, grants, investments, and "other" (see Figure 9.2).

Over 92 percent of AARP's $800 million in annual expenditures in 2004 was for membership development, management, member programs, field services, publications, and other revenue-generating activities. However, the organization also spent $61 million on public policy research and legislative lobbying. This level of expenditure on aging policy activities, together with a membership of approximately 36 million, makes it dominant among old-age interest groups in framing age-related policy issues.

In the political arena AARP's incentive system has long dictated that it should clearly establish a record that it is "fighting the good fight" with respect to policy proposals affecting old-age programs. However, as with all mass membership organizations, there is always the danger that its political positions and tactics might jeopardize the stability of the organization's membership and, thereby, its financial resources.

Two episodes in the late 1980s and early 1990s antagonized some of AARP's members and eroded some of its political standing in Washington. One episode was AARP's endorsement of a bill that became the Medicare

Catastrophic Coverage Act (MCCA) of 1988. This legislation levied a progressive income surtax on Medicare participants to pay for new catastrophic hospital insurance benefits. The MCCA was unpopular among many middle and upper income Medicare enrollees who thought (for the most part, erroneously) that they already had protection for financially catastrophic hospital costs. Because of strong protests from within this group, even though they were a minority of older persons, it was repealed the next year.[53] The other episode was AARP's support for the Democratic leadership's 1994 health care reform bills, introduced in both the Senate and the House but never passed.[54]

On both occasions a number of AARP members resigned. And following the ineffectual endorsement of the health reform bills, the president of AARP publicly acknowledged that his membership had widely divergent and strongly held views on the issue and that representing a diverse membership in public policy affairs is an ongoing struggle for the organization.[55] A membership of 35 million persons recruited on the basis of age, not ideology, will inevitably have large numbers of Democrats, Republicans, and Independents.

Subsequently, from about 1995 to 2003, AARP assumed a withdrawn public posture. During this period, the organization became sufficiently cautious in its policy stances that a staff member for a Democrat in the House of Representatives observed, "I've almost stopped thinking of them as a lobby. They have all kinds of valuable member services and do really good research work. But in terms of being a tough lobby, they're not what they used to be."[56]

AARP Flexes Some Muscle On Drug Benefits. But all this changed during the legislative process that resulted in the enactment of the Medicare Prescription Drug, Improvement, and Modernization Act (MMA) of 2003. Led by a new CEO—a widely experienced public relations professional, William D. Novelli—AARP's support for this legislation at a critical point in the process was the most influential that any old-age interest group has ever had in American politics over the years.

Given that the most broadly publicized feature of MMA was to provide Medicare coverage for outpatient prescription drugs—a critical gap in the existing program—it would have been difficult for AARP to continue its relatively low visibility of the preceding years. Indeed, as an organization purporting to represent the needs of older Americans, how could AARP do anything but support such an expansion of Medicare, and do so prominently?

But the MMA legislation also contained a number of provisions to further the privatization of Medicare. These provisions concerned AARP, as well as other members of the LCAO and substantial segments of the social policy community. It was feared that these provisions would undermine the overall Medicare program, while achieving little in the way of program efficiency or savings.[57]

Yet, AARP sided with the Bush administration and the Republicans in Congress, supporting the legislation. Moreover, it played a decisive role in the MMA's passage.

A clear signal as to AARP's stance emerged 2 weeks before the MMA achieved final passage in the Senate. AARP sponsored rallies in five major cities, which included the transmission of a televised speech by President Bush calling for passage of the MMA. In addition, five high-level White House surrogates—the Administrator of the Centers for Medicare and Medicaid Services, the Surgeon General, the Director of the National Institutes of Health, the Commissioner of the Food and Drug Administration, and the Commissioner of the Centers for Disease Control and Prevention—were present at the five AARP rallies to introduce the President's speech and to answer questions following it.[58] Four days later, AARP endorsed the bill and announced that it would spend $7 million on newspaper and television advertising during the week to support passage of the legislation[59]—a promise on which it delivered.

By all accounts AARP's endorsement was likely decisive in enabling the bill to pass the Senate.[60] Some Democratic Senators who might have been prepared to sustain a filibuster against the bill were clearly concerned that it would be difficult for them to explain to their constituents in subsequent campaigns how they could be against legislation which AARP, the "800 pound gorilla" representing the interests of older people, had strongly supported.[61]

Democrats were particularly disappointed and angry with AARP because many of them had come to view AARP as basically in harmony, politically, with their party. Over the years, the Republicans had generally agreed with that assessment. In 2002, for example, Republican Senator Trent Lott characterized AARP as a "wholly owned subsidiary of the Democratic party."[62]

In contrast, following AARP's endorsement and the passage of MMA, Democratic Congressman Pete Stark, a leading health policy spokesman, sent a letter to House Democrats in which he said, "AARP—what does it stand for? Always Advocating for the Republican Party."[63] Eighty-five House Democrats proclaimed that they "would either resign from AARP, or refuse to join it," and Democrat Nancy Pelosi, minority leader in the House, complained that AARP was "in the pocket of Republicans."[64] In addition, Congressional Democrats (and many other commentators) charged AARP with a conflict of interest in supporting the MMA because a large percentage of the organization's income is derived from selling insurance, and the new legislation provided tens of billions in subsidies to insurance companies.[65]

Although the conflict-of-interest accusations suggested that AARP endorsed the MMA in order to increase its income (an accusation that the organization strongly denied), its decision probably turned on other factors. One obvious explanation for the organization's decision was that the new drug coverage, though far from perfect, would be of *some* assistance to most older Americans, of *great* assistance to many of them, and *a good first step* toward better coverage. This was, in fact, an argument that AARP made at the time in newspaper advertisements throughout the country and in other venues as well.

Another explanation for the AARP decision is that the endorsement made sense from an organizational maintenance perspective. For AARP, maintaining and growing its membership is a prime directive that underlies all of its activities, since the size and quality of its offerings is related to the size of its mass membership—including developing volunteer programs to help the elderly, marketing and providing products and services, and "representing" older people in public policy affairs. AARP's Director of Policy and Strategy, John Rother, says that "the organizational maintenance concern was never a factor."[66] From our vantage, however, organizational maintenance had to be a major consideration (whether explicit or implicit) at some level of the organization. In deciding whether to endorse or oppose the MMA—a choice that AARP could not avoid—surely an important factor was which choice would be likely to alienate the fewest members. A rationale *for endorsing* the bill could be readily conveyed to AARP members and the larger community. Most of the rationales *for opposing* the bill would have been much more impersonal, abstract, and difficult to convey—centered on arguments regarding future erosion of Medicare's traditional fee-for-service reimbursement program.

Given the political heterogeneity of its membership, AARP's endorsement of the MMA did create some member backlash. According to AARP's CEO, following the endorsement at least 45,000 members resigned in anger over the next 8 weeks.[67] Yet, one wonders how many resignations there would have been if AARP had opposed a bill that provided prescription drug coverage under Medicare for the first time. It is probably safe to say that the number would have been far, far more than 45,000. It is quite possible that millions of members were at stake.

In any event, AARP moved swiftly to contain whatever damage had been done to its image. Novelli immediately disseminated defensive "op-eds" to major newspapers.[68] In the next issue of AARP's newsletter to members he carefully explained the organization's decision.[69] And in the following issue of the newsletter, he outlined AARP's agenda for reforming the Medicare law it had endorsed just 3 months earlier.[70]

More Muscle Displayed on Privatization Proposals. In 2005, AARP flexed some political muscle again, but this time aligned with Democrats and against the White House and Congressional Republicans. As we have noted in earlier chapters, President Bush launched a vigorous campaign early in 2005 to reform Social Security by creating private or "personal accounts" to be financed by diverting a portion of the payroll tax revenue that presently generates revenue for the public Social Security program.[71] He touted personal accounts as a centerpiece of "the ownership society" that he was attempting to create.

AARP immediately countered the President's efforts with a nationwide campaign of television commercials and full-page color newspaper ads, raising strong objections to "privatization" of Social Security. In addition, it took out state and local ads to thank specific Democratic Senators in swing states for holding the line against private accounts that take money out of Social Security. The AARP ads were effective enough to provoke counterattacks from a conservative organization named USA Next, which hired the same consultants that had shaped the campaign to "swift-boat" Senator John Kerry during the 2004 presidential campaign. In their nationwide advertisements they slurred and depicted AARP as an organization that favored gay marriage and was not supportive of the American troops in Iraq.[72]

AARP, however, was not deterred. By mid-decade it had revived its reputation as a powerful interest group and, in reality, had established itself as far more of a force in the politics of old-age policies than it had been in the past. AARP's willingness, under Novelli's leadership, to spend millions of dollars of the organization's wealth on ads in nationwide and state media venues had a great deal to do with this reversal of image and the enhancement of power that imagery can confer.

BABY BOOMERS AND THE POLITICS OF AGING

This review of what we know about the modern politics of aging puts us in position to undertake informed speculation regarding what the political milieu will be like when baby boomers have joined the ranks of older voters. On the one hand, we have emphasized that present and past generations of older persons have shown no signs of voting as a bloc in response to self-interests in old-age benefit programs. On the other hand, we argued that politicians do perceive older voters as an electoral constituency, attempt to appeal to them, and fear retribution from them. This, in turn, gives various types of old-age interest groups opportunities for exercising some degrees of influence regarding a variety of old-age policies.

In the case of AARP, those opportunities have very recently been exploited in relation to major policy decisions regarding Medicare and Social Security. The organization's support for the MMA at a strategic moment in the 2003 legislative process may have been decisive in creating the largest benefit expansion in Medicare since it was originally enacted in 1965. And the ever-increasing popular distaste among all age groups for proposals to privatize Social Security may have been fueled considerably by AARP's 2005 public relations campaign against President Bush's proposal.

How will these patterns in the politics of aging play out in the decades immediately ahead? Will the political characteristics and behavior of elderly baby boomers be different from today's and yesterday's elders? Will they band together as an electoral force? Will politicians pander to them—voluntarily or in response to pressures from old-age-based interest groups—by increasing government old-age benefits? Is intergenerational political warfare likely? What broader social forces may shape the future politics of aging?

In general, a reading of the modern history of the politics of aging would support the view that Social Security old-age benefits will be maintained for baby boomers in a form and level comparable to today's benefits. Moreover, despite the revenue demands necessary to do this, the history of age-group politics suggests that there will not be severe intergenerational warfare. In no small part, these outcomes would be due to politicians' concerns about the old-age vote and the strong political presence that AARP has established in the early years of this century.

But extrapolation from past and current trends is often a poor mode of prediction in the public policy arena, especially when anticipating the state of affairs several decades hence.[73] The prevailing economic and political contexts could be radically different from those of today, giving rise to new forms of age group politics. Some are predicting just such a change.

Baby Boomers and Voting Participation. How accurate is Lester Thurow's suggestion that older persons will become "a voting majority"?[74] When all baby boomers are age 65 and older, they will still only be 27 percent of voting age Americans.[75]

But that may not be the most meaningful number. The percentage of votes cast by older Americans could be even higher because older voters have tended to turn out to vote at a higher rate than younger voters. Two models we have generated, extrapolating from past trends in age-group participation, suggest *that older persons might cast from 33 to 41 percent of the votes in presidential elections.*[76]

However, for a variety of reasons, neither these nor similar projections can be counted on. The various age brackets of voters in the future will be composed of different mixtures of generations than in the past, and those mixtures will continue to change in the years ahead. Consequently, age-category voting participation rates and trends may differ substantially from those in the past as different generations enter the respective age categories.

The voting turnout rate for older persons, by far the highest for any age group, has been about 69 percent in the last five presidential elections.[77] Sociologist John Williamson of Boston College suggests that the participation rate for baby boomers when they reach old age may even be greater because, on average, they will have better health and higher levels of education and income than the generations of older persons that preceded them.[78] But it is also possible that participation rates in younger age groups will increase considerably as the Internet and other communication technologies are used to facilitate voting participation.

Even if rates or trends should prove to be generally stable over time, the specific political context of elections—such as a campaign that is highly focused on age-related issues to the virtual exclusion of others—could also alter trends in age-group voting participation. Given the fiscal challenges of sustaining old-age benefit programs, one can easily imagine a presidential election in which the candidates take starkly opposed policy positions regarding the future of Social Security and Medicare. Depending on the details, such a political context might substantially affect age-group turnout rates and thereby sharply alter the long-term patterns in percentages of total votes cast by particular age categories.

In short, *all that one can confidently predict* regarding voting participation is that when all members of the baby boom are aged 65 and older, the proportion of the total vote that is cast by older people in national elections will probably be significantly higher than it is today.

Will Aged Baby Boomers Be Politically Cohesive? Unlike preceding generations of older Americans, will aged baby boomers cast a notably cohesive "senior vote"? That is, is it conceivable that Thurow's specter of class warfare between the old and the young will materialize?

During the late 1960s and early 1970s, baby boomers were popularly characterized as a monolithic political group, notable for its liberal activism. As political scientist Paul Light notes, its members had much in common: "They shared the great economic expectations of the 1950s and the fears that came with Sputnik and the dawn of the nuclear era. They shared the hopes of John F. Kennedy's New Frontier and Lyndon Johnson's Great Society, and the disillusionment that came with the assassinations, Vietnam, Watergate, and the resignations."[79] Yet, as Light also notes, not all of the baby boomers were liberal protesters on college campuses. Some went to Vietnam instead, and others went straight from high school to work.

Regardless of stereotypes of the baby boom in this earlier period, it is clear that its members have not been politically homogenous. Demographer Duane Alwin reports that from 1968 through 1978 about 50 percent of boomers identified themselves as Independents, 35 percent as Democrats, and 15 percent as Republicans.[80] Since 1980 the proportion that has said they are Democrats has remained stable, but there has been a systematic decline in Independent identification, and an increase in Republican identification. By 1994 about 30 percent of baby boomers had declared themselves to be Republicans. So the baby boom generation seems to have become somewhat more conservative as it grew older.

In terms of socioeconomic characteristics, members of the baby boom cohort are diverse just like members of previous generations. In some respects they are more so. As John Williamson notes, baby boomers are made up of two, what he calls, mini-generations—those born between 1946 and 1954 and those born between 1955 and 1964. He points out that the economic experiences of these two groups have been different. The demand for jobs and housing was not exceptional when the older boomers entered those markets. But both markets were tight and difficult for the younger boomers.[81]

In addition, the baby boom will be more racially and ethnically diverse in old age than is today's older population. Between the years 2000 and 2030 the proportion of persons aged 65 and older who are of Hispanic origin will have doubled from 5 percent to 11 percent, and the proportion of Black older persons will increase by nearly one-sixth, from 8 to 10 percent.[82]

Given the partisan attachments and diverse individual characteristics of the boomer generation, it should not be surprising that its voting behavior during the past 30 years has been similar to that of other generations. As baby boomers have passed through various age ranges they have distributed their votes among candidates in roughly the same proportions as have other age groups in the many different elections over these years.[83] That is, they have not been a cohesive electoral constituency.

When baby boomers reach old age they are likely to continue splitting their votes among candidates in patterns similar to those of younger age groups unless the political context of election campaigns is radically different from what it has been in the last 25 years. Although boomers will come to share characteristics of old age, this will only be one set of characteristics that members of the group will have.

Yet, it is possible under certain circumstances that old age could become the most important characteristic influencing electoral decisions of baby boomers. As national politicians come to grips more fully with the fiscal challenges of sustaining Social Security and Medicare, for instance, Republican and Democratic candidates could espouse drastically different positions regarding government benefits for older persons. Such a development might especially emerge in the broader context of a prevalent pessimistic viewpoint regarding the country's economic future. For ultimately, the challenge of sustaining our large governmental expenditures on old-age benefits will depend on whether our nation has enough wealth to do so, as well as on its political will.

In the context of a gloomy economic outlook, for instance, one party might propose substantial cuts in Social Security benefits, as well as retrenchments in existing Medicare coverage and a moratorium on authorizing coverage for expensive newly developed diagnostic tests and medical procedures. The platform of the other party could be to preserve the programs, with minor changes, and to oppose the notion that older Medicare recipients should be denied coverage for the fruits of advances in medical technology and procedures. In such circumstances the votes of baby boomers might tend to coalesce as never before, in favor of the latter party, as the self-interest of depending on old-age benefits might well transcend other issues and partisan attachments for a great many (if not all) of them.

If an "old-age political consciousness" develops among baby boomers it might even be built on and magnified by the creation of a political party to protect their interests. To be sure, no major old-age parties have yet developed in Western democracies. But a minor precursor of what could develop occurred in the Netherlands in the early 1990s. Controversial Dutch national policies relevant to older people led to the establishment of two national parties, the General Senior Citizen's Union and Union 55+. Together, in 1994, they won 7 of the 150 seats in parliament.[84] If radical proposals for revising Social Security and Medicare are seriously entertained or implemented—and supported by both the Democratic and Republican parties—one could imagine the creation of a Seniors' Rights party in the United States and the development of the type of intergenerational warfare envisioned by Lester Thurow, Peter Peterson, and some of the other Merchants of Doom.

All this is possible but in our opinion not likely. Barring a seriously negative economic situation, the policy reforms proposed and acted upon to affect the old-age benefits available to baby boomers are unlikely to involve radical changes. The prime reason is that the political parties and candidates are well aware of the very large latent constituency of older voters that boomers will comprise. And they are likely to both court them and be wary of making them enemies. Because of this, the recent political strength of AARP puts it in a key position to prevent radical old-age policy proposals from being enacted, reducing the likelihood of intergenerational political clashes, and sustaining the governmental benefits that will be essential for most baby boomers in their old age.

. . . .

CHAPTER 10

Framing the Issues for an Aging Nation

Politics is not the art of the possible; it is the art of making possible what is necessary.

—Jacques Chirac[1]

The world of poor houses and elderly parents moving in with adult children has been replaced by an era of financial independence and dignity in old age.

—Nancy Altman[2]

There is no doubt that we are an aging nation. Our country is easing into a new demographic pattern characterized by a smaller number of young people, a declining proportion of people in the labor force, and an increasing proportion of people who are old.

About seven decades ago the nation began another, but related, transition. That was the shift in how people were to be economically supported in old age and how they were to pay for health care. The shift was away from family and public welfare support for the elderly (neither of which worked well or were liked) to group pension programs sponsored by employers and government. The system that resulted has been in place for many years, is familiar to us all, and generally well accepted.

The result of these various private and public sector supports, as we observed in Chapter 1, is that today's seniors enjoy a kind of "golden age of retirement." Not that there are no problems; far from it. But unlike generations of old people in the early years of our country, most of today's elderly have obtained:

- A modest but adequate income to live on.[3]
- A promise from Social Security that a basic part of this income will be relatively secure.
- Employer-sponsored pensions (for many), providing a significant amount of supplemental income.
- Substantial health insurance coverage from employers, Medicare, and Medicaid.
- Much greater respect and attention as a result of (1) their relatively high participation in political affairs, (2) growing numbers of advocates for the elderly, and (3) laws against age discrimination.
- The benefits of a growing national realization that the latter years of life can be years of opportunity and challenge, not years of inactivity and misery.

But now, as we are becoming an aging nation, things are changing. We see the scaffolding of private and public sector policies and programs that helped to bring about a golden age of retirement becoming rickety. Measures need to be taken to ensure that baby boomers and generations that follow them will experience (like the elderly of today) an adequate amount of income, independence, and control over their lives in old age. Undertaking these measures surely presents challenges. But the Merchants of Doom have, unnecessarily, articulated these challenges as alarming crises that call for radical solutions.

THE SOCIAL SECURITY "CRISIS"

On the evening of January 31, 2006, President George W. Bush stood before Congress and gave his sixth "State of the Union" address. He began with strong declarations about the war in Iraq, the defense of democracy, and the fight against terrorism. He then made brief references to tax relief, a growing economy, and his cutting of "nonsecurity discretionary spending."

What topic did he address next? The Israeli–Palestinian conflict? Soaring war expenditures? Huge deficits and a mushrooming national debt? Global warming? National medical care costs that defy imagination? Or, despite the huge health care expenditures, the tens of millions of people without basic health insurance coverage?

No, his next concern was the baby boomers and the financial burden they would impose on the nation as they became older. With the greatest sense of urgency, he warned:

The retirement of the baby boom generation will put unprecedented strains on the federal government. By 2030, spending for Social Security, Medicare and Medicaid alone will be almost 60 percent of the entire federal budget. And that will present future Congresses with impossible choices: staggering tax increases, immense deficits or deep cuts in every category of spending.

Congress did not act last year on my proposal to save Social Security. Yet the rising cost of entitlements is a problem that is not going away. And with every year we fail to act, the situation gets worse.[4]

In the previous year, President Bush had given top priority to dealing with this issue. Early in 2005, he crisscrossed the country in Air Force 1 to educate the American people to the dangers of America's national retirement benefit program—Social Security. In an intensive presidential tour that was historically unique, he visited one state after another, day after day, to argue that the Social Security old-age pension program was *imminently faced with disaster*.[5] The Bush solution? To privatize some of it, using a portion of the money from payroll taxes to finance individual retirement accounts.

But as we have argued in this book, of all the "aging problems" we have discussed, the Social Security old-age benefits program financing problem is the one that can be fixed most easily. We have explained that much more important are concerns regarding health care costs, the current push toward individual responsibility for old age security through personal investment accounts, and the privatization of all or part of Social Security. The result, if this trend is allowed to continue, will be a major shift in our approach to the economics of old age. And that shift will result in a significant weakening of America's *successful* approach, to date, for dealing with many major economic risks all of us must confront as we grow older.

The ingenious solution of the Social Security approach was (and still is) the national pooling of risks through insurance mechanisms, a solution that has produced meaningful financial security with dignity for most older Americans. At the present time, the Social Security old-age pension program keeps over 15 million people out of poverty and keeps millions more from near poverty.[6] And for the rest of Americans, it provides a solid foundation on which to build a satisfactory financial retirement situation—although, many of the Merchants of Doom have been eager to undermine our trust in the system.

Given the uncertainty about Social Security's future, *most Americans want to make the system financially secure for the future, not eliminate it or pull it apart*. This is why, we think, President Bush has not been able to convince the American people that Social Security should be radically changed.

THE HEALTH CARE COSTS/ACCESS CRISIS: BLAMING THE VICTIM

In April 2006, President Bush's Assistant for Economic Policy, Allan B. Hubbard, wrote an op-ed that appeared in the *New York Times*. First he addressed the high and growing costs of American health care. And then he articulated an incredible diagnosis for what ails the system.

Hubbard, also the President's Director of the National Economic Council, began with an excellent summary of unfortunate developments in employer-sponsored health insurance:

> In the past five years, private health insurance premiums have risen 73 percent. Some businesses have responded by dropping healthcare coverage, leaving employees uninsured. Other employers pass the costs on to workers, both by raising co-payments and premiums and by denying workers the wage increases they need to afford these higher prices.[7]

Then Hubbard went on to consider "what is driving this unsustainable run-up in health care costs." He blamed it on Americans—on "us"—because of our wanton and irresponsible behavior in seeking health care. "*Health care*," he said, "*is expensive because the vast majority of Americans consume it as if it were free*" (emphasis added).

Hubbard's explanation for the explosion in health care costs totally ignored the fact (as we discussed in Chapter 8) that new, expensive medical technology and drugs are key forces driving health care expenses upwards. He also ignored the fact that health insurance companies try very hard to avoid covering "high-risk" individuals who need coverage, with the consequence that health care is not "free" to those persons. And he ignored the fact that at least one-fifth of every health care dollar in private sector insurance goes for administrative costs (as compared with 3% in the administration of Medicare).

Hubbard deserved a scathing response to his diagnosis of the problem. And he got it from many critics. One of the best responses, in our opinion was by journalist Hendrik Hertzberg, in an article published in *The New Yorker*. Hertzberg wrote:

> Can this really be the Administration's view of the health-care crisis? That its root cause is that Americans are (a) malingerers and (b) freeloaders who perversely refuse to go comparison-shopping when illness strikes? That we're *over*insured? Hard as it is to believe that this is what they say, it's even harder to believe that this is what they believe.[8]

Hertzberg went on to point out that the word "consumers" was used by Hubbard ten times in his op-ed to refer to Americans who are seeking health care; the word "patient" appeared but once! By consistently referring to seekers of health care in the United States as consumers, rather than patients, Hubbard rhetorically seeks to set us up for the Merchants of Doom's typical response: That the social and economic risks that we face as Americans are best solved by reliance on individual responsibility and the free market.

Once again, there was little room in President Bush's administration for the collective spreading of risk with the aid of governmental action. Instead, the solution Hubbard offered was Health Savings Accounts (HSAs), a health care reform policy that President Bush had already been championing for several years. Early on in his presidency Bush had endorsed HSAs that allow people to save money tax-free to pay their out-of-pocket health care costs, combined with high deductible health insurance policies to cover catastrophic expenses.

Characteristic of the market "solutions" put forward these days, HSAs will do little to help the working poor and other low- and moderate-income Americans who already find it difficult to save in any form and who pay relatively little in taxes, anyway.

Hubbard, on behalf of the President, envisioned a world in which consumers, "armed with information about the price and quality of health care, set out to find the best available value." In doing so, he and the President ignored two obvious facts—that consumers are not well informed about complex medical options and health care provider alternatives and that they don't behave as rationally calculating entrepreneurs when seeking health care and making medical decisions. The contemporary economics profession is finally beginning to recognize this with the growing subspecialty of "behavioral economics"—comparing traditional economic assumptions with actual behavior in a wide range of economic arenas. Behavioral economics is especially relevant in areas of individual behavior related to risk. Using this broader perspective, the weaknesses of the "shopping for medical care" perspective become readily apparent.

THE SWISS CHEESE SOCIETY AND SOCIAL INSURANCE[9]

The financial risks people face throughout their lifetimes are many. Why then would we want to be developing policies and programs that increase these risks? For that is the direction we are heading if government and employers continue to shift more and more responsibility for retirement security back onto individuals and their families with measures such as converting Social Security into personal private accounts and relying on individual Health Savings Accounts to pay medical bills. Gene Sperling, an economist at the Center for American Progress, concludes: "our upside-down saving system has helped create a Swiss cheese retirement landscape, with tens of millions of Americans falling through gaping holes with no support to pull themselves out."[10]

Speaking in 1938, President Franklin Roosevelt expressed well the situation we have today when he said, "We must face the fact that, in this country, we have a rich man's security and a poor man's security and that the government owes equal obligations to both. National security is not a half-and-half matter. It is all or none."[11]

The uneven distribution of security from risks is why insurance was invented—to deal with the unexpected by spreading the risks. As expressed by Yale political scientist, Jacob Hacker, "the genius of insurance, especially when coupled with the power of the state to require participation, was that it could transform individual misfortunes into social costs distributed broadly across the citizenry. 'Social insurance,' as it came to be called, transformed the dislocations of modern capitalism into risks that could be managed and redistributed, rather than blows of fate that could only be feared and suffered."[12]

YES! THERE'LL BE SOME CHANGES MADE

There is no doubt that the aging of America presents special issues and problems, many of which (because of the new demographics) we have not confronted before. We need to understand better these issues and problems; that was one of the major purposes of this book. With better understanding, we can more sensibly establish priorities among all the matters requiring change. And hopefully we can also find an appropriate balance among the many demands on our personal and our governments' income.

It does not help, we think, to overdramatize the changes in demography and the resulting issues. And certainly we should not (and need not) undertake actions that will negate much of the progress to date with regard to making life in old age not only bearable but also enjoyable for most. Achieving that reality, however, certainly requires that we address the fiscal challenges of government entitlement programs that benefit older persons.

Throughout this book we have expressed our view that privatizing Social Security into personal accounts would be unwise—principally because it would put many of today's and tomorrow's elderly at far greater risk of having inadequate income in old age than has been the case in recent decades. In Chapter 4 we deliberately chose to limit our discussions of alternatives for dealing with the challenges of financing Social Security—a variety of possible tax increases, benefit reductions, and combinations thereof. Proposals for such alternatives abound in excellent treatises written by a number of highly respected economists and other policy analysts.[13] In our judgment, many of them are sensible and politically feasible. In this volume, however, our central intent regarding Social Security has been to explain why the radical approach of privatizing the program can be dangerous for older people, and why preserving the social insurance approach is so important.

The many problems associated with defined contribution plans should give pause to any thoughts that they are "the solution of the future." This does not mean that the problems arising in connection with DC plans cannot be reduced. For example, some have pointed to lessons that can be learned from the "Thrift Savings Plans" that are currently a part of the retirement package for federal employees. Employee participation in optional DC plans may increase due to the Pension Protection Act of 2006 which encourages employers to automatically cover employees unless they explicitly decide to opt out. Still another possibility is limiting DC investment plan options and offering workers "packages" of investing alternatives (such as a "conservative approach" vs. a more risky one)—reducing the complexity of the investment decision making DC plan participants confront.

We have also discussed at length why we think "putting the elderly back to work" is not the "magic bullet" that would solve most of the Social Security financing problem. Americans want a meaningful choice in old age between work and retirement. Overwhelming numbers, however, want to retire as soon as possible.

Escalating health care costs is probably the biggest domestic issue we face. As we have pointed out, the problems faced by Medicare must be seen in the context of an overall American health care system that has many flaws— soaring costs, unequal access to care, inadequate results by some measures, and growing public dissatisfaction. Sustaining Medicare for the old age of the baby boom will require that these broader problems of the system be addressed. No one, at the moment, has any miracle cure for these problems. As we noted in Chapter 8, health economist Uwe Reinhardt of Princeton University has suggested a reasonable start—a gradual nationwide switch from the high cost styles of medical practice in some regions of the country to the more conservative lower-cost practice styles in other regions. In our opinion, this is a far more useful approach than the Health Savings Accounts championed by President Bush and his surrogates; they are essentially just another tax shelter for wealthier Americans.

We have also argued that paying for long-term care is an extraordinary challenge for the majority of Americans—a challenge that is growing because of cutbacks in Medicaid, as well as the ever-increasing costs of care. It is an issue that needs considerable public debate regarding how the responsibilities of paying for long-term care should be divided between individuals (and their families) and the public sector. Consider, for example, the possibility that government could finance long-term care for middle-class families so that they do not have to spend down their assets and become Medicaid wards of the state. Sounds good? Well, look at it another way. Why should you pay taxes so that somebody else can inherit the assets of his or her parents?

The President's Council on Bioethics had a chance to address this and other issues in a meaningful way when it issued its report on long-term care to the president in 2005. But as we indicated in Chapter 8, the Council totally avoided discussions of major reforms to deal with the costs of care. The issue of how to pay for long-term care through some combination of private and public resources surely needs to be on our national agenda.

REFRAMING THE ISSUES FOR AN AGING NATION

In his book, *Don't Think of an Elephant: Know Your Values and Frame the Debate*,[14] George Lakoff highlights principles for making effective political and policy arguments. Lakoff, a professor of cognitive science and linguistics at the University of California, Berkeley, illustrates the role of metaphors in framing issues, and the ongoing influence of rhetorical frameworks in the policy arena.

Certainly, the rhetoric of the Merchants of Doom is a case in point. In the arena of Social Security they have successfully framed much of the public policy dialogue in terms of whether privatization of Social Security into personal accounts is good or bad. There is very little attention (except among policy wonks) to whether other, public sector solutions to Social Security issues are good or bad.

In the arena of health care the Merchants have portrayed Medicare as a fiscal black hole that will ruin the nation economically. Accordingly, most solutions are perceived as cuts in Medicare coverage and spending rather than alternatives for overhauling our health care system, which is badly in need of reform. At the same time, drumbeats regarding the unsustainability of Medicare have drowned out attention to issues of paying for long-term care.

In the political arena the Merchants have framed older people as greedy geezers whose self-interested pursuit of government benefits will crowd out almost everything else worthwhile and strain the fabric of democracy. Out of the picture are the many and varied interests among current and future generations of the elderly, their political diversity, and, for many, an inclination toward altruism.

Framing a White House Conference. In December, 2005, 1,200 delegates from throughout the United States assembled at the Marriott Wardman Park Hotel in Washington, DC, for a White House Conference on Aging. The members of President Bush's administration that planned the conference demonstrated that they very well understood the importance of framing issues.[15] For one thing, they prepackaged resolutions for delegates to vote on. By the rules laid down for the conference, delegates were not allowed to offer additional or substitute resolutions of their own. And there were no opportunities allowed for the delegates to even discuss the resolutions before they were instructed to vote on them by paper ballot.

Thematically, the concept of collective responsibility for spreading risks was little seen or heard at the conference. As reported by Abigail Trafford of the *Washington Post*, "the agenda was carefully scripted to emphasize the Bush themes of personal responsibility, healthy lifestyle, technological innovation and entrepreneurial solutions."[16]

President Bush did not appear personally at the conference. This, in itself, is interesting from a framing point of view. He became the first sitting

President during five White House Conferences on Aging, dating from 1961, who did not speak to the delegates. Instead, during the midst of the conference, he visited an upscale retirement community in nearby Virginia. When asked why the President didn't show up at the White House Conference, a White House spokesman replied that President Bush "could not attend all the conferences he's invited to."[17]

Nonetheless, the President's philosophy of limited government and individual responsibility was well represented by his surrogates at the conference. A bevy of opening day speakers selected by the administration consistently sounded these themes.

Not even the opening prayer was left out of the framing. In his invocation on the first official day of the conference, the U.S. Senate Chaplain, Barry Black, took as his text, "They shall still bear fruit in old age." From this opening he developed the message that the elderly should work until nearly the end of their lives. "We should be productive throughout the seasons of life. And one of the purposes of a conference on aging should be to ensure that people have a chance even in life's evening to live productively."[18]

This sentiment of "let's put the old folks back to work" (which we discussed in Chapter 7) was then echoed in the speech of David Walker, Comptroller General of the United States. Walker presented a dramatic slide show that delivered a strong message that the economics of sustaining Social Security and Medicare in the decades ahead are formidable. After providing this context he told the delegates that the elderly are "our most underutilized resource." To underline the value of older persons as a productive resource, he recommended that the term "senior citizens" should be replaced by "seasoned citizens."[19]

The Assistant to the President for Domestic Policy, Claude Allen, focused his talk on "the President's *compassion agenda*," which he described in such terms as "individual responsibility," "ownership," and "choices." He also urged elders to look to their families and communities for support.

Michael Leavitt, U.S. Secretary of Health and Human Services, elaborated on this theme of supportive family ties. He called for adult children of older Americans to become involved in the day-to-day details of their parent's health, urging the use of contemporary technology, specifically the Internet and "instant messaging," for this purpose. Perhaps Leavitt's emphasis on the family getting involved in elder health care was intended to substitute for a substantial and growing shortage of health professionals trained in geriatrics—the medical specialty for diagnosing and treating older people. For, during the White House Conference on Aging, the U.S. House of Representatives removed from the federal budget a program that had funded education in geriatrics throughout the nation for 20 years. This, despite the fact that conference delegates selected support for geriatric education and training as the sixth highest priority among the seventy-three resolutions on which they voted.

The Power of Issue-Framing. Those who frame issues are sometimes so successful that they can even get their opponents to buy into the message. This is often true among political and policy opponents "inside the Washington Beltway."

In early 2006, for example, about a dozen professionals and students in the field of aging, from "outside the Beltway"—all of them adamantly opposed to the privatization of Social Security—held a small, informal strategy session during a conference in Anaheim, California. They were joined in their meeting room by a "Washington insider," a high-level employee of an old-age interest group based in the nation's capital.

The group reviewed with satisfaction the apparent failure of President Bush to sell the American public on the virtues of privatizing Social Security during his blitzkrieg campaign to do so in 2005. However, they noted with concern that the President's budget for 2007 provided funding for "transition costs" to privatized personal accounts, and that various Republican members of Congress seemed determined to push ahead with the agenda of privatizing Social Security.

The sympathetic "insider" from Washington attempted to reassure the group by observing that he didn't expect any serious Congressional action for privatizing Social Security during the remainder of 2006. It was to be an election year, so Representatives and Senators would obviously be wary of moving forward with something as controversial as Social Security privatization until 2007.

At that point in the conversation, one of the group's members (a university professor) suggested that now—during this 2006 hiatus in the efforts of the privatization proponents—would be the ideal time to fill the vacuum with a widely publicized proposal for legislation that would effectively cope with the projected shortfall in Social Security several decades hence—an alternative to privatization. But the insider pooh-poohed the suggestion. He proclaimed that "the only game in town [Washington] is privatization. What we have to do is focus on fighting privatization."

FRAMING NEW ISSUES: WE'RE ALL IN THIS TOGETHER

We strongly disagree. In our opinion, it is critical that old-age policy issues be reframed in ways that counter the apocalyptic visions and radical solutions put forward by the Merchants of Doom. To do so, one must effectively question the widely accepted assumptions and declarations of the Merchants, established in their campaign to shape the challenges of our aging nation and public opinion concerning them.

The Merchants of Doom have repeatedly declared Medicare and Social Security to be unsustainable and asserted that they must be changed. They propose radical solutions such as old-age-based health care rationing and the dismantling of Social Security into private personal accounts—a reform that would place workers at risk and generate tremendous uncertainty regarding their income in old age. And they argue that such changes should be enacted now, before the massive numbers of baby boomers are old and can politically prevent such policies.

If the Merchants have their way, the circumstances of daily life for baby boom older Americans in the future might well resemble the situation in the past. We are likely to see a return of many difficult economic and health care situations that earlier generations of the elderly experienced prior to the establishment of Social Security and Medicare as pillars of support in old age.

If we want to prevent this, who or what organization might undertake leadership in framing new issues for our aging nation? AARP, of course, is a potential candidate. The organization is a far more influential force in the politics than it was in its earlier years. Under the leadership of CEO William Novelli, a longtime public relations specialist, AARP is likely to continue drawing on its large resources and its standing as a massive membership organization of older persons to play a visible and active policy role. Since Novelli took charge of the organization in early 2002, "positive social change" has become an explicitly avowed priority of the organization.[20] Moreover, it appears that it is his intention to make the organization a major "player" in Washington politics, by continuing to spend millions to influence public opinion.

In response to Democratic complaints that AARP had cooperated with the Republicans on the Medicare prescription drug legislation of 2003, he acknowledged that these actions had realigned AARP politically. Shortly after the legislation passed he opined that, "AARP was taken for granted" by Democratic leaders in the past. And he then observed that "the best thing we can do is not be aligned with either party."[21] This intent was demonstrated clearly when 12 months later his organization mounted its vigorous war of words, images, and dollars in opposition to the push for partially privatizing Social Security.

Perhaps the most effective issue-framing strategy to counter the Merchants of Doom and minimize conflict among generations would be for AARP to form a coalition with advocates for children (such as the Children's Defense Fund) and other key organizations concerned with the welfare of family members of all ages. Banding together its resources, the coalition could launch a sustained media campaign. The campaign should portray the aging of the baby boomers as *a challenge confronting baby boomers themselves, their families, and society—rather than as a Social Security crisis and a Medicare crisis.*

The central focus of this coalition's campaign should be on *people rather than programs.* The key is to convey the consequences of radical policy changes in terms of what they would mean tomorrow for older people, the nature of family obligations and lifestyles, and the fabric of familiar social institutions that are integral to the daily life of Americans of all ages.

Such a campaign could be initially targeted to the 76 million baby boomers, and be strong enough to compete with antiaging marketing campaigns that tell this audience how to avoid growing old.[22] Its initial goal might be to convey to boomers (perhaps in a congratulatory fashion) that they will live as older Americans for many, many, years. An important complementary aspect of this first "congratulatory" phase would be to effectively inform baby boomers about the existing array and financing of various benefit programs that reduce the risks of old age, making clear their roles, and also their limitations.

A next element would be to develop and convey scenarios that depict what life will be like for aged baby boomers *and their families* if nothing is done to maintain Social Security and Medicare in forms that sustain government supports at a level that is reasonably comparable to what older Americans experienced in the last three decades of the twentieth century and the first years of the twenty-first.

What will the budgets of elderly couples and aged widows be like in terms of how much they have to spend on food, shelter, clothing, utilities, transportation, medical care, and long-term care? For those who are less than wealthy, what limits might exist on their access to medical care—including high-cost and high-tech medical interventions—particularly at advanced old ages? How many older persons will have to be financially supported by their children, including the catastrophic expenses of acute health care and long-term care? Will American society witness, due to the necessity of family economics, the return of three- and perhaps four-generation households? Will the constant stream of emerging medical miracles be available to all of us, or only the very wealthy and "connected" in American society? Many such questions could be vividly posed.

The generation and promulgation of scenarios that answer these questions might be enough to help baby boomers and their families feel that sufficient problems loom in societal support for the basic needs of tomorrow's older people to warrant remedial, but not radical, policy action in the near future. If an issue as abstract, unfamiliar, and seemingly distant in consequences as Global Warming can reach public attention, then our vision of the challenges of population aging surely could, especially if the not-too-distant consequences are conveyed in terms of *daily lives for persons of all ages* rather than projected program deficits.

Of course, in the visions of our aging nation put forward by the Merchants of Doom, we are a country of age groups, divided from one another. Some of them depict the nation as engaged in intergenerational political conflict, young against old. Most promote the breakup of our universal social insurance program, a system that pools the many financial risks of old age. This they would replace (in whole or in part) with personal private accounts that put us individually at risk and promote the view of "every man and woman for themselves." Similarly, some Merchants encourage the breakup of Medicare, our only *national* health insurance risk pool that covers the well and sick alike. As an alternative, they promote the creation of so-called "competitive" private health plans with smaller and smaller risk pools, managed by companies that have no financial incentive to serve the sickest people. If that were not bad enough, a growing number of these reformers talk about the need to deny to the oldest among us many of the advances of modern American medicine.

But as we have explained above, the issues confronting older people— individually and collectively—are not now, and will not in the future, be hermetically sealed from the rest of society. Perhaps the way to gain widespread political support among all generations is to package policy options for our aging nation as *family policies*.[23] In effect, this is what they will be. We should not forget that the beneficiaries of the future would be all of us.

NOTES

CHAPTER ONE: BABY BOOMERS AND THE MERCHANTS OF DOOM

1. S. Maugham, *The Summing Up*. London: Heinemann, 1938.

2. F. Cairncross, "Forever Young." *The Economist* (March 27, 2004): 3–18, Special Supplement.

3. P. C. Light, *Baby Boomers*. New York: W.W. Norton & Company, 1988.

4. Social Security and Medicare Boards of Trustees, *Status of the Social Security and Medicare Programs: A Summary of the 2006 Annual Reports*. Retrieved May 2, 2006, from http://www.socialsecurity.gov/OACT/TRSUM/trsummary.html

5. R. Toner and M. Connelly, "Poll Finds Broad Pessimism on Social Security Payments." *New York Times* (June 6, 2005): A18.

6. Social Security and Medicare Boards of Trustees, *Status of the Social Security and Medicare Programs: A Summary of the 2006 Annual Reports*.

7. R. Weiss, "Medicare to Cover Cardiac Device: Plan Raises Issue of Line between Care and Research." *Washington Post* (January 20, 2005): A1.

8. See D. P. Goldman, B. Shang, J. Bhattacharya, A. M. Garber, M. Hurd, G. F. Joyce, D. N. Lakdawalla, C. Panis, and R. Shekelle, *Consequences of Health Trends and Medical Innovation for the Future Elderly. Health Affairs—Web Exclusive* (September 26, 2005): W5, R5–R16. Retrieved September 27, 2005, from http://content.healthaffairs.o9rg/cgi/reprint/hlthaff.w5.r5v1

9. U.S. Government Accountability Office (GAO), *Retiree Health Benefits: Options for Employment-Based Prescription Drug Benefits under the Medicare Modernization Act*. Washington, DC: GAO, 2005.

10. M. Maynard, "United Air Wins Right to Default on Its Employee Pension Plans." *New York Times* (May 11, 2005). Retrieved May 11, 2005, from http://www.nytimes.com/2005/05/11/business/11air.html?pagewanted=print

11. R. A. Kalish, "The New Ageism and the Failure Models: A Polemic." *Gerontologist* 19 (1979): 398–407.

12. R. J. Samuelson, "Aging America: Who Will Shoulder the Growing Burden?" *National Journal* 10 (1978): 1712–1717.

13. N. R. Gibbs, "Grays on the Go." *Time* 131(8) (1980): 66–75.

14. H. Fairlie, "Talkin' 'Bout My Generation." *New Republic* 198 (1988): 19–22.

15. See, for example, E. Salholz, "Blaming the Voters: Hapless Budgeteers Single Out "Greedy Geezers." *Newsweek* (October 29, 1990): 36.

16. L. Smith, "The Tyranny of America's Old." *Fortune* 125(1) (1992): 68–72.

17. S. Chapman, "Meet the Greedy Grandparents." *Slate* (December 10, 2003). Retrieved on December 17, 2005, from http://slate.msn.com/id/2092302/%20

18. See R. B. Hudson, "The 'Graying' of the Federal Budget and Its Consequences for Old Age Policy." *Gerontologist* 18 (1978): 428–440.

19. D. Broder, "Budget Funds for Elderly Grow Rapidly." *Washington Post* (January 30, 1973): A-16.

20. Barbara Boyle Torrez, "Guns vs. Canes: The Fiscal Implications of an Aging Population." *American Economics Association Papers and Proceedings* 72 (1982): 309–313.

21. See J. Quinn, "The Economic Status of the Elderly: Beware the Mean." *Review of Income and Wealth* 33(1) (1987): 63–82.

22. P. G. Peterson, "The Morning After." *Atlantic Monthly* 260(4) (1987): 43–49.

23. M. Carballo, "Extra Votes for Parents?" *Boston Globe* (December 17, 1981): 35.

24. S. H. Preston, "Children and the Elderly in the U.S." *Scientific American* 51(6) (1984): 44–49. Government support (money and services) for poor children in the United States has always been low, given the fear of many people that the provision of benefits to them might create strong work disincentives, encouraging many parents to go on welfare.

25. See R. H. Binstock and S. G. Post, eds., *Too Old For Health Care? Controversies in Medicine, Law, Economics, and Ethics*. Baltimore, MD: Johns Hopkins University Press, 1991.

26. D. Callahan, *Setting Limits: Medical Goals in an Aging Society*. New York: Simon and Schuster, 1987.

27. See, for example, L. J. Kotlikoff, *Generational Accounting: Knowing Who Pays, and When, for What We Spend*. New York: Free Press, 1992.

28. See R. Haveman, "Should Generational Accounts Replace Public Budgets and Deficits?" *Journal of Economic Perspectives* 8 (Winter 1994): 95–111.

29. J. Quadagno, "Generational Equity and the Politics of the Welfare State." *Politics and Society* 17 (1989): 353–376.

30. P. Longman, *Born to Pay: The New Politics of Aging in America*. Boston, MA: Houghton Mifflin, 1987.

31. The Concord Coalition, *About Us*. Retrieved on December 3, 2005, from www.concordcoalition.org/about.html

32. Third Millennium, *Declaration of Beliefs*. Retrieved on August 21, 2005, from www.thirdmil.org/publications/declare.html

33. F. L. Cook, V. M. Marshall, J. E. Marshall, and J. E. Kaufman, "The Salience of Intergenerational Equity in Canada and the United States." In T. R. Marmor, T. M. Smeeding, and V. L. Greene, eds., *Economic Security and Intergenerational Justice: A Look at North America*. Washington, DC: Urban Institute Press, 1994, pp. 91–129.

34. R. M. Rosenzweig, address at the president's opening session, *43rd Annual Meeting of the Gerontological Society of America*, Boston, MA, November 16, 1990.

35. Ford Foundation, Project on Social Welfare and the American Future, Executive Panel, *The Common Good: Social Welfare and the American Future*. New York: Ford Foundation, 1989.

36. A. Pifer and L. Bronte, eds., *Our Aging Society: Paradox and Promise*. New York: W.W. Norton & Company, 1986.

37. National Center for Health Statistics, *Health, United States, 2004: With Chartbook on Trends in the Health of Americans*. Hyattsville, MD, 2004. Retrieved September 28, 2005, from http://www.cdc.gove/nchs/data/hus/hus04trend.pdf

38. D. Callahan, *Setting Limits: Medical Goals in an Aging Society*.

39. L. C. Thurow, "The Birth of a Revolutionary Class." *New York Times Magazine* (May 19, 1996): 46–47.

40. P. G. Peterson, *Gray Dawn: How the Coming Age Wave Will Transform America—and the World*. New York: Times Books, 1999.

41. Bipartisan Commission on Entitlement and Tax Reform, *Commission Findings*. Washington, DC: U.S. Government Printing Office, 1994.

42. See, for example, E. Bumiller, "Bush Presses His Argument for Social Security Change." *New York Times* (January 12, 2005): A18.

43. See, for example, G. W. Bush, "Transcript: President Bush's State of the Union Address." *New York Times* (February 3, 2005). Retrieved on February 4, 2005, from http://www.nytimes.com/2005/02/03/politics/03btext.html?pagewanted-print& position=

44. W. Vieth and R. Simon, "President Casts Doubt on Trust Fund: Promoting His Private Account Plan, Bush Calls the Social Security Bonds Held for Future Beneficiaries "Just IOUs" Sitting In A Filing Cabinet." *Los Angeles Times* (April 6, 2005). Retrieved on April 6, 2005, from http://www.latimes.com/news/printedition/asection/ la-na-bush6apr06,1,4700653,print.story

45. Editorial, "For the Record." *New York Times* (January 10, 2005): A22.

46. See J. B. Williamson, "A Critique of the Case for Privatizing Social Security." *Gerontologist* 37 (1997): 561–571.

47. Y. Tsurumi, "Hail to the Robber Baron?" *The Harvard Crimson* (April 6, 2005). Retrieved on April 8, 2005, from http:///www.thecrimson.com/ printerfriendly.aspx?ref=506836

48. D. D. Eisenhower, Personal and confidential correspondence with Edgar Newton Eisenhower, November 8, 1954. *The Papers of Dwight David Eisenhower*. Vol. XV Document #1147. Retrieved on April 5, 2006, from http://www. eisenhowermemorial.org/presidential-papers/first-term/documents/1147.cfm

49. See Paul C. Light, 1985, *Artful Work: The Politics of Social Security Reform*.

50. 1994–1996 Advisory Council on Social Security, *Report of the 1994–1996 Advisory Council on Social Security, Volume I: Findings and Recommendations*. Washington, DC: U.S. Government Printing Office, 1997.

51. R. W. Stevenson, "Privatization of Social Security Is Gaining Ground." *New York Times* (April 6, 1998): A1.

52. R. W. Stevenson, "Clinton May Use Wall Street to Ease Social Security Ills." *New York Times* (July 28, 1998): A9.

53. President's Commission to Strengthen Social Security. (2001). Retrieved on September 27, 2005, from http://www.csss.gov/reports/

54. Among the coalition's members were the Business Roundtable, the U.S. Chamber of Commerce, the National Association of Manufacturers, the Alliance of Automobile Manufacturers, the Associated General Contractors of America, the National Restaurant Association, and the National Retail Federation. See Judy Sarasohn, "Coalition Pushes Social Security Accounts." Retrieved on April 7, 2005, from http://www.washingtonpost.com/ac2/wp-dyn/A32781-2005Apr6?language=printer

55. J. White, *False Alarm: Why the Greatest Threat to Social Security and Medicare Is the Campaign to "Save" Them*. Baltimore, MD: Johns Hopkins University Press, 2001.

56. R. B. Friedland and L. Summer, *Demography Is Not Destiny, Revisited*. Washington, DC: Center on an Aging Society, Georgetown University, 2005.

57. H. J. Aaron, "Budget Estimates: What We Know, What We Can't Know, and Why It Matters." In S. H. Altman and D. I. Schactman, eds., *Policies for an Aging Society*. Baltimore, MD: Johns Hopkins University Press, 2000, pp. 63–80.

58. See the discussion and review of research on this question in L. K. George, "Perceived Quality of Life." In R. H. Binstock and L. K. George, eds., *Handbook of Aging and the Social Sciences*, 6th ed. San Diego, CA: Academic Press, 2006, pp. 320–336.

59. Quoted in L. M. Ireland and K. Bond, "Retirees of the 1970s." In G. S. Kart and B. B. Manard, eds., *Aging in America—Readings in Social Gerontology*. Sherman Oaks, CA: Alfred, 1976, pp. 231–251.

60. AARP, *Reimagining America: AARP's Blueprint for the Future*. Washington, DC: AARP, 2005.

CHAPTER TWO: THE PHONY THREAT OF POPULATION AGING

1. J. Flint, "The Old Folks." *Forbes* (February 18, 1980): 1.

2. T. R. Marmor, F. L. Cook, and S. Scher, "Social Security Politics and the Conflict Between Generations." In E. R. Kingson, and J. H. Schulz, eds. *Social Security in the 21st Century*. New York: 1997, pp. 195–207.

3. L. Kotlikoff and S. Burns, *The Coming Generational Storm—What You Need to Know about America's Economic Future*. Cambridge, MA: MIT Press, 2004.

4. R. J. Samuelson, "Generational Economics." *Boston Globe* (April 19, 1994): 46.

5. D. Price, "Of Population and False Hopes: Malthus and His Legacy." *Population and Environment* 19(3) (January 1998): 1–10.

6. D. Warsh, *Knowledge and the Wealth of Nations*. New York: W. W. Norton & Company, 2006.

7. A. J. Coale, "How a Population Ages or Grows Younger." In R. Freedman, ed., *Population: The Vital Revolution* Garden City, NY: Anchor Books, 1964, pp. 47–58.

8. U.S. Census Bureau, *65+ in the United States: 2005*. Current Population Reports P23-209. Washington, DC: U.S. Government Printing Office, 2005.

9. S. N. Chakravaty and K. Weisman, "Consuming Our Children?" *Forbes* (November 14, 1988): 222–232.

10. E. C. Steuerle and C. Spiro, "What Does Fixing Social Security Actually Fix?" *Straight Talk*. Briefs from the Retirement Project, No. 1. Washington, DC: Urban Institute Press, 1999.

11. R. B Friedland and L. Summer, *Demography Is Not Destiny*. Washington, DC: National Academy on an Aging Society, 1999.

12. U.S. Census Bureau, *Demographic Trends in the 20th Century*. Census 2000 Special Reports, Series CENSR-4. Washington, DC: U.S. Government Printing Office, 2002.

13. "The Downturn." *The Economist* (January 7, 2006): 37.

14. "Half a Billion American?" *The Economist* (August 24, 2002): 20–22.

15. "Incredible Shrinking Countries." *The Economist* (January 7, 2006): 12.

16. Both the 4 million and 19–21 million statistics are from N. Eberstadt, *The Russian Federation at the Dawn of the Twenty-first Century*. Seattle, WA: National Bureau of Asian Research, 2004.

17. F. Weir, "Russia Begins to Reconsider Wide Use of Abortion," *Christian Science Monitor* (August 28, 2003): 1.

18. N. Eberstadt, *The Russian Federation at the Dawn of the Twenty-first Century*.

19. "Charlemagne: Europe's Population Implosion." *The Economist* (July 19, 2003): 42.

20. Ibid.

21. "Incredible Shrinking Countries," 12.

22. Social Security Advisory Board, *Social Security: Why Action Should Be Taken Soon*. Washington, DC: SSAB, September 2005.

23. Ibid.

24. H. J Aaron, "When Is a Burden Not a Burden? The Elderly in America." *The Brookings Review* (Summer 1986): 17–24.

25. For a good explanation of this phenomenon, see D. O. Cowgill, *Aging Around the World*. Belmont, CA: Wadsworth, 1986.

26. J. H. Schulz, A. Borowski, and W. H. Crown, *Economics of Population Aging: The "Graying" of Australia, Japan, and the United States*. Westport, CT: Auburn House, 1991.

27. See, for example, P. G. Peterson, *The Age Way*. New York: Crown, 1999.

28. J. H. Schulz, A. Borowski, and W. Crown, *Economics of Population Aging*, 1991. The basic projections were carried out using a real growth rate of 3.0 percent. Sensitivity testing was then carried out using lower and higher rates, demonstrating that burdens are very sensitive to economic growth rates but not to assumptions regarding population growth rates or labor force participation rates.

29. Other research supports this conclusion. For example, Richard Easterlin concludes from his research that "the outlook for the total dependency burden, when viewed against the experience of the past century, is not unprecedented." R. A. Easterlin, "Implications of Demographic Patterns." In R. H. Binstock and L. K George, eds. *Handbook of Aging and the Social Sciences*, 4th ed. San Diego: Academic Press, 1996, pp. 73–93.

30. These are estimates by economist Robert Eisner, reported in R. C. Leone, "Why Boomers Don't Spell Bust." *American Prospect* (January–February 1997): 68–71.

31. Most of Easterlin's many research studies on this topic are summarized in R. A. Easterlin, "Implications of Demographic Patterns."

32. J. M. Buchanan, "We Should Save More In Our Own Economic Interest." In L. M. Cohen, ed., *Justice across Generations: What Does It Mean?* Washington, DC: American Association of Retired Persons, 1993, pp. 269–282.

33. R. A. Blecker, book review of *Macroeconomic Policy after the Conservative Era: Studies in Investment, Saving and Finance* by G. A. Epstein and H. M. Gintis, *Journal of Economic Literature* 35 (March 1997): 131–132.

34. E. M. Gramlich, "How Does Social Security Affect the Economy?" In E. R. Kingson and J. H. Schulz, eds., *Social Security in the 21st Century*. New York: Oxford University Press, 1997, pp. 147–155.

35. The literature is very extensive on this point. See, for example, the review article by W. Cohen and R. Levin, "Empirical Studies of Innovation and Market Structure." In R. Schmalensee and D. Levinthal, eds., *Handbook of Industrial Organization*. New York: North Holland, 1989, pp. 1059–1107. See also D. Warsh, *Knowledge and the Wealth of Nations*. New York: W. W. Norton & Company, 2006, and E. Helpman, *The Mystery of Economic Growth*. Cambridge: Belknap Press, 2004.

36. M. Feldstein, *Transition to a Fully Funded Pension System: Five Economic Issues*. NBER Working Paper no. 6149. Cambridge, MA: National Bureau of Economic Research, 1997.

37. R. Nelson, "How New Is New Growth Theory?" *Challenge* 40(5) (September–October 1997): 29–58.

38. A. Marshall, *Principles of Economics: An Introductory Volume*. New York: Macmillian, 1948.

39. "Silicon Valley." *The Economist* (March 29, 1997): 5–20.

40. Ibid.

41. D. Warsh, *Knowledge and the Wealth of Nations*.

42. The famous Solow model of economic growth (that has dominated growth theory over the years) included "exogenously increasing knowledge as a kind of public good," that is, empirically the model found that "fully 85 percent of the increase in output was unexplained by what was in the model." D. Warsh, *Knowledge and the Wealth of Nations*.

43. R. R. Nelson, *The Sources of Economic Growth*. Cambridge, MA: Harvard University Press, 1996.

44. "Education and the Wealth of Nations." *The Economist* (March 29, 1997): 15–16.

45. I. M. Kirzner, "Entrepreneurial Discovery and the Competitive Market Process: An Austrian Approach." *Journal of Economic Literature* 35 (March 1997): 60–85.

46. R. Disney, *Can We Afford to Grow Older?* Cambridge, MA: MIT Press, 1996.

CHAPTER THREE: THE SEARCH FOR SECURITY WITH DIGNITY

1. R. B. Reich, "Good for Granddad, Good for My Sons." *USA Today* (March 10, 2005): 19A.

2. J. D. Brown, *An American Philosophy of Social Security*. Princeton, NJ: Princeton University Press, 1972.

3. E. McClure, "An Unlamented Era—County Poor Farms in Minnesota." *Minnesota History Magazine* 38(8) (December 1963): 365–377.

4. B. Gratton, "The New History of the Aged: A Critique." In D. Van Tassel and P. N. Stearns, eds., *Old Age in a Bureaucratic Society.* New York: Greenwood Press, 1986, pp. 3–29.

5. W. I. Trattner, *From Poor Law to Welfare State*, 4th ed. New York: Free Press, 1989.

6. "The Poorhouse Story," Web site at http://www.poorhousestory.com. Downloaded on October 5, 2004.

7. J. Quadagno, "The Transformation of Old Age Security." In D. Van Tassel and P. N. Stearns, eds., *Old Age in a Bureaucratic Society:* New York: Greenwood Press, 1986, pp. 129–155.

8. B. C. Vladeck, *Unloving Care: The Nursing Home Tragedy.* New York: Basic Books, 1980.

9. L. W. Squier, *Old Age Dependency in the United States.* New York, 1912. Quoted in J. Quadagno's article in D.Van Tassel and P. N. Stearns, eds., *Old Age in a Bureaucratic Society.* New York: Greenwood Press, 1986.

10. One other important alternative for poor old people without family help was charitable private "homes," typically built and run by organizations helping immigrants or mental hospitals. See D. S. Smith, "Accounting for Change in the Families of the Elderly in the United States, 1900–Present." In D. Van Tassel and P. N. Stearns, eds., *Old Age in a Bureaucratic Society.* New York: Greenwood Press, 1986, pp. 87–109.

11. The events of the evening are reported in O. Pflanze, *Bismarck and the Development of Germany*, vol. 3. Princeton, NJ: Princeton University Press, 1990.

12. The discussion in this paragraph relies heavily on H. Beck, *The Origins of the Authoritarian Welfare State in Prussia.* Ann Arbor, MI: University of Michigan Press, 1995.

13. "The Revolutions of 1848 in the German States." *Wikipedia.* Retrieved on October 14, 2004, from http://en.wikipedia.org/wiki/The_Revolutions_of_1848_in_the_German_States

14. M. Stürmer, *The German Empire, 1870–1918.* New York: Modern Library, 2000.

15. L. Gall, *Bismarck: The White Revolution*, vol. 1. London, UK: Unwin Hyman, 1986.

16. O. Pflanze, *Bismarck and the Development of Germany.*

17. Quoted in W. Vogel, *Bismarck's Arbeiterversicherung.* Braunschweig, Germany: G. Westerman, 1951.

18. G. Rimlinger, *Welfare Policy and Industrialization in Europe, America, and Russia.* New York: Wiley, 1971.

19. O. Pflanze, *Bismarck and the Development of Germany.*

20. H. Beck, *The Origins of the Authoritarian Welfare State in Prussia.*

21. Van D. Ooms, M. C. Macguiness, J. L. Mashaw, W. Niskanen, and J. H. Langbein, "Perspectives on Individual Responsibility and Social Insurance." In T. Ghilarduici, Van D. Oons, J. L. Palmer, and C. Hill, eds., *In Search of Retirement Security.* New York: Century Fund Publications, 2005, pp. 82–113.

22. R. L. Clark, L. A. Craig, and J. W. Wilson, *A History of Public Sector Pensions in the United States.* Philadelphia, PA: University of Pennsylvania Press, 2003.

23. Quoted in A. J. Altmeyer, *The Formative Years of Social Security*. Madison, WI: University of Wisconsin Press, 1968.

24. The Union for Social Justice led by Father Charles E. Coughlin, "The End of Poverty in California" plan devised by Upton Sinclair, and the "Ham and Eggs" scheme promoted by Robert Noble.

25. The story of the three old women and the quotation are from J. MacGregor Burns, *The Lion and the Fox*. New York: Harcourt, Brace and Company, 1956.

26. J. MacGregor Burns, *The Lion and the Fox*; and A. Holtzman, *The Townsend Movement: A Political Study*. New York: Bookman Associates, 1963.

27. A. Holtzman, *The Townsend Movement: A Political Study*.

28. Ibid.

29. M. Roth, "Forgotten Doctor Planted Social Security's Seed," *Pittsburg Post-Gazette* (February 6, 2005). Retrieved on May 2, 2005, from http//:www.post-gazette.com/pg/05037/453041.stm

30. J. D. Brown, *An American Philosophy of Social Security*.

31. A. Holtzman, *The Townsend Movement: A Political Study*.

32. Quoted in A. M. Schlesinger, Jr., *The Coming of the New Deal*. Boston, MA: Houghton Mifflin, 1959.

33. Ibid.

34. J. O. Parsson, *Dying of Money: Lessons of the Great German and American Inflations*. Boston, MA: Wellspring Press, 1974.

35. *The Nightmare German Inflation*. Retrieved on May 2 from http://www.usagold.com/GermanNightmare.html

36. Ibid.

37. J. Frerich and M. Frey, "Rentenversicherungsrecht." In J. Schulin, ed., *Handbuch des Sozialversicherungsrechts*, vol. 3. Munich, Germany: C. H. Beck, 1999, p. 11.

38. In 2001, however, Germany legislated a major Social Security reform with a *partial shift* from (mandatory) public pay-as-you-go to (voluntary) private (capital funded) pensions and from defined benefit towards a defined contribution scheme.

39. Retrieved on July 6, 2006, from http://en.wikipedia.org/wiki/Hyperinflation#Hyperinflation_around_the_world

40. R. Ball, "Social Insurance and the Right to Assistance." Reprinted from *The Social Service Review* 21 (1947). In T. N. Bethell, ed., *Insuring the Essentials: Bob Ball on Social Security*. New York: Century Foundation Press, 2000.

41. K. de Schweinitz, *People and Process in Social Security*. Washington, DC: American Council on Education, 1948.

42. T. Leavitt and J. H. Schulz, *The Role of the Asset Test in Program Eligibility and Participation: The Case of SSI*. Publication No. E-2, Washington, DC: American Association of Retired Persons, 1988.

43. L. D, Melinda Upp, and V. Reno, "Low Income Aged: Eligibility and Participation in SSI." *Social Security Bulletin* 45 (1982): 28–35.

44. Quoted in D. Milbank, "Social Security Debate Has Echoes of 1935," *Washington Post*. Retrieved on April 26, 2005, from http://www.washingtonpost.com/wp-dyn/content/article/2005/04/25/AR2005042501445.html

45. Ibid.

46. Quoted in D. A. Moss, *When All Else Fails: Government as the Ultimate Risk Manager*. Cambridge, MA: Harvard University Press, 2002.

47. This point is made, for example, by economist K. Boulding in *Principles of Economic Policy*. Englewood Cliffs, NJ: Prentice-Hall, 1958.

48. A. Epstein, *Insecurity: A Challenge to America*. New York: H. Smith & R. Hess, 1936.

49. M. Derthick, *Policymaking for Social Security*. Washington, DC: Brookings Institution, 1979.

50. Prior to 1978, a quarter of coverage was defined as a calendar quarter in which the worker in covered employment was paid at least $50. In 1978 the reporting of Social Security wages was changed from a quarterly to annual basis. The original 1935 legislation required covered work for only twenty quarters, but the number of required quarters was increased over the years, up to the current forty quarters today.

51. An alternative view receiving little attention in the early years of Social Security is that building reserves increases national saving, and this saving may have the effect of promoting greater economic growth.

52. Quoted in M. Derthick, *Policymaking for Social Security* from the *Congressional Record*, March 17, 1937.

53. Quoted in M. Derthick. *Policymaking for Social Security* from the *Transactions of the Actuarial Society of America*, 36 (1935).

54. A. M. Schlesinger Jr., *The Coming of the New Deal*.

55. See the surveys cited in V. Reno and R. B. Friedland, "Strong Support but Low Confidence," In E. R. Kingson and J. H. Schulz, eds. *Social Security in the 21st Century*. New York: Oxford University Press, 1997, pp. 178–194.

56. Ibid.

57. Ibid.

58. T. L. Friedman, *The World Is Flat*. New York: Farrar, Straus, and Giroux, 2005.

59. G. Sperling, *The Pro-Growth Progressive*. New York: Simon & Schuster, 2005, reporting on research published in N. Nohria, D. Dyer, and F. Dalzill, *Changing Fortunes: Remaking the Industrial Corporation*. Hoboken, NJ: John Wiley & Sons, 2004.

60. G. Sperling, *The Pro-Growth Progressive*.

CHAPTER FOUR: DEALING WITH RISK

1. Quoted in A. E. Hotchner, *Papa Hemingway*. New York: Caroll & Graf, 1999.

2. J. Hacker, "False Positive." *The New Republic* (August 16, 23, 2004): 14–16.

3. The description of this event in history is taken from U.S. Social Security Administration, "Historical Background and Development of Social Security." History section of *Social Security Online*. Retrieved on February 28, 2006, from http://www.socialsecurity.gov/history

4. J. Fallows, "America's Changing Economic Landscape." *Atlantic Monthly* (March 1985): 47–68.

5. See, for example, A. Okun, *Equality and Efficiency: The Big Tradeoff*. Washington, DC: Brookings Institution, 1975.

6. AARP, *Baby Boomers Envision Retirement II*. Washington, DC: AARP, May 2004.

7. K. Holden and C. Hatcher, "Economic Status of the Aged." In R. H. Binstock and L. K. George, eds., *Handbook of Aging and the Social Sciences*, 6th ed. San Diego, CA: Academic Press, 2006, pp. 219–137.

8. K. Boulding, *Principles of Economic Policy*. Englewood Cliffs: Prentice Hall, 1958.

9. U.S. Social Security Administration, "Historical Background and Development of Social Security. History section of *Social Security Online*. Retrieved on February 28, 2006, from http://www.socialsecurity.gov/history

10. L. Hartz, *The Liberal Tradition in America*. New York: Harcourt Brace, 1955.

11. J. A. Pechman, H. J. Aaron, and M. K. Taussig, *Social Security: Perspectives for Reform*. Washington, DC: Brookings Institution, 1968.

12. K. Boulding, *Principles of Economic Policy*.

13. P. A. Diamond, "A Framework for Social Security Analysis," *Journal of Public Economics* 8 (December 1977): 275–298; and L. J. Kotlikoff, A. Spivak, and L. Summers, "The Adequacy of Savings," *American Economic Review* 72 (December 1982): 1056–1069.

14. D. D. Bernheim, *Is the Baby Boom Generation Preparing Adequately for Retirement?* (Summary Report). New York: Merrill Lynch, 1993.

15. National Committee to Preserve Social Security. "Disability Insurance & Survivors' benefits. Retrieved on July 8, 2006, from http://www.ncpssm.org/news/archive/vp_surviors bene/

16. J. D. Brown, *An American Philosophy of Social Security*. Princeton, NJ: Princeton University Press, 1972.

17. See J. H. Schulz, *Old-Age Income Security: Australia Tries a Different Way*. AARP Policy Institute Report #2005-21. Washington, DC: AARP, December 2005.

18. A. M. Schlesinger, Jr., *The Coming of the New Deal*. Cambridge, MA: Houghton Mifflin, 1959.

19. P. G. Gosselin, "If America Is Richer, Why Are Its Families So Much Less Secure?" Retrieved on April 22, 2005, from http://www.latimes.com/business/specials/la-fi-riskshift30ct10,0,908738,print.story

20. J. Hacker, "False Positive."

21. P. G. Gosselin, "If America Is Richer . . ."

22. M. W. Walsh, "Many Companies Ending Promises for Retirement." *New York Times* (January 9, 2006): A1, A20.

23. U.S. Department of Labor, Pension Welfare & Benefits Administration, *Abstract of 1998 Form 5500 Annual Reports* (Winter 2001–2002). Washington, DC: Pension Welfare & Benefits Administration, 2002.

24. U.S. Census Bureau, "Health Insurance Coverage: 2004. Retrieved on June 23, 2006 at http//www.census.gov/hhes/www/

25. Kaiser Commission on Medicaid and the Uninsured, *The Uninsured and Their Access to Health Care*. Publication # 1420-07. California: The Commission, November 2004.

26. Kaiser Family Foundation and Health Research and Education Trust, "Summary of Findings." *Employer Health Benefits 2004*. Retrieved on April 27, 2005, from http://www.kff.org

27. M. W. Walsh, "U.S. to Pay Big Employers Billions Not to End Their Retiree Health Plans." *New York Times* (February 24, 2006): C3.

28. Kaiser Family Foundation and Health Research and Educational Trust, *Employee Health Benefits, 2002 Annual Survey*. Washington, DC: Kaiser Foundation, 2002.

29. The statistics are reported in P.G. Gosselin, "If America is Richer ..."

30. P. G. Gosselin, "Experts Are at a Loss on Investing." *Los Angeles Times* (May 11, 2005). Retrieved on May 20, 2005, from http://www.latimes.com/news/printedition/fron/la-na-nobel11may11,1,1607625.story?coll=la-headlines-frontpage

31. S. Diamond, "Testimony." In U.S. Senate Special Committee on Aging. *How Secure Is Your Retirement: Investments, Planning, and Fraud?* Washington, DC: U.S. Government Printing Office, 1993. pp. 44–45.

32. Senator William S. Cohen, prepared statement. In U.S. Senate Special Committee on Aging, *How Secure Is Your Retirement: Investments, Planning, and Fraud?* Washington, DC: U.S. Government Printing Office, 1993, pp. 4–5.

33. B. Stein, *How to Ruin Your Financial Life*. Carlsbad, CA: Hay House, 2004.

34. J. R. Macey, *Regulation of Financial Planners – A White Paper Prepared for the Financial Planning Association*. Denver, CO: Financial Planning Association, 2002.

35. Certificate in Financial Gerontology, Certified Senior Advisor Certificate, Registered Financial Gerontologist, Certified Retirement Financial Adviser, Chartered Advisor for Senior Living Certificate, and Certified Financial Planner.

36. S. Z. Berg. "For Older Americans, Money Advice Is Just a Start." *New York Times* (July 2, 2006): BU6.

37. National Center on Women & Aging, *Financial Challenges for Mature Women*. Waltham, MA: Heller Graduate School, Brandeis University, 1988.

38. AARP, *Baby Boomers Envision Retirement II*.

39. See, for example, P. A. Diamond and P. R. Orszag, *Saving Social Security: A Balanced Approach*. Washington, DC: Brookings Institution, 2004; M. J. Graetz and J. L. Mashaw, *True Security: Rethinking American Social Insurance*. New Haven, CT: Yale University Press, 1999; C. E. Steuerle and J. M. Bakija, *Retooling Social Security for the 21st Century*. Washington, DC: Urban Institute Press, 1994; N. J. Altman, *The Battle for Social Security*. Hoboken, NJ: Wiley, 2005; G. Sperling, *The Pro-Growth Progressive*. New York: Simon & Schuster, 2005; and E. R. Kingson and J. H. Schulz, eds., *Social Security in the 21st Century*. New York: Oxford University Press, 1997.

40. Trustees of the Social Security and Medicare Trust Funds, *Status of the Social Security and Medicare Programs: A Summary of the 2006 Annual Reports*. Retrieved May 2, 2006, from http://www.socialsecurity.gov/OACT/TRSUM/trsummary.html

41. These options were recommended by delegates at the White House Conference on Aging of 2005; See R. H. Binstock, "Social Security and Medicare: President Bush and the Delegates Reject Each Other," *Public Policy and Aging Report* 16(1) (2006): 9–12.

42. The 3 percent tax is proposed by Gene Sperling in *The Pro-Growth Progressive*.

43. Robert M. Ball. *The Social Security Protection Plan*. Mitchellville , MD: reproduced, January 2006.

44. L. Bilmes and J. E. Stiglitz, "The Economic Costs of the Iraq War." Retrieved on March 22, 2006, from http://www2.gsb.columbia.edu/faculty/jstiglitz/cost_of_war_in_iraq.pdf

45. A. Munnell, "The Case for Retaining Defined Benefit Programs. In S. H. Altman and D. I. Shactman, eds., *Policies for an Aging Society*. Baltimore, MD: Johns Hopkins University Press, 2002, pp. 236–265.

CHAPTER FIVE: THE COMPANY PENSION: ALTRUISM OR SELF-INTEREST?

1. M. C. Bernstein and J. B. Bernstein, *Social Security: The System that Works*. New York: Basic Books, 1988.

2. B. Stein and P. Demuth, *Yes, You Can Still Retire Comfortably!* Carlsbad, CA: New Beginnings Press, 2005.

3. M. S. Chambers, *Reviewing and Revising Wal-Marts Benefits Strategy*. Memorandum to the Board of Directors (undated). Retrieved on October 26, 2005, from http://walmartwatch.com/docs/susan_chambers_memo_to_walmart_board.pdf

4. Who bears what risk (worker or employer) is a more complicated question than we suggest in the main text. See the discussion in J. A. Turner and N. Watanabe, *Private Pension Policies in Industrialized Countries*. Kalamazoo, MI: W. E. Upjohn Institute for Employment Research, 1995.

5. Usually the plan formula is one of three types: flat-benefit, career-average, or final-pay.

6. W. Graebner, *A History of Retirement*. New Haven, CT: Yale University Press, 1980.

7. J. Quadagno, *The Transformation of Old Age Security: Class and Politics in the American Welfare State*. Chicago, IL: University of Chicago Press, 1988.

8. W. Graebner, *A History of Retirement*.

9. "Replacement rate" is a technical term used in the pension literature. The replacement rate is the ratio of retirement income to preretirement income. The definition (or measure) of both numerator and denominator varies from one analyst to another. One of the most important measures is the ratio of pension income (or Social Security income) to the worker's preretirement earnings (measured in various ways).

10. U.S. General Accounting Office (GAO), *Private Pensions: Improving Coverage and Benefits*. Washington, DC: GAO, April 2002.

11. A. H. Munnell, J. G. Lee, and K. B. Meme, "An Update on Pension Data." *Issue Brief* #20. Newton, MA: Center for Retirement Research at Boston College, July 2004. Munnell et al. point out that "coverage" is not necessarily the same as actual "participation" in a pension plan. For example, about one-fifth of workers covered by 401(k) plans, where coverage is generally optional, choose not to participate.

12. U.S. Department of Labor, *Private Pension Plan Bulletin*. No. 8. Washington, DC: Pension and Welfare Benefits Administration, Office of Policy and Research, 2000.

13. A. H. Munnell, J. G Lee, and K. B. Meme, "An Update on Pension Data."

14. J. R. Woods, "Pension Coverage among Private Wage and Salary Workers: Preliminary Findings from the 1988 Survey of Employee Benefits," *Social Security Bulletin* 52 (October 1989): 2–19.

15. Many of the issues are discussed in E. S. Andrews, *Pension Policy and Small Employers: At What Price Coverage?* Washington, DC: Employee Benefit Research Institute, 1989.

16. "Sears Ends Defined Benefit Plan." Retrieved on January 15, 2006, from http://www.benefitnews.com/detail.cfm?id=7479

17. U.S. Congressional Budget Office, *True Profit-sharing Plans*. Retrieved on February 23, 2006, from http://www.cbo.gov/OnlineTaxGuide/Text_1E1b1.cfm.

18. National Center for Employee Ownership (NCEO), *A Statistical Profile of Employee Ownership*. Retrieved on February 24, 2005, from http://www.nceo.org/library/eo_stat.html

19. E. M. Coates, "Profit Sharing Today: Plans and Provisions." *Monthly Labor Review* 114 (April 1991): 19–25.

20. Not discussed are Employee Stock Ownership Plans (ESOP), in which companies make employee retirement contributions that are primarily in the form of the company's stock and Section 403(b) plans for certain nonprofit organizations and public schools.

21. S. Sass, "Crisis in Pensions," *Regional Review* (Spring 1993): 13–18.

22. K. E. Cahill and M. Soto, "How Do Cash Balance Plans Affect the Pension Landscape?" *Issue Brief* #14. Newton, MA: Center for Retirement Research at Boston College, December 2003.

23. C. Copeland, "IRA and Keogh Assets Contributions." EBRI Notes, 27(1) (January 2006): 2–5.

24. See, for example, the survey of research in J. Skinner, "Individual Retirement Accounts: A Review of the Evidence." Tax Notes 54(2)(January 13, 1992): 201–212.

25. C. Mikkelsen, "A Corporate Response to Pension Reform." In R. V. Burkhauser and D. L. Salisbury, eds., Pensions in a Changing Economy. Washington, DC: EBRI and Syracuse University, 1993, pp. 107–108.

26. See, for example, C. Copeland, "IRA and Keogh Assets and Contributions."

27. White House Task Force on Older Americans, *Report to the President from the White House Task Force on Older Americans*. Washington, DC: White House Task Force on Older Americans, 1968.

28. "Red and Redder." *The Economist* (January 15, 2005): 68–69.

29. Statement made in a July 4, 2006 interview on the PBS television show NewsHour with Jim Lehrer. Retrieved on July 6, 2006, from http://www.pbs.org/newshour/bb/business/july-dec06/pension_07-04.html

30. Comment by Hedrick Smith on the same television program. Ibid.

31. Ibid.

32. M. W. Walsh, "U.S. Moves to Take Over a United Air Pension Plan." *New York Times* (March 12, 2005): C2.

33. K. Yamanouchi, "Pilots Bristle at Pension Cuts." *Denver Post*. Retrieved on April 5, 2006, from http://us.f841.mail.yahoo.com/ym/ShowLetter?MsgId=8212_13542949_8664_1956_1731_0_2293_3519_3441449588&Idx=4&YY=89523&inc=200&order=down&sort=date&pos=0&view=a&head=b&box=Inbox

34. Ibid.

35. Pension Benefit Guaranty Corporation (PBGC), *Pension Insurance Data Book*. Retrieved on March 24, 2005, from http://www.pbgc.gov/publications/databook/databook03.pdf

36. Ibid.

37. S. Cohen, "White House Unveils Plan to Shore Up Pension Agency." *CBS MarketWatch* (January 10, 2005). Retrieved on March 13, 2006, from http://www.freerealtime.com/dl/frt/N?tmn_id={683538CE-183D-497F-A66E-A12AB88DA373}

38. M. W. Walsh, "Pension Board Says Deficit Is Steady for Now." *New York Times* (November 16, 2005): A2; B. D. Bovbjerg, *Pension Benefit Guaranty Corporation: LongTerm Financing Risks to Single-Employer Insurance Program Highlight. Need for Comprehensive Reform.* Testimony before the U. S. Senate Special Committee on Aging (October 14, 2003). Retrieved on March 24, 2005, from http://www. gao.gov/new.items/do4150t.pdf

39. U.S. Senate Special Committee on Aging, *Developments in Aging, 1986*, Vol. 1. Washington, DC: U.S. Government Printing Office, 1987.

40. "IRS Hears Pension Witnesses Sing the 'Plan Dropout Blues.'" *Tax Notes* (October 1, 1990): 9.

41. P. H. Jackson, "Philosophical Basis of the Private Pension Movement." In D. M. McGill, ed., *Social Security and Private Pension Plans: Competitive or Complementary?* Homewood: Richard D. Irwin, 1977, pp. 14–28.

CHAPTER SIX: THE PENSION LOTTERY: PERSONAL PENSION ACCOUNTS

1. J. C. Dash and E. Dash, "New York State Sues H&R Block Over I.R.A. Sales." *The New York Times* (March 16, 2006): A1, C2.

2. F. Modigliani and A. Muralidhar, *Rethinking Pension Reform.* Cambridge, U.K.: Cambridge University Press, 2004.

3. Quoted in R. Wild, "Now You See It, Now You Don't." *AARP Bulletin* (November 2005): 12–14.

4. For a more detailed statement of Representative Sanders' view of this issue, see his full statement on the Internet, Retrieved on December 15, 2005, from http://www. uschamber.com/NR/rdonlyres/e6rj7stzvslcrvofsdflnmzi6pfr6ck5qvbm7ucqc62uial2 xd7fjquzngtxi7ayjxjpaxrhxqqyxe/Sandersamendment.pdf#search='IBM%20had% 20enough%20money%20Sanders'

5. Memorandum and Order of the United States District Court for the Southern District of Illinois entered on July 31, 2003, in the action titled Kathi Cooper, Beth Harrington, and Matthew Hillesheim, Individually and on Behalf of All Those Similarly Situated vs. IBM Personal Pension Plan and IBM Corporation (Civil No. 99-829-GPM).

6. M. W.Walsh, "I.B.M. to Freeze Pension Plans to Trim Costs." *The New York Times* (January 6, 2006): A1, A10.

7. M. W. Walsh, "Many Companies Ending Promises for Retirement." *The New York Times* (January 9, 2006): A1, A20.

8. M. W. Walsh, "When Your Pension Is Frozen." *The New York Times* (January 22, 2006): A3.

9. Employee Benefit Research Institute (EBRI), *History of 401(k) Plans—An Update* (2005). Retrieved on March 16, 2006, from http://www.ebri.org/pdf/ publications/facts/0205fact.a.pdf

10. Estimate provided by Employee Retirement Research Institute.

11. The limits for contributions in general are about $40,000 a year.

12. A. Munnell and A. Sundén, *401(K) Plans Are Still Coming Up Short.* Issue Brief #43. Newton, MA: Boston College Center for Retirement Research, March 2006. The Employee Benefits Research Institute, using the same data, reports that

noncoverage is one-quarter of "eligible family heads." See C. Copeland, "Individual Account Retirement Plans." *EBRI Issue Brief* No. 293. Washington, DC: Employee Benefit Research Institute, May 2006.

13. Ibid.

14. Employee Benefit Research Institute, "401(k) Accounts Balances, Asset Allocations by the Numbers." *Fast Facts from EBRI* (October 3, 2005). Retrieved on March 16, 2006, from http://www.ebri.org/pdf/publications/facts/fastfacts/fastfact100405.pdf

15. Munnell and Sundén, *Coming Up Short: The Challenge of 401(k) Plans.* Washington, DC: Brookings Institution Press, 2004.

16. Munnell and Sundén, *401(K) Plans Are Still Coming Up Short.*

17. There are very few exceptions to the penalty.

18. From P. G. Gosselin, "Experts Are at a Loss on Investing." *Los Angeles Times* (May 11, 2005). Retrieved on May 20, 2006, from http://www.latimes.com/news/printedition/fron/la-na-nobel11may11,1,1607625.story?coll=la-headlines-front-page. Quotes are from (in order) Clive W. J. Granger, George A. Akerlof, Harry M. Markowitz, and Daniel Kahneman.

19. Ibid.

20. British Department for Work and Pensions, *Security in Retirement: Towards a New Pensions System.* White Paper. Norwich, England: The Stationery Office, May 2006.

21. A. Atkinson, S. McKay, E. Kempson, and S. Collard, *Levels of Financial Capability in the UK: Results of a Baseline Survey.* Retrieved on June 5, 2006, from www.fsa.gov.uk/pubs/consumer-research/crp47.pdf

22. Gosselin, "Experts Are at a Loss on Investing."

23. R. P. Hinz and J. Turner, "Why Don't Workers Participate?" In O. S. Mitchell and S. J. Schieber, eds., *Living with DC Plans: Remaking Responsibility.* Philadelphia, PA: University of Pennsylvania Press, 1998, pp. 17–37.

24. Munnell and Sundén, *Coming Up Short.*

25. Both the Lawson quote and the Sharp figure are reported in B. Brubaker, "Verdict Stirs Up Mix of Emotion for Employees." *Washington Post* (March 15, 2005): A13.

26. Quoted in C. Noble, "Workers Rethink Retirement Savings." *Reuters* (December 2002). Retrieved on June 5, 2004, from http://dailynews.yahoo.com/h/nm/ 20011230/bs/yearendbizfinancial_fund_401k_dc_1.html

27. S. Braunstein and C. Welch, "Financial Literacy: An Overview of Practice, Research, and Policy." *Federal Reserve Bulletin* (November 2002): 445–457.

28. Ibid.

29. Statistics reported in C. Dugar, "Retirement Crisis Looms as Many Come Up Short." *USA Today* (July 19, 2002): 4.

30. P. Orszag and J. E. Stiglitz, "Rethinking Pension Reform." In R. Holzmann and J. E. Stiglitz, eds., *New Ideas About Old Age Security.* Washington, DC: World Bank, 2001, pp. 17–56.

31. GE Center for Financial Learning, *Financial Literacy Project* (1999). Retrieved from www.financiallearning.com/ge/researchstudies.jsp?c=getResearchHtml1; National Center on Women & Aging, *Financial Challenges for Mature Women.* Waltham, Massachusetts: The Center, Brandeis University, 1998.

32. Investor Protection Trust, *Investor Knowledge Survey 1996*. Retrieved on June 24, 2004, from http://www.investorprotection.org

33. A. Lusardi and O. S. Mitchell, "Financial Literacy and Planning: Implications for Retirement Wellbeing." *Working Paper WP 2005-108*. Ann Arbor, MI: University of Michigan Retirement Research Center, 2005.

34. Z. Bodie, "An Analysis of Investment Advice to Retirement Plan Participants." In O. Mitchell and K. Smetters, eds., *The Pension Challenge*. Oxford: Oxford University Press, 2003, pp. 19–32.

35. I. S. Gill, T. Packard, and J. Yermo, *Keeping the Promise of Social Security in Latin America*. Palo Alto, CA: Stanford University Press, 2005.

36. Disciplined Capital Management, "401k Plan Participants Want Help with Investment Decisions." Syracuse, NY: Disciplined Capital Management, March 25, 2004 (press release).

37. Ibid. For a discussion of the experience of another 401(k) financial advice firm and also an on-line help line, see J. Agnew, "Personalized Retirement Advice and Managed Accounts." *CRR Working Papers 2006-9*. Newton, MA: Boston College Center for Retirement Research, March 2006.

38. "IRS Ends Exempt Status for Some Credit Counselors." *The New York Times* (May 16, 2006): B6

39. U.S. Department of Labor, *Retirement Benefits of American Workers*. Washington, DC: U.S. Pension and Welfare Administration, 1995.

40. The result depends on job tenure. The DC benefits are likely to be better for those who separate from the employer and the plan when they have less than 15 years tenure. Munnell and Sundén, *Coming Up Short*. Also see S. Holden and J. VanDerhei, *Can 401(k) Accumulations Generate Significant Income for Future Retirees?* Issue Brief #251. Washington, DC: Employee Benefit Research Institute, November 2002; A. A. Samwick and J. Skinner, "How Will 401(k) Pension Plans Affect Retirement Income?" *American Economic Review* 94(1) (March 2004): 329–343.

41. U.S. Congressional Budget Office, *Administrative Costs of Private Accounts in Social Security*. (March 2004). Retrieved on January 23, 2006, from http://www.cbo.gov/showdoc.cfm?index=5277&sequence=1&from=0

42. Editorial, "Fleecing American Soldiers." *The New York Times* (July 21, 2004): A18.

43. "Fleecing American Soldiers." The articles complementing the editorial and documenting its conclusions are D. B. Henriques, "Going Off to War, and Vulnerable to the Pitches of Salesmen." *The New York Times* (July 20, 2004): A1, C6–7 and D. B. Henriques, "Insurers Rely on Congress to Keep Access to G.I.'s." *The New York Times* (July 21, 2004): A1, C4.

44. F. Kaplan, "Bubble Bursts for Russian Investors." *Boston Globe* (July 30, 1994): 2.

45. B. Richards, "High Flying Ponzi Scheme Angers and Awes Alaskans." *Wall Street Journal* (August 13, 1998): B1.

46. A detailed account of the fraud and the puny restitution to investors is found in K. Eichenwald, *Serpent on the Rock*. New York: Broadway Books, 2005.

47. AFL/CIO, "WorldCom's Collapse and the Consequences for Workers' Retirement Security." www.afl/cio.org/mediacenter/resource/upload/worldcom401-kreport.pdf

48. Ibid.

49. C. Dugas, "Spotlight Hits Whistle Blower." *USA Today* (December 9, 2003). Retrieved on February 2, 2006, from www.usatoday.com/money/perfi/funds/2003-12-09-whistleblow_x.htm

50. J. C. Bogle, *The Battle for the Soul of Capitalism.* New Haven, CT: Yale University Press, 2005.

51. J. Williamson, "Assessing the Notional Defined Contribution Model," *Issues in Brief* #24. Newton, MA: Center for Retirement Research, Boston College, 2004.

52. J. H. Schulz and A. Borowski, "Economic Security in Retirement: Reshaping the Public-Private Pension Mix," In R. H. Binstock and L. K. George. Eds. *Handbook of Aging and the Social sciences,* 6th ed. San Diego, CA: Academic Press, 2006, pp. 360–379.

53. Quoted by T. Lieberman, "Social Insecurity: The Campaign to Take the System Private." *Nation* (January 27, 1997). Retrieved on April 9, 2006, from http://www.ourfuture.org/issues_and_campaigns/socialsecurity/key_issues/money_trail_and_wall_street/readarticle52.cfm

54. Quoted in L. Rohter, "Chile's Candidates Agree to Agree on Pension Woes." *The New York Times* (January 10, 2006): A3.

55. R. J. Myers, Quoted in J. H. Schulz, "Chile's Approach to Retirement Income Security Attracts Worldwide Attention." *Aging International* (September 1993): 51–52.

56. Ibid.

57. J. Williamson, *An Update on Chile's Experience with Partial Privatization and Individual Accounts.* AARP Public Policy Institute Publication #2005-19. Washington, DC: AARP, 2005.

58. The research is summarized and discussed in I. S. Gil, T. Packard, and J. Yermo, *Keeping the Promise of Social Security in Latin America.* Palo Alto, CA: Stanford University Press and the World Bank, 2005.

59. Rohter, "Chile's Candidates Agree to Agree on Pension Woes."

60. S. Edwards and A. Edwards, *Social Security Privatization Reform and Labor Markets: the Case of Chile.* Working Paper 8924. Cambridge: National Bureau of Economic Research, 2002.

61. Rohter, "Chile's Candidates Agree to Agree on Pension Woes."

62. R. Holzmann and J. E. Stiglitz, eds., *New Ideas about Old Age.* Washington, DC: World Bank, 2001.

63. "Chile: Pondering Pensions: Aging Model Requires Facelift." *The Economist* (November 12, 2005): 40.

64. For a discussion of the approach and performance to date, see J. H. Schulz and A. Borowski, "Economic Security in Retirement: Reshaping the Public-Private Pension Mix."

65. Pensions Commission, *A New Pension Settlement for the Twenty-First Century.* London: The Commission, November 2005.

66. "Reforming Pensions: A Way Out of the Mess." *Economist* (May 27, 2006): 53–54.

67. The financial institutions have been lobbying the Government to increase the fee. See E. Philip Davis, *Is There a Pension Crisis in the UK?* Discussion Paper PI-0401. London: The Pensions Institute, City University, 2004.

68. See the discussion in J. H. Schulz, *Older Women and Private Pensions in the United Kingdom*. Waltham, MA: National Center on Women & Aging, 2000.

69. Pensions Commission, *A New Pension Settlement for the Twenty-First Century*.

70. British Department for Work and Pensions, *Security in Retirement*.

71. M. W. Walsh, "I.B.M. to Freeze Pension Plans To Trim Costs." *The New York Times* (January 6, 2006): A1.

72. M. W. Walsh, "Many Companies Ending Promises for Retirement." *The New York Times* (January 9, 2006): A1, A20.

73. "The Pension Deep Freeze." *The New York Times* (January 14, 2006): A30.

CHAPTER SEVEN: TO WORK OR NOT TO WORK: THAT IS THE QUESTION

1. S. A. Teicher, "White-Collar Jobs Moving Abroad." *The Christian Science Monitor* (July 29, 2003): 1, 9.

2. "65 Not Out." *Economist* (November 2005): 16.

3. L. Uchitelle, *The Disposable American Layoffs and Their Consequences*. New York, Knopf, 2006.

4. J. Martin, *Greenspan: The Man Behind the Money*. Cambridge, MA: Perseus, 2001.

5. Quoted in Martin, *Greenspan: The Man Behind the Money*.

6. S. Davis, J. Haltiwanger, and S. Schuh, *Job Creation and Destruction*. Cambridge, MA: The MIT Press, 1996.

7. See the discussion of this point in J. H. Schulz, *The Economics of Aging*, 7th ed. Westport, CT: Auburn House, 2001.

8. A. R. Herzog, R. I. Kahn, J. N. Morgan, J. S. Jackson, and T. C. Antonucci, "Age Differences in Productive Activities." *Journal of Gerontology: Social Sciences* 44 (1989): S129–S138.

9. See an expanded discussion of this topic in Schulz, *The Economics of Aging*.

10. Not everyone agrees with this conclusion. See, for example, the discussion of alternative views in N. Tucker, "Leisure Overload? Nothing Doing." *Washington Post* (February 19, 2006): D01

11. J. B. Schor, *The Overworked American: The Unexpected Decline of Leisure*. New York: Basic Books, 1991.

12. R. G. Niemi, J. Mueller, and T. W. Smith, *Trends in Public Opinion: A Compendium of Survey Data*. New York: Greenwood, 1989.

13. See, for example, E. Larrabee and R. Meyerson, eds., *Mass Leisure*. Glencoe, IL: Free Press, 1958.

14. Schor, *The Overworked American: The Unexpected Decline of Leisure*.

15. W. Donahue, H. Orbach, and O. Pollak, "Retirement: The Emerging Social Pattern." In C. Tibbitts, ed., *Handbook of Social Gerontology*. Chicago, IL: University of Chicago Press, 1960.

16. E. A. Friedman and H. L. Orbach, "Adjustment to Retirement." In S. Ariete, ed., *The Foundation of Psychiatry, vol. 1: American Handbook of Psychiatry*, 2nd ed. New York: Basic Books, pp. 609–645.

17. Profit statistic and quote retrieved on March 27, 2006, from http://phx. corporate-ir.net/phoenix.zhtml?c=84530&p=irol-earnings

18. M. Mayard, "G. M. Will Offer Buyouts to All Its Union Workers." *New York Times* (March 23, 2006): 1, C4.

19. N. Bunkley, "47,600 Take Offer of Buyouts." *The New York Times* (June 27, 2006): C1.

20. J. M. Kreps, "Age, Work, and Income." *Southern Economic Journal* 43 (1977): 1423–1437.

21. P. A. Diamond, *Pensions for an Aging Population.* NBER Working Paper No. 11877. Cambridge, MA: National Bureau of Economic Research, 2005. See also J. Gruber and D. A. Wise, eds., *Social Security and Retirement Around the World.* Chicago, IL: University of Chicago Press, 1999.

22. See the discussion in Schulz, *The Economics of Aging.*

23. C. E. Uccello, *Factors Influencing Retirement.* Publication #9810. Washington, DC: AARP, October 1998.

24. See Schulz, *The Economics of Aging.*

25. R. Havighurst and E. Friedmann, *The Meaning of Work and Retirement.* Chicago, IL: University of Chicago Press, 1954.

26. I. Mothner, *Children and Elders: Intergenerational Relations in an Aging Society.* New York: Carnegie Foundation, 1985.

27. Two groups dominate: the disabled and persons eligible for early pensions. See R. E. Smith, *Disability and Retirement: The Early Exit of Baby Boomers from the Labor Force* (November 2004). Retrieved on March 2, 2006, from http://www.cbo.gov/ showdoc.cfm?index=6018&sequence=0

28. S. E. Rix, "The Older Worker in a Graying America." In R. N. Butler, L. K. Grossman, and M. R. Oberlink, eds., *Life in an Older America.* New York: Century Foundation, 1999, pp. 187–215.

29. Ibid.

30. R. Clark and J. Quinn, "Patterns of Work and Retirement for a New Century." *Generations* 26(11) (2002): 17–24.

31. Unpublished data from the U. S. Bureau of Labor Statistics.

32. AARP, *Staying Ahead of the Curve 2003: The AARP Working In Retirement Study.* Washington, DC: AARP, 2003.

33. R. Hutchens, *The Cornell Study of Employer Phased Retirement Policies (2003).* Retrieved on March 1, 2006, from http://www.ilr.cornell.edu/extension/files/ 20031219112155-pub1251.pdf#search='robert%20hutchens%20cornell%20study'

34. M. Hurd, *The Effect of Labor Market Rigidities on the Labor Force Behavior of Older Workers.* Working Paper No. 4462. Cambridge, MA: National Bureau of Economic Research, 1993.

35. R. Clark, R. Burkhauser, M. Moon, J. Quinn, and T. Smeeding, *The Economics of an Aging Society.* Malden, MA: Blackwell, 2004.

36. 6. AARP, *The State of 50+ America.* Washington, DC: AARP, 2004.

37. Reported in A. H. Munnell, *Policies to Promote Labor Force Participation of Older People.* CRR WP 2006-2. Chestnut Hill, MA: Center for Retirement Research at Boston College, January 2006.

38. See, for example, the data and discussion in J. H. Schulz, "What Can Japan Teach Us about an Aging U.S. Work Force?" *Challenge* (November/December): 56–60.

39. Reported in L. Uchitelle, "Retraining, But for What?" *New York Times* (March 26, 2006): 1BU, 8–9BU.

40. Uchitelle, *The Disposable American: Layoffs and Their Consequences*.

41. K. G. Abraham, "Work and Retirement Plans among Older Americans." Upjohn Institute Staff Working Paper No. 04-105 (July 2004).

42. NCOA (National Council on the Aging), *The Myth and Reality of Aging in America*. Washington, DC: NCOA, 1975.

43. U. S. Bureau of Labor Statistics, *Employment and Earnings*. Washington, DC: U.S. Bureau of Labor Statistics, 2004, Table 35. Data for later years can be found at http://www.bls.gov/cps/cpsaat35.pdf

44. Reported in *Economist*, "Turning Boomers into Boomerangs." (February 18, 2006): 65–67.

45. P. Cappelli, "Will There Really Be a Labor Shortage?" Retrieved on February 26, 2006, from http://www.nga.org/cda/files/wf03Cappelli.pdf#search='peter%20cappelli%20shortage'

46. S. Rai, "India Becoming a Crucial Cog in the Machine at I. B. M." *The New York Times* (June 5, 2006): C4.

47. Uchitelle, "Retraining, But for What?"

48. "Now for the Hard Part: A Survey of Business in India." *Economist* (June 3, 2006): Special Section.

49. "Relocating the Back Office." *Economist*, (December 13, 2003): 67–69.

50. D. McGinn, "Help Not Wanted." *Newsweek* (March 1, 2004): 31–33.

51. T. L. Friedman, *The World Is Flat*. New York: Farrar, Straus, and Giroux, 2005.

52. Cappelli, "Will There Really Be a Labor Shortage?"

53. O. S. Mitchell, "As the Workforce Ages." In O. S. Mitchell, ed., *As the Workforce Ages*. Ithaca, NY: ILR Press, 1993, pp. 3–15.

54. Gary Burtless, "An Economic View of Retirement." In H. J Aaron, ed., *Behavioral Dimensions of Retirement Economics*. Washington, DC: Brookings Institution Press, 1999, pp. 7–42.

55. U.S. Department of Labor, *The Older American Worker*. Washington, DC: U.S. Department of Labor, 1965.

56. This phenomenon is consistent with discrimination but could also be the result of other factors, such as obsolescent skills and lower job mobility with age. Statistics presented are from tabulations by the U.S. Bureau of Labor Statistics, Department of Labor. Retrieved on February 1, 2006, from http://www.bls.gov/cps/#charunem

57. M. E. Kite and B. T. Johnson, "Attitudes toward Older and Younger Adults: A Meta-Analysis." *Psychology and Aging* 3 (1988): 233–244.

58. R. Lewis, "For Whom the Job Bell Doesn't Toll." *AARP Bulletin* 55 (February, 1994): 2, 12.

59. J. N. Lahey, "Do Older Workers Face Discrimination?" *Issue in Brief #33*. Newton, MA: Center for Retirement Research, Boston College, 2005.

60. R. Posner, *Aging and Old Age*. Chicago, IL: Chicago: University of Chicago Press, 1995.

61. Towers Perrin, *The Business Case for Workers 50+*. A report prepared for AARP, December 2005. Retrieved on January 5, 2006, from assets.aarp.org/rgcenter/econ/workers_fifty_plus.pdf

62. E. L. Andrews, "Health Care Heights: Soaring Rates Leave Little Companies in a Bind." *New York Times* (February 24, 2004): B1, B8.

63. S. E. Rix, "The Older Worker in a Graying America."

64. R. Abelson, "Everyday High Health Costs." *New York Times* (October 29, 2005): B1, B4, B5.

65. Towers Perrin, *The Business Case for Workers*.

66. Ibid.

67. "Economic Focus: Re-engineering Retirement." *Economist* (December 14, 2002): 70.

68. Friedman, *The World Is Flat*.

69. Ibid.

70. United Nations Economic Commission for Europe, *Trends in Europe and North America: The Statistical Yearbook of the Economic Commission for Europe.* Geneva, Switzerland: The Commission, 2003.

71. R. M. Kanter, "U.S. Competitiveness and the Aging Workforce: Toward Organizational and Institutional Change." In J. A. Auerbach and J. C. Welsh, eds., *Aging and Competition: Rebuilding the U.S. Workforce.* Washington, DC: National Council on Aging, 1994.

72. Structural unemployment is the loss of a job as a result of structural changes in the patterns of production and skill requirements—arising from new products and shifting consumer preferences, technological change, changes in regional or international competitiveness, and so forth.

73. E. L. Groshen and S. Potter, "Has Structural Change Contributed to a Jobless Recovery?" *Current Issues in Economics and Finance* 9(8) (August 2003): 1–7.

74. D. McGinn, "Help Not Wanted." *Newsweek* (March 1, 2004): 31–33.

75. As quoted in T. Costlow, "A Short Circuit for US Engineering Careers." *The Christian Science Monitor* (December 25–26, 2002): 2–3.

76. Ibid.

77. U.S. Department of Labor, 1994, Communication and Report of the Secretary of Labor to Senator David Pryor, Chairman, U.S. Senate Special Committee on Aging. Reproduced, 1994.

78. See the discussion in U.S. General Accounting Office, "Older Workers: Employment Assistance Focuses on Subsidized Jobs and Job Search, but Revised Performance Measures Could Improve Access to Other Services." GAO-03-350. Washington, DC: U.S. General Accounting Office, 2003.

79. Retrieved on April 11, 2005, from http://www.doleta.gov/Seniors/other_docs/agingBoomers.pdf

80. *Experience Works* Web site. Retrieved on October 25, 2005, from http://www.experienceworks.org

81. Commonwealth Fund, *Older Workers Are Good Investments.* New York: The Commonwealth Fund, 1991.

82. B. A. Hirshorn and D. T. Hoyer, "Private Sector Hiring and Use of Retirees: The Firm Perspective." *Gerontologist* 34(1) (1994): 50–58.

83. Information on the alliance can be retrieved on the Internet at http://www.experiencedworkforce.org/mission/index.shtml

84. World Health Organization (WHO). *Health and Ageing—A Discussion Paper.* Geneva: WHO Department of Health Promotion, undated.

85. W. D. Novelli, "A Blueprint for Change." *Harvard Generations Policy Journal* 1 (Winter 2004): 11–23.

86. AARP. *Staying Ahead of the Curve 2003: The AARP Working in Retirement Study.* Washington, DC: AARP, 2003.

87. S. Rix, "The Aging Workforce: Will We Ever Be Ready for It?" *Gerontologist* 46 (2006): 404–409.

88. Ibid.

89. M. Freedman, *Prime Time: How Baby Boomers Will Revolutionize Retirement and Transform America.* New York, Public Affairs, 1999.

90. M. Martinson and M. Minkler, "Civic Engagement and Older Adults: A Critical Perspective." *Gerontologist* 46(3) (2006): 318-324.

91. M. Kohli, M. Rein, A.M. Buillemand, and Herman van Gunsteren, eds., *Time for Retirement.* New York: Cambridge University Press, 1991.

92. T. Piketty and E. Saez, "The Evolution of Top Income," Working Paper #11955. Cambridge, MA: National Bureau of Economic Research, 2006.

CHAPTER EIGHT: HEALTH AND LONGEVITY: WHAT LIES AHEAD?

1. The President's Council on Bioethics, *Taking Care: Ethical Caregiving in Our Aging Society.* Washington, DC: The President's Council on Bioethics, 2005.

2. S. Ferraro, "An Aching Jaw Leads to a World of Medical Uncertainty." *New York Times* (April 4, 2006): D5.

3. B. Sibley, "A Year to Remember: My Mother's Story." Retrieved on April 15, 2006, from http://www.zarcrom.com/users/yeartorem/

4. T. DeBaggio, *Losing My Mind.* New York: Simon & Schuster, 2003.

5. Ibid.

6. Alzheimer's Association, *Statistics about Alzheimer's Disease* (undated). Retrieved on April 15, 2006, from http://www.alz.org/aboutad/statistics.asp

7. Alzheimer's Association, "The States of Alzheimer's Disease." Information pamphlet (reproduced).

8. Federal Interagency Forum on Aging Related Statistics, *Older Americans 2004: Key Indicators of Well Being.* Washington, DC: U.S. Government Printing Office, 2004.

9. R. I. Stone, *Long-Term Care for the Elderly with Disabilities.* New York: Milbank Memorial Fund, 2000.

10. Federal Interagency Forum on Aging Related Statistics, *Older Americans 2004: Key Indicators of Well Being.*

11. MetLife Mature Market Institute, *The MetLife Market Survey of Nursing Home and Home Care Costs.* New York: Metropolitan Life Insurance Company, September 2005.

12. See W. G. Weissert, "Strategies for Reducing Home Care Expenditures." *Generations* 14(2) (1990): 42–44.

13. 3. U.S. Census Bureau. *Health Insurance Coverage: 2004.* Retrieved on June 28, 2006, from http://www.census.gov/hhes/www/hlthins/hlthin04/hlth04asc.html

14. U.S. Congressional Budget Office, *Financing Long-Term Care for the Elderly.* Washington, DC: U.S. Congressional Budget Office, 2004.

15. S. Coronel, *Long-Term Care Insurance in 2002*. Washington, DC: America's Health Insurance Plans, 2004.

16. U.S. General Accountability Office (GAO), *Long-Term Care Insurance: Federal Program Compared Favorably with Other Products, and Analysis of Claims Trend Could Inform Future Decisions*, GAO-06-401. Washington, DC: GAO, 2006.

17. Ibid.

18. B. Hogan and T. Nicholson, "A Surprise in the Fine Print." *AARP Bulletin* (April 2004): 20.

19. Stone, *Long-Term Care for the Elderly with Disabilities*.

20. R. I. Stone, "Emerging Issues in Long-Term Care." In R. H. Binstock and L. K. George, eds., *Handbook of Aging and the Social Sciences*, 6th ed. San Diego, CA: Academic Press, 2006, pp. 397–418.

21. A. A. Bove, Jr., *The Medicaid Planning Handbook: A Guide to Protecting Your Family's Assets from Catastrophic Nursing Home Costs*, rev. ed. Boston, MA: Little, Brown Inc., 1996.

22. See L. C. Walker and B. Burwell, "Access to Public Resources: Regulating Asset Transfers for Long-Term Care." In L. C. Walker, E. H. Bradley, and T. Wetle, eds., *Public and Private Responsibilities in Long-Term Care: Finding the Balance*. Baltimore, MD: Johns Hopkins University Press, 1998, pp. 165–180.

23. A study published in 2006 estimated that sheltered assets totaled about 1 percent of Medicaid spending, or about $1 billion in fiscal year 2004. See T. Waidmann and K. Liu, *Asset Transfer and Nursing Home Use*. Washington, DC: Kaiser Commission on Medicaid and the Uninsured, Issue Paper, April, 2006.

24. D. M. Walker, *Long-Term Care: Aging Baby Boom Generation Will Increase Demand and Burden on Federal and State Budgets*. Washington, DC: U.S. Government Printing Office, 2002.

25. A. E. Cuellar and J. M. Wiener, "Can Social Insurance for Long-Term Care Work? The Experience of Germany." *Health Affairs* 19(3) (2000): 8–25.

26. The White House Domestic Policy Council, *The President's Health Security Plan: The Clinton Blueprint*. New York: Times Books, 2003.

27. Statistics reported in Stone, "Emerging Issues in Long-Term Care."

28. R. H. Binstock, "The Financing and Organization of Long-Term Care." In L. C. Walker, E. H. Bradley, and T. Wetle, eds., *Public and Private Responsibilities in Long-Term Care*. Baltimore, MD: Johns Hopkins University Press, pp. 1–24.

29. D. L. Yee, "Long-Term Care Policy and Financing as a Public or Private Matter in the United States." *Journal of Aging & Social Policy* 13(2/3) (2001): 35–51.

30. D. A. Wolf, "Population Change: Friend or Foe of the Chronic Care System?" *Health Affairs* 20(6) (2001): 28–42.

31. The President's Council on Bioethics, *Taking Care: Ethical Caregiving in Our Aging Society*. Washington, DC: The President's Council on Bioethics, 2005.

32. L. S. Paige. Retrieved on February 8, 2006, from http://motd.ambians.com/quotes.php/name/linux_wisdom/toc_id/1-1-35

33. L. Cornaro, *The Art of Living Long*, 1903 translation by W. Butler. New York: Springer Publishing Company, 2005.

34. L. Hayflick, "La Dolce Vita vs. La Vita Sobria." *The Gerontologist* 46 (2006): 423–426.

35. Cornaro, *The Art of Living Long.*

36. Quoted in L. Hayflick, *How and Why We Age.* New York: Ballantine Books, 1994.

37. U.S. General Accounting Office, *Health Products for Seniors: "Anti-Aging" Products Pose Potential for Physical and Economic Harm.* Washington, DC: U.S. Government Printing Office, 2001, GAO-01-1129.

38. See, for example, D. Chopra, *Grow Younger, Live Longer: 10 Steps to Reverse Aging.* New York: Harmony Books, 2001.

39. Youngevity, *Youngevity Product Highlights.* Retrieved on May 29, 2005, from http://youngevity.com/brochure/brochure_p1.htm

40. FIND/SVP, *New Anti-Aging Market Creates Opportunities for Marketers.* Retrieved on May 31, 2005, from http://www.findsvp.com/about/2003-04-08antiaging.cfm

41. A4M (American Academy of Anti-Aging Medicine), *The Fleecing of Academic Integrity by the Gerontological Establishment.* Retrieved on June 13, 2002, from http://www.worldhealth.net/html/fleecing_of_academic_integrity.htm

42. A4M (American Academy of Anti-Aging Medicine), *The American Academy of Anti-Aging Medicine.* Retrieved on May 31, 2005, from http://www.worldhealth.net/p/96.html

43. R. Klatz, ed., *Ten weeks to a Younger You.* Chicago, IL: Sport Tech Labs, Inc., 1999.

44. A4M (American Academy of Anti-Aging Medicine), *The American Academy of Anti-Aging Medicine.* Retrieved on May 31, 2005, from http://www.worldhealth.net/p/96.html

45. Guidestar, *U.S. IncomeTax Return of the American Academy of Anti-Aging Medicine for 2003, Internal Revenue Service Form 990.* Retrieved on April 17, 2006, from http://www.guidestar.org/pqShowGsReport.do?finId=101258767&npoId=598448&gotoNext=/reports/partners/guidestar/showDocuments.jsp

46. C. Haber, "Anti-Aging: Why Now?—A Historical Framework for Understanding the Contemporary Enthusiasm." *Generation* 25(4) (2001–2002): 9–14.

47. M. J. Mehlman, R. H. Binstock, E. T. Juengst, R. S. Ponsaran, and P. J.Whitehouse. "Anti-Aging Medicine: Can Consumers Be Better Protected?" *Gerontologist* 44 (2004): 304–310.

48. See M. R. Blackman, J. D. Sorkin, T. Munzer, M. F. Bellantoni, J. Busby-Whitehead, T. E. Stevens, J. Jayme, K. G. O'Connor, C. Christmas, J. D. Tobin, K. J. Steward, E. Cottrell, C. St. Clair, K. M. Pabst, and S. M. Harman, "Growth Hormone and Sex Steroid Administration in Healthy Aged Women and Men: A Randomized Controlled Trial." *Journal of the American Medical Association* 288 (2002): 282–292.

49. J. M. Chan, M. J. Stampfer, E. Giovannucci, P. H. Gann, J. Ma, P. Wilkinson, C. H. Hennekens, and M. Pollak, "Plasma Insulin-Like Growth Factor I and Prostate Cancer Risk: A Prospective Study." *Science* 279 (1998): 563–566.

50. Blackman et al., "Growth Hormone and Sex Steroid Administration in Healthy Aged Women and Men: A Randomized Controlled Trial."

51. M. L. Vance, "Can Growth Hormone Prevent Aging?" *New England Journal of Medicine* 348 (2003): 779–780.

52. E. Pope, "51 Top Scientists Blast Anti-Aging Idea." *AARP Bulletin* 23(43) (2002): 3–5.

53. U.S. GAO (General Accounting Office), *Health Products for Seniors: "Anti-aging" Products Pose Potential for Physical and Economic Harm.* Washington, DC: U.S. Government Printing Office, 2001.

54. National Institute On Aging (NIA), *Life-Extension. Science or Science Fiction?* (2002). Retrieved on July 8, 2002, from http://www.nia.nih.gov/health/agepages/lifeext.htm

55. NIA (National Institute On Aging) (2002b), *Looking for the Fountain of Youth?* Retrieved on July 3, 2002, from http://www. nia.nih.gov/health/ads/fount1.git

56. U.S. Senate Special Committee on Aging, "Swindlers, Hucksters and Snake Oil Salesmen: The Hype and Hope of Marketing Anti-Aging Products to Seniors." Hearing held in Washington, DC, September 10, 2001.

57. Mehlman et al., "Anti-Aging Medicine: Can Consumers Be Better Protected?"

58. R. H. Binstock, J. R. Fishman, and T. E. Johnson. "Anti-Aging Medicine and Science: Social Implications." In R. H. Binstock and L. K. George eds., *Handbook of Aging and the Social Sciences*, 6th ed. San Diego, CA: Academic Press, 2006, pp. 436–455.

59. E. J. Masoro, ed., (2001), "Caloric Restriction's Effects on Aging: Opportunities for Research on Human Implications." *Journal of Gerontology: Biological Sciences* 56A(1) (Special Issue, 2001).

60. L. K. Heilbronn, L. de Jonge, M. I. Frisard, J. P. DeLany, D. E. Larson-Meyer, J. Rood, T. Nguyen, C. K. Martin, J. Volaufova, M. M. Most, F. L. Greenway, S. R. Smith, W. A. Deutsch, D.A. Williamson, and E. Ravussin, "Effect of 6-Month Calorie Restriction on Biomarkers of Longevity, Metabolic Adaptation, and Oxidative Stress in Overweight Individuals: A Randomized Controlled Trial." *Journal of the American Medical Association* 295 (2006): 1539–1548.

61. See, for example, D. K. Ingram, R. M. Anson, R. de Cabo, J. Mamczarz, M. Zhu, J. Mattison, M. A. Lane, and G. S. Roth, "Development of Calorie Restriction Mimetics As A Prolongevity Strategy." *Annals of the New York Academy of Science* 1019 (2004): 412–423.

62. National Center for Health Statistics, *Deaths: Preliminary Data for 2004.* Retrieved on April 20, 2006, from http://www.cdc.gov/nchs/products/pubs/pubd/hestats/prelimdeaths04/preliminarydeaths04.htm

63. Houston Chronicle News Services, *"Believed to Be World's Oldest, Woman in France Dies at 122." Retrieved on April 17, 2006, from http://www.chron.com/content/chronicle/page1/97/08/05/calment.html*

64. R. A. Miller "Extending Life: Scientific Prospects and Political Obstacles." *Milbank Quarterly* 80 (2002): 155–174.

65. Binstock, Fishman, and Johnson. "Anti-Aging Medicine and Science: Social Implications."

66. A. Pollack, "Forget Botox. Anti-Aging Pills May Be Next. *New York Times* (September 23, 2003) Section 3: 1, 10.

67. A. D. N. J. de Grey, B. N. Ames, J. K. Andersen, A. Bartke, J. Campisi, C. B. Heward, R. J. M. McCarter, and G. Stock, "Time to Talk SENS: Critiquing the Immutability of Human Aging." *Annals of the New York Academy of Science* 959 (2002): 452–462.

68. A. D. N. J. de Grey, "Gerontologists and the Media: The Dangers of Over-Pessimism." *Biogerontology*1 (2002): 355–368.

69. See A. L. Bonnicksen, *Crafting a Cloning Policy: From Dolly to Stem Cells:* Washington, DC: Georgetown University Press, 2002.

70. E. T. Juengst, R. H. Binstock, M. J. Mehlman, and S. G. Post. "Antiaging Research and the Need for Public Dialogue." *Science* 299 (2003): 1323.

71. See, for example, S. G. Post and R. H. Binstock eds., *The Fountain of Youth: Cultural, Scientific, and Ethical Perspectives on a Biomedical Goal.* New York: Oxford University Press, 2004.

72. NIA (National Institute on Aging), *Action Plan for Aging Research: Strategic Plan for Fiscal Years 2001–2005* (2001). Retrieved on May 31, 2005, from http://www.nia.nih.gov/AboutNIA/StrategicPlan/ResearchGoalB/Subgoal1.htm

73. J. Schulte, "Terminal Patients Deplete Medicare, Greenspan Says." *Dallas Morning News* (April 26, 1983): 1.

74. Studies over the years have consistently indicated that the proportion of Medicare expended on enrollees who are in their last year of life is about 27 to 28 percent, not the 30 percent figure used by Greenspan. See, for example, J. D. Lubitz and G. F. Riley. "Trends in Medicare Payments in the Last Year of Life." *New England Journal of Medicine* 328 (1993): 1092–1096.

75. W. Slater, "Latest Lamm Remark Angers the Elderly." *Arizona Daily Star* (March 29, 1984): 1.

76. See, for example, R. D. Lamm, "The Moral Imperative of Limiting Elderly Health Entitlements." In S. H. Altman and D. Shactman eds., *Policies for an Aging Society* Baltimore, MD: Johns Hopkins University Press, 2002, pp. 199–216.

77. C. Smith, C. Cowan, S. Heffler, A. Catlin, and the National Health Accounts Team, "National Health Spending in 2004: Recent Slowdown Led By Prescription Drug Spending." *Health Affairs* 25(1) (2006): 186–196.

78. T. M. Smeeding, ed., *Should Medical Care Be Rationed By Age?* Totowa, NJ: Rowman & Littlefield, 1987.

79. See N. Daniels, *Am I My Parents' Keeper?* New York: Oxford University Press, 1988; P. T. Menzel, *Strong Medicine: The Ethical Rationing of Health Care,* New York: Oxford University Press, 1990.

80. D. Callahan, *Setting Limits: Medical Goals in an Aging Society,* New York: Simon and Schuster, 1987, p. 171.

81. D. Callahan, "Death and the Research Imperative." *New England Journal of Medicine* 342 (2000): 654–656.

82. See, for example, R. L. Barry and G. V. Bradley, eds., *Set No Limits: A Rebuttal to Daniel Callahan's Proposal to Limit Health Care for the Elderly.* Urbana, IL: University of Illinois Press, 1991; R. H. Binstock and S. G. Post, eds., *Too Old for Health Care: Controversies in Medicine, Law, Economic, and Ethics.* Baltimore, MD: Johns Hopkins University Press, 1991.

83. Daniels, *Am I My Parents' Keeper?*.

84. L. R. Kass, "L'Chaim and Its Limits: Why Not Immortality?" *First Things* 13 (May 2001): 17–24.

85. Alliance for Aging Research, *Seven Deadly Myths: Uncovering the Facts About the High Cost of the Last Year of Life.* Washington, DC: Alliance for Aging Research, 1997.

86. Ibid.

87. A. M. Wilkinson and J. Lynn, "The End of Life." In R. H. Binstock and L. K. George eds., *Handbook of Aging and the Social Sciences*, 5th ed. San Diego, CA: Academic Press, 2001, pp. 444–461.

88. E. H. Erikson, *Insight and Responsibility: Lectures on the Ethical Implications of Psychoanalytic Insight*. New York: Norton, 1964.

89. C. Smith et al., "National Health Spending in 2004: Recent Slowdown Led by Prescription Drug Spending."

90. Social Security and Medicare Boards of Trustees, Status of the Social Security and Medicare Programs: A Summary of the 2006 Annual Reports. Retrieved May 2, 2006, from http://www.socialsecurity.gov/OACT/TRSUM/trsummary.html

91. Medicare Payment Advisory Commission, *Report to the Congress: Medicare Payment Policy*. Washington, DC: U.S. Government Printing Office, 2006.

92. See U. E. Reinhardt, "Does the Aging of the Population Really Drive the Demand for Health Care?" *Health Affairs* 22(6) (2003): 27–39; R. H. Binstock. "Older Persons and Health Care Costs." In R. N. Butler, L. K. Grossman, and M. R. Oberlink eds., *Life in an Older America*. New York: Century Foundation Press, 1999, pp. 75–95.

93. D. J. Gross, L. Gross, S. W. Schondelmeyer, and S. O. Raetzman, *Trends in Manufacturers Drug Prices of Brand Name Prescription Drugs Used by Older Americans—2005 Year End Update*. Washington, DC: AARP Public Policy Institute, 2005.

94. "Going Broke to Stay Alive," *Business Week* (January 30, 2006). Retrieved on February 17, 2006, from http://yahool.businessweek.com/magazine/content/06_05/b3969051.htm

95. "Price Gouging on Cancer Drugs?" *New York Times* (February, 17, 2006): A22.

96. J. Abramson, *Overdosed America: The Broken Promise of American Medicine*. New York: HarperCollins, 2004.

97. J. Abramson, *Overdosed America*.

98. C. Smith et al., "National Health Spending in 2004: Recent Slowdown Led by Prescription Drug Spending."

99. M. Moon, *Medicare: A Policy Primer*. Washington, DC: The Urban Institute Press, 2006.

100. R. Pear, "Fewer People on Medicare Are Dropped By H.M.O's." *New York Times* (September 9, 2003): A21.

101. U. E. Reinhardt, "Does the Aging of the Population Really Drive the Demand for Health Care?"

102. C. Smith et al., "National Health Spending in 2004: Recent Slowdown Led by Prescription Drug Spending."

103. Medicare Payment Advisory Commission, *Report to the Congress: Medicare Payment Policy*.

104. C. Smith et al., "National Health Spending in 2004: Recent Slowdown Led By Prescription Drug Spending."

105. Organisation for Economic Cooperation and Development, *Health Data 2005*. Paris, France: OECD, 2005.

106. Ibid.

107. U.S. Centers for Disease Control and Prevention, *QuickStats: Life Expectancy at Birth, By Sex—Selected Countries, 2001*.

108. G. E. Anderson and J.-P. Poullier, "Health Spending, Access, and Outcomes: Trends in Industrialized Countries." *Health Affairs* 18(3) (1999): 178–192.

109. U.S. Census Bureau, *Health Insurance Coverage: 2004.* Retrieved on April 24, 2005, from http://www.census.gov/hhes/www/hlthins/hlthin04/hlth04asc.html

110. K. Donelan, R. J. Blendon, C. Schoen, K. Davis, and K. Binns, "The Cost of Health System Change: Public Discontent In Five Nations." *Health Affairs* 18(3) (1999): 206–216.

111. P. Belluck, "Massachusetts Sets Health Plan for Nearly All." *New York Times* (April 5, 2006): A1.

112. A different approach for achieving near-universal health insurance coverage, legislated in by Vermont in 2006, will also bear watching. In contrast to the mandatory provisions in the Massachusetts plan, Vermont will be providing a new *voluntary*, standardized plan for uninsured residents. The plan will be offered through private insurers, but with costs defined by the state. See P. Barry, "Coverage for All." *AARP Bulletin* 47(7) (2006): 8–10.

113. M. Tanner, "Individual Mandates for Health Insurance: Slippery Slope to National Health Care." *Policy Analysis* 565 (April 5, 2005).

CHAPTER NINE: A GERONTOCRACY? THE POLITICS OF AGING

1. P. G. Peterson, *Gray Dawn: How the Coming Age Wave Will Transform America—and the World.* New York: Times Books, 1999.

2. H. Heclo, "Generational Politics." In J. L. Palmer, T. Smeeding, and B. B. Torrey, eds., *The Vulnerable.* Washington, DC: Urban Institute Press, 1988, pp. 381–411.

3. L. C. Thurow, "The Birth of a Revolutionary Class." *New York Times Magazine* (May 19, 1996): 47.

4. R. J. Samuelson, "AARP's America Is a Mirage." *Washington Post* (November 16, 2005): A19.

5. D. J. Stewart, "Disfranchise the Old: The Lesson of California." *New Republic* 163(8/9) (1970): 20–22.

6. M. Carballo, "Extra Votes for Parents?" *Boston Globe* (December 17, 1981): 35.

7. P. G. Peterson, *Gray Dawn.*

8. U.S. Census Bureau, *Reported Voting and Registration by Race, Hispanic Origin, Sex, and Age Groups: November 1964 to 2004* (2005). Retrieved on July 7, 2005, from http://www.census.gov/population/www/socdemo/voting.html

9. See R. H. Binstock and Y. Riemer, "Campaigning for 'The Senior Vote': A Case Study of Carter's 1976 Campaign." *Gerontologist* 18 (1978): 517–524.

10. Currently Social Security's normal retirement age is slowly increasing over time, from the long-established traditional age of 65, to reach age 67 in 2027.

11. D. Street, "Special Interests or Citizens' Rights? 'Senior Power,' Social Security, and Medicare." In M. Minkler and C.L. Estes, eds., *Critical Gerontology: Perspectives from Political and Moral Economy.* Amityville, NY: Baywood, 1999, pp. 109–130.

12. M. Connelly, "How Americans Voted: A Political Portrait." *New York Times* (November 7, 2004): 4wk.

13. Ibid.

14. Ibid.

15. "The Third Rail of Politics." *Newsweek* (November 24, 1982): 24.

16. M. Connelly, "How Americans Voted: A Political Portrait."

17. G. Naegele and A. Walker, "Conclusion." In A. Walker and G. Naegele, eds., *The Politics of Old Age in Europe.* Buckingham, PA: Open University Press, 1999, pp. 197–209.

18. See, e.g., D. Street and J. S. Cossman, "Greatest Generation or Greedy Geezers?" *Social Problems* 1 (2006): 75–96.

19. Federal Interagency Forum on Aging-Related Statistics, *Older Americans 2004: Key Indicators of Well-Being.* Federal Interagency Forum on Aging-Related Statistics. Washington, DC: U.S. Government Printing Office, 2004.

20. See M. J. Schlesinger and K. Kronebush (1994), "Intergenerational Tensions and Conflict: Attitudes and Perceptions about Social Justice and Age-Related Needs." In V. L. Bengtson and R. A. Harootyan, eds., *Intergenerational Linkages: Hidden Connections in American Society.* New York: Springer Publishing Company, 1994, pp. 152–184.

21. B. R. Levy and M. J. Schlesinger, "When Self-interest and Age Stereotypes Collide: Elders Opposing Increased Funds for Programs Benefiting Themselves." *Journal of Aging and Social Policy* 17(2) (2005): 25–39.

22. S. A. Peterson and A. Somit, *Political Behavior of Older Americans.* New York: Garland, 1994.

23. A. L.Campbell, *How Policies Make Citizens: Senior Political Activism and the American Welfare State.* Princeton, NJ: Princeton University Press, 2003.

24. R. D. Arnold, *The Logic of Congressional Action.* New Haven, CT: Yale University Press, 1992.

25. M. Derthick, *Policymaking for Social Security.* Washington, DC: The Brookings Institution, 1979.

26. A. Holtzman, *The Townsend Movement: A Political Study.* New York: Bookman Associates, 1963. Also see S. L. Messinger, "Organizational Transformation: A Case Study of a Declining Social Movement." *American Sociological Review* 20 (1995): 3–10; F. A. Pinner, P. Jacobs, and P. Selznick, *Old Age and Political Behavior.* Berkeley, CA: University of California Press, 1959; J. Quadagno, *The Transformation of Old Age Security.* Chicago, IL: University of Chicago Press, 1988.

27. C. L. Day, L. A. Powell, K. J. Branco, and J. B. Williamson, *The Senior Rights Movement: Framing the Policy Debate in America.* New York: Twayne Publishers, 1996; H. J. Pratt, *Gray Agendas: Interest Groups and Public Pensions in Canada, Britain, and the United States.* Ann Arbor, MI: University of Michigan Press, 1993.

28. J. H. Birnbaum, "Washington's Power." *Fortune* (December 8, 1997). Retrieved on January 2004 from http://www.pathfinder.com/fortune/1997/971208/was 1.htm; F. L. Cook and E. J. Barrett, *Support for the American Welfare State.* New York: Columbia University Press, 1992; Day et al., *The Senior Rights Movement*; C. R. Morris, *The AARP: America's Most Powerful Lobby and the Clash of Generations.* New York: Times Books, 1996.

29. J. L. Walker, "The Origins and Maintenance of Interest Groups in America." *American Political Science Review* 77 (1983): 390–406; C. L. Estes, *The Aging Enterprise*. San Francisco, CA: Jossey-Bass, 1979.

30. On Social Security see M. Derthick, *Policymaking for Social Security*; on Medicare see R. M. Ball, "What Medicare's Architects Had in Mind." *Health Affairs* 14(44) (1995): 62–72, and W. J. Cohen, "Reflections on the Enactment of Medicare and Medicaid." *Health Care Financing Review*, Annual Supplement (1985): 3–11.

31. See, for example, R. H. Binstock, "Interest-Group Liberalism and the Politics Of Aging." *Gerontologist* 12 (1972): 265–280; Estes, *The Aging Enterprise*; and B. A. Lockett, *Aging, Politics, and Research: Setting the Federal Agenda for Research on Aging*. New York: Springer Publishing Company, 1983.

32. See Campbell, *How Policies Make Citizens*.

33. Leadership Council of Aging Organizations, *LCAO Mission and Purpose*. Washington, DC, 2004. Retrieved on March 26, 2004, from http://lcao.org/himssion.htm

34. Leadership Council of Aging Organizations, *Social Security Privatization*. Washington, DC, 2004. Retrieved on March 26, 2004, from http://lcao.org/legagenda/ss_private.htm

35. R. Himmelfarb, *Catastrophic Politics: The Rise and Fall of the Medicare Catastrophic Coverage Act of 1988*. University Park, PA: Pennsylvania State University Press, 1995.

36. C. L. Day, *What Older Americans Think*. Princeton, NJ: Princeton University Press, 1990; also see Pratt, *Gray Agendas*.

37. K. Dumas, "Budget Buster Hot Potato: The Earnings Test." *Congressional Quarterly Weekly Report* (January 11, 1992): 52–55.

38. J. Kosterlitz, "Golden Silence?" *National Journal* (April 3, 1993): 800–804.

39. The Seniors Coalition, *About TSC* (2004). Retrieved on March 26, 2004, from http://www.senior.org/bin/view.fpl/10142/article/327/cms_article/327.html

40. R. C. Adelman, "The Alzheimerization of Aging." *The Gerontologist* 35 (1995): 526–532.

41. "Senior Power Rides Again." *Newsweek* (February 20, 1995): 31.

42. Lockett, *Aging, Politics, and Research: Setting the Federal Agenda for Research on Aging*.

43. National Association of Retired Federal Employees, *About NARFE* (2004). Retrieved on March 28, 2004, from http://www.narfe.org/guest/about_narfe_guest.cfm

44. See P. C. Light, *Artful Work: The Politics of Social Security Reform*. New York: Random House, 1985.

45. National Committee to Preserve Social Security and Medicare, *Message from the President*, 2004. Retrieved on March 27, 2004, from http://www.ncpssm.org/about/index.html

46. M. Richtman, Personal telephone communication to Robert Binstock from the Executive Director of the National Committee to Preserve Social Security and Medicare (February 5, 2004).

47. National Committee to Preserve Social Security and Medicare, "Join Us." (2004). Retrieved on March 27, 2004, from http://www.ncpssm.org/join/indes/html

48. Alliance for Retired Americans, "About Us." (2004). Retrieved on March 27, 2004, from http://www.retired americans.org/indes.php?tg=topusn&cat=2

49. S. Greenhouse, "A.F.L.-C.I.O. Forms Retiree Advocacy Group." *New York Times* (May 24, 2001): A14.

50. The union movement in the 1960s saw the enactment of Medicare as a means of making retiree health benefits less important to bargain for as part of compensation packages; without them, there might be greater room to bargain for wage increases and other benefits. See J. Quadagno, *One Nation, Uninsured: Why the U.S. Has No National Health Insurance*. New York: Oxford University Press, 2005.

51. See J. H. Birnbaum, "Washington's Power." and C. R. Morris, *The AARP: America's Most Powerful Lobby and the Clash of Generations.*

52. *AARP Annual Report 2004* and *Consolidated Financial Statements as of December 31, 2004*. Retrieved on January 8, 2006, from http://www.aarp.org/about_aarp/aarp/_overview/a2003-06-24-annualreport-03.html

53. Himmelfarb, *Catastrophic Politics.*

54. "Endorsement Riles Members of Retiree Group." *New York Times* (August 12, 1994): A10.

55. E. I. Lehrman, "Health-Care Reform at the Crossroads." *Modern Maturity* 12 (January/February, 1995).

56. S. A. Holmes, "The World According to AARP." *New York Times* (March 21, 2001), D1.

57. See J. S. Hacker and T. Marmor, "Medicare Reform: Fact, Fiction and Foolishness." *Public Policy & Aging Report* 13(4) (2003): 1, 20–23; J. K. Iglehart, "The New Medicare Prescription-Drug-Benefit—A Pure Power Play." *New England Journal of Medicine* 350 (2004): 826–833; J. White, "The Social Security and Medicare Debate Three Years after the 2000 Election." *Public Policy and Aging Report* 13(4) (2003): 15–19.

58. America's Future, *Coordinated Events by Bush, Trade Association, and AARP* (2004). Retrieved on November 12, 2003, from http://action@action.ourfuture.org

59. R. Pear and R. Toner, "Medicare Plan Covering Drugs Backed by AARP." *New York Times* (November 18, 2003): A21.

60. See Iglehart, "The New Medicare Prescription-Drug-Benefit—A Pure Power Play"; R. Pear, "Sweeping Medicare Change Wins Approval in Congress; President Claims a Victory." *New York Times* (November 26, 2003): A1; R. Toner, "An Imperfect Compromise." *New York Times* (November 25, 2003): A1.

61. S. G. Stolberg, "An 800-Pound-Gorilla Changes Partners over Medicare." *New York Times* (November 23, 2003): wk5.

62. Ibid.

63. R. Pear, "AARP, Eye on Drug Costs, Urges Change in New Law." *New York Times* (January 17, 2004): A12.

64. Stolberg, "An 800-Pound-Gorilla Changes Partners over Medicare."

65. See J. Drinkard and W. M. Welch, "AARP Accused of Conflict of Interest." *USA Today* (November 24, 2003): 11A; P. Krugman, "AARP Gone Astray." *New York Times* (November 21, 2003): A31.

66. J. Rother, e-mail message to James Schulz on March 27, 2006.

67. Pear, "AARP, Eye on Drug Costs, Urges Change in New Law."

68. W. D. Novelli, "AARP Stays Sharp." *Wall Street Journal* (December 4, 2003): A16.

69. W. D. Novelli, "Now, the Next Phase." *AARP Bulletin* 45(1) (2004): 28.

70. P. Barry, "Pushing Down Drug Costs: AARP Opens Drive to Lower Drug Prices with a Range of Fixes to New Medicare Law." *AARP Bulletin* 45(2) (2004): 8.

71. In fact, Bush never presented a specific proposal for consideration, and critics had to guess (based on past events) exactly what the details might be.

72. 3. W. M. Welch and J. Drinkard. "USA Next campaign targets AARP." Retrieved March 14, 2005, from http://www.usatoday.com/news/washington/2005-02-27-soc-security-aarp_x.htm

73. See H. J. Aaron, "Budget Estimates: What We Know, What We Can't Know, and Why It Matters." In S. H. Altman and D. I. Schactman, eds., *Policies for an Aging Society*. Baltimore, MD: Johns Hopkins University Press, 2002, pp. 63–80.

74. Thurow, "The Birth of a Revolutionary Class."

75. U.S. Census Bureau, *Current Population Reports, Series P2* (Middle Series Projections). Washington, DC: U.S. Government Printing Office, 1998.

76. R. H. Binstock, "Older People and Voting Participation: Past and Future." *The Gerontologist* 40 (2000): 18–31.

77. U.S. Census Bureau, *Reported Voting and Registration by Race, Hispanic Origin, Sex, and Age Groups: November 1964 to 2004* (2005). Retrieved on July 7, 2005, from http://www.census.gov/population/www/socdemo/voting.html

78. J. B. Williamson, "Political Activism and the Aging of the Baby Boom." *Generations* 22(1) (1998): 55–59.

79. Light, *Artful Work*.

80. D. F. Alwin, "The Political Impact of the Baby Boom: Are There Persistent Generational Differences in Political Beliefs and Behavior?" *Generations* 22(1) (1998): 46–54.

81. J. B. Williamson, "Political Activism and the Aging of the Baby Boom."

82. F. B. Hobbs, *65+ in the United States*. U.S. Bureau of the Census, Current Population Reports, Special Studies, P23-190. Washington, DC: U.S. Government Printing Office, 1996.

83. M. Connelly, "How Americans Voted: A Political Portrait."

84. T. Schuyt, L. L. García, and K. Knipscheer. "The Politics of Old Age in the Netherlands." In A. Walker and G. Naegele, eds., *The Politics of Old Age in Europe*. Buckingham, PA: Open University Press, 1999, pp. 123–134.

CHAPTER TEN: FRAMING THE ISSUES FOR AN AGING NATION

1. As quoted in R. D. Lamm, "The Moral Imperative of Limiting Elderly Health Entitlements." In S. H. Altman and D. I. Shactman, eds., *Policies for an Aging Society*. Baltimore, MD: Johns Hopkins University Press, 2002, pp. 199–216.

2. N. J. Altman, *The Battle for Social Security: From FDR's Vision to Bush's Gamble*. Hoboken, NJ: John Wiley & Sons, 2005.

3. Based on statistics from the U.S. Census Bureau's Current Population Survey. We have pointed out elsewhere that government poverty statistics are an underestimate, given their derivation. See J. H. Schulz, *The Economics of Aging*, 7th ed., Westport, CT: Auburn House, 2001.

4. Retrieved on February 20, 2006, from http://www.washingtonpost.com/wp-dyn/content/article/2006/01/31/AR2006013101468.html

5. W. Vieth and R. Simon. "President Casts Doubt on Trust Fund: Promoting His Private Account Plan, Bush Calls the Social Security Bonds Held for Future Beneficiaries. Just IOUs Sitting In A Filing Cabinet." *Los Angeles Times* (April 6, 2005). Retrieved on April 6, 2005, from http://www.latimes.com/news/printedition/asection/la-na-bush6apr06,1,4700653,print.story

6. T. N. Bethell, ed., *Insuring the Essentials—Bob Ball on Social Security.* New York: Century Foundation Press, 2000.

7. A. B. Hubbard, "The Health of a Nation." *New York Times* (April 3, 2005): A21.

8. H. Hertzberg, "Comment: Consumption." *The New Yorker* (April 17, 2006): 25–26.

9. The descriptive term "Swiss cheese" that is used here comes from a book by G. Sperling. *The Pro-Growth Progressive.* New York: Simon & Schuster, 2005.

10. G. Sperling, *The Pro-Growth Progressive.*

11. Quoted in J. S Hacker, "Reviving the Social Safety Net; Insurance Policy" *The New Republic Online.* Retrieved on March 25, 2006, from http://www.tnr.com/doc.mhtml?i=20050704&s=hacker070405

12. J. S. Hacker. "Reviving the Social Safety Net; Insurance Policy."

13. See, for example, P. A. Diamond and P. R. Orzag, *Saving Social Security: A Balanced Approach.* Washington, DC: The Brookings Institution, 2004.

14. G. Lakoff. *Don't Think of an Elephant: Know Your Values and Frame the Debate—The Essential Guide for Progressives.* White River Junction, VT: Chelsea Green Publishers, 2004.

15. See R. H. Binstock, "Social Security and Medicare: President Bush and the Delegates Reject Each Other." *Public Policy and Aging Report* 16(1) (2006): 9–12.

16. A. Trafford, "Bush on Aging: Not Now." *Washington Post* (December 20, 2005): F1.

17. Ibid.

18. 2005 White House Conference on Aging. "Remarks of Barry C. Black, Ph.D., Chaplain, U.S. Senate." Retrieved on March 25, 2006, from http:www.whcoa.gov/press/speakers/Remarks_Barry_Black.pdf

19. R. H. Binstock, Notes taken while delegate-at-large to the 2005 White House Conference on Aging.

20. AARP, *Annual Report, 2002* (2003). Retrieved on March 27, 2004, from http://assets.aarp.org/www.aarp.org-articles/aboutaarp/annualreports2002-f.pdf

21. D. Cook, "The Point Man on AARP's Controversial Move." *Christian Science Monitor* (December 11, 2003). Retrieved on December 29, 2003, from http://www.christiansciencemonitor.com/2003/12/11/p03s01-supo.hmtl

22. M. J. Mehlman, R. H. Binstock, E. T. Juengst, R. S. Ponsaran, and P. J. Whitehouse, "Anti-Aging Medicine: Can Consumers Be Better Protected?" *The Gerontologist* 44 (2004): 304–310.

23. See M. Harrington, *Care and Equality: Inventing a New Family Politics.* New York: Alfred A. Knopf, 1999.

INDEX

About the Author

JAMES H. SCHULZ is Emeritus Professor of Economics, Brandeis University. A former president of the Gerontological Society of America, and recipient of numerous awards—including the Kleemier Award for outstanding research in the field of aging—he has written extensively on aging, pensions, retirement, and social policy. His 17 books include *Social Security in the Twenty-First Century, The Economics of Population Aging, Providing Adequate Retirement Income When Life-Time Employment Ends*, and seven editions of *The Economics of Aging*.

ROBERT H. BINSTOCK is Professor of Aging, Health, and Society at Case Western Reserve University. A former president of the Gerontological Society of America, and recipient of numerous awards, he has served as director of a White House Task Force on Older Americans and as chairman and member of many advisory panels to the U.S., state, and local governments. He is the author of more than 250 articles and book chapters, primarily on the politics and policies affecting aging, and has published 24 books, including *America's Political System, Too Old for Health Care?, The Future of Long-Term Care*, and six editions of the *Handbook of Aging and the Social Sciences*.

DATE DUE

12/13/19			
GAYLORD			PRINTED IN U.S.A.